Double
Your Money
In Real
Estate
Every
2 Years

DOUBLE YOUR MONEY IN REAL ESTATE EVERY 2 YEARS

By Dave Glubetich

Impact Publishing Co.
Pleasant Hill, CA.

Double Your Money in Real Estate Every 2 Years.
Copyright © 1980 Impact Publishing Co.

First printing 1980
Second printing 1981

ISBN 0-9601530-4-7
Library of Congress No. 80-142122

Published by

America's Number-One Source of
Books, Reports, and Newsletters
for Rental Property Investors.

1601 Oak Park Boulevard, Pleasant Hill, California 94523
Customer Service and Order Telephone: (415) 935-4370

CONTENTS

Acknowledgments

My sincere thanks to the following friends for their help, encouragement and advice. Without these people my task would have been nearly impossible and this book might not have ever been written: John Beck, Joan Gardner, Judy Maddy, Judy Moretz, Howard Pierce, Mark Shih, Joe Vanis, Dave Wigginton and last, but not least, my wife Janet.

Illustrations by Dave Patton
Cover by Wayne Pope

To Jon, Erick

and Debra.

May they someday be free

"Buying real estate is not only the best way, the quickest way, but the only way to become wealthy."   *—Marshall Field*

INTRODUCTION

It's called the *Great American slide* . . . and you're on it whether you want to be or not.

Picture yourself on a gigantic slide which is forever taking you and your family downhill. With each passing year you slip farther down as goods and services cost more and your dollars buy less. And when you get a raise or make a few extra bucks Uncle Sam comes along and takes a big portion of that away by a clever device known as tax bracketing.

Tax bracketing means that when you make more money you step up into a higher and more costly tax bracket. It's how the government robs people without most of them knowing what "hit them." Our entire economy is indexed in such a way that when prices rise, wage scales increase to compensate the worker for the additional income he will need just to stay even. But many a person has ended up with less money than he made the year before after a raise *raised* him into a higher tax bracket.

The reason this happens is that our federal income tax structure is not indexed to change. It is stationary and has been for many years. Because of this, the downhill slide you and I are on hurts a little more than it should. As our dollars buy less and we struggle to make ends meet, along comes Uncle Sam with his hand out for *more, more* and *more*. No wonder people are frustrated!

Unless you take the specific action that I am going to recommend in this book, don't expect things to get any better. As you probably know, the inflation rate (as measured by the Cost of Living Index which is compiled by the U.S. Labor Department) in 1979 was over 13 percent. And at this writing in the Spring of '80 the index is headed for even higher figures. Only a steep recession, according to some, *might* turn things around.

Wouldn't it be nice, for instance, if the overall inflation rate settled down to something like 6 percent annually? Let's take a look and see what might happen to prices with a steady 6 percent inflation rate.

With an average annual rate of 6 percent, in just twenty more years you will be paying $1.76 for the 5-cent Hershey bar; or $2.10 for a pack of cigarettes from the corner grocery store; or $3.60 for a Big Mac hamburger.

And that no-frills single-family home that's selling for $65,000 in 1980 (the same one you thought was over-priced at $15,000 in 1960) will be worth $234,000 in the year 2000. And remember—that's only if the inflation rate averages 6 percent!

Here is the first lesson that you'll get from this book. You don't have to ride the great American slide all the way to the poor house. There is a way to fight back so that you can deservedly keep more of your hard-earned income—so that you can better cope with whatever inflation rate we get stuck with in the future.

Consider, for instance, that if a well-meaning friend convinced you to invest in a Big Mac because they were assuredly going up in price, each dollar spent on one today would return you zero (0) by the end of the century. Big Macs obviously can't last that long.

What if instead you invested in something more durable—like a new automobile? You reason that today's modest car which sells for $5,000 will be selling for over $17,000 in twenty more years. But in twenty years the car will be that many years old and it won't be in vogue. It won't be an antique either, so even if you managed to put very few miles on it in that time span, you'll be lucky to get one-tenth of your original $5,000 back.

But a house—now that's a horse of a different color. The $65,000 house that you buy today will be worth $234,000 in twenty years. And you probably won't pay all cash for the home, but spend something closer to $10,000 and finance the balance. So for a $10,000 investment you'll reap something in excess of $179,000 in twenty years. This amount could really be a lot higher, but I am not considering tax shelter benefits, equity pay-down or any fancy creative financing or pyramiding plans which could greatly expand the profit outlined.

Now just for a moment, imagine what could happen if you bought two homes instead of one . . . or how about four or five?

I know that most of my readers don't need this analogy to muster the confidence one needs to have in real estate before they boldly invest their life savings and then some. Millions of Americans are already doing so . . . and these are the people who have climbed off the great American slide. Heck, I won't mind buying my large family a round of $3.60 Big Macs with all the trimmings if I've got a few million dollars worth of property, plus an income of $250,000 a year which is sheltered from the tax collector. And that's the way it'll be for me—and possibly you too, if you get a piece of the action.

And that *piece of action* is a chunk of real estate for you and your family. I don't mean just your personal residence—that's a good start—but a rental home or two, or perhaps a small apartment building. In this book I'll show you how you can double your money every two years . . . or at least to the point where either you feel you have enough or you've got *so much* that further doubling becomes physically impossible. And that's a nice problem to have, because you'll be a multi-millionaire by that time.

It doesn't take a lot of "smarts" to realize that inflation is a two-edged sword. It can kill you if you don't have any protection against it. Again consider the family whose purchasing power is constantly eroded by inflation. Each year they make more but they also pay more in taxes. And with prices constantly rising, they're getting caught in the middle of a closing vice. This family probably owns their home . . . good! At least that's some protection. Like a lot of Americans these people may have invested in a T-Bill account when rates exceeded 16 percent. But that wasn't a move which will get them off the great American slide. If they are in the forty-percent tax bracket, for example, Uncle Sam will be helping himself to 6.4 percent of that earned interest. That leaves an effective net return of 9.6 percent, which is then gobbled up by inflation. If the inflation rate were at 10 percent, for instance, the effective return would be *minus* 0.4 percent.

On the other hand, this family might have bought an additional home. With a 10 percent inflation rate the value of that home would have increased dramatically during the course of a year. On an $80,000 purchase the value would have increased to about $88,000 at the end of a year. They would have increased their net worth by over $8,000; and because this investment affords a legal tax shelter which will provide $2,000 to $3,000 in additional deductions, they will pay a lot less in taxes. Granted, this family will not have the $8,000 profit to use this year—but neither will they be paying any taxes on it. After a few years they will be able to get the money out of their investment and still not pay any taxes.

Does inflation have to keep going at 6 or 10 or 13 percent for this investment program to work? The answer is no. Inflation just helps you make money a little faster and isn't really a necessity for making money in real estate. The principles in this book will help you make money regardless of what the inflation rate is. Inflation just sweetens the pot. But in times of high inflation, you almost have to buy property just to keep ahead. That's because real estate is just like a little wooden boat in a bathtub filling with water. Its value keeps rising as the water level goes up.

And will inflation continue? Asked recently why he believed inflation would soar to the statistical mountaintops, an economist participating in a panel discussion answered, "Because it's here," reported the Associated Press.

"Pardon me," asked a member of the audience, "Because it's here?"

"Yes," he replied. "Because we have inflation, we'll have inflation. It discourages saving. It encourages spending. It entices people to borrow money for purchases that otherwise might be postponed."

"Explain," he was asked, and he replied:

"Why save at 5.25 percent when value declines at 9 percent? Why not spend now and avoid higher prices later? Why not borrow to buy now when you're fairly certain of repaying in cheaper dollars?"

Most people don't know what to make of inflation. If you let it, it can push you back and pin you against the proverbial poorhouse wall. Or you can roll with it (like buying real estate) and let it help make you rich. It's only an obstacle if you let it be one.

YOU CAN *DOUBLE YOUR MONEY EVERY TWO YEARS*

The effects inflation has on you and your family is ultimately up to you. Think about that for a moment! You have two roads you can take . . . one leads down the great American slide and the other leads to riches and reasonable financial independence. It's your choice.

I am not saying it will be easy . . . but I am saying you can do as I and literally hundreds of other people I communicate with are doing. You can actually lift yourself above the daily problems of recession, high interest rates and inflation. In fact you can even benefit from these nemeses.

That's what this book is basically all about. It's a continuation and expansion of my first book, *THE MONOPOLY GAME*, which is now in the fourth edition. *DOUBLE YOUR MONEY IN REAL ESTATE EVERY TWO YEARS* goes beyond the basics discussed in the first book and shows the reader how he or she can do just what the title says—double your money (your equities) every two years for as long as it is physically possible or financially rewarding.

DOUBLE YOUR MONEY was written for today's difficult and cyclical market. It goes thoroughly into techniques for searching for property, negotiating favorable contracts, creative financing ploys and methods of eliminating negative cash flows despite problems like high interest rates and recession.

Every concept, principle or idea written about in this book is both practical and workable. If a method for buying or financing a property will work only for one in a thousand people or only once in each thousand times it's employed, then I simply don't write about it.

I have always prided myself on presenting workable information—information which can be successfully implemented by almost anyone, regardless of where they might live. So the only real question that the reader will have is: "Do I want to succeed badly enough to get off my duff and go out and start buying real property?"

The plan is here—it's in this book, just waiting for you to take the ideas which best apply to you and your community. A little practical field experience will "work out the bugs" and in no time at all you'll be a successful property owner.

In the first part of the book I go into ways of raising investment capital, with many even applicable to the person who has no money of his own but a lot of desire to be successful. In Part 1 I thoroughly discuss partnerships, joint ventures and syndications.

In the second part of *DOUBLE YOUR MONEY* the subject is *the property*—how to find it, how to inspect it and how to buy it. This includes a chapter on finding and buying distressed properties.

Part III goes into creative financing and covers such topics as assumptions, second mortgages, purchase money loans, wrap-arounds and contracts of sale, and ways to either reduce or eliminate negative cash flow.

The final section of the book goes into problem solving techniques and provides a workable plan, using all the knowledge you'll accumulate over the first 16 chapters, where you can use advanced pyramiding methods to own and control millions of dollars worth of real estate in a few short years.

Note: If you purchased *THE MONOPOLY GAME* with this book, I recommend that you start by reading *THE MONOPOLY GAME* first, as it is more basic and covers the entire single-family home investment scene from beginning to end. It also goes into management, tenant selection, selling and refinancing—subjects which this book does not cover in any detail.

TODAY'S UNIQUE OPPORTUNITIES

I am often asked if today is a good time to buy real estate. My answer is the same now as it was two years or five years ago. Yes! One reason for my answer can be found in this Associated Press article:

WASHINGTON—A time bomb is set to go off in the early 1980's that could send home prices sky high, and the detonator may be the new surge of high interest rates, say numerous housing experts.

Ironically, the rapidly rising interest rates are aimed at dampening inflation and reducing excessive credit that has infected most markets, including housing.

These experts, interviewed last week, believe home prices should stabilize and, in some instances, fall slightly as a result of the board's tight-money policies.

But only temporarily. For as mortgages become too expensive for most people, and completely dry up for others, the pressure for housing will intensify, ready to burst as soon as interest rates begin to decline once again.

"People in the prime home buying ages, between 25 and 34, will increase over the next decade at about 660,000 a year," said William Young, an analyst for the National Association of Home Builders.

This is the post-World War II baby-boom generation coming of age.

In recent years, they have been bidding for homes faster than builders could supply them. This helped increase housing prices 13 to 14 percent a year, economists say.

Now this group will be expanding in size, but the building of new houses will slump dramatically. Government officials and private economists say the board's new actions may reduce housing starts next year by as much as 25 percent.

Once the market opens up again, probably in 1981 and no later than 1982, buyers will come flying in, said Ken Kerin, an economist for the National Association of Home Builders.

"That worries me," he added. "But that's what happens when you use housing as the flywheel to keep the economy straight and narrow. Policies designed to solve problems for the next six months affect long-run price stability."

Tough times may be here for awhile . . . but with them will come exciting opportunities for many investors. And almost as sure as the "sun comes up in the morning" these tough times will be followed by a brisk economy. Again opportunities, albeit different ones, will present themselves to the alert investor.

For the past 10-plus years now the American economy has suffered through a series of cycles. And during these times interest rates, the supply of money, number of foreclosures, inflation, etc. has jumped up and down. Many have learned to make financial killings in these cycles . . . using the traditional concepts of buying low and selling high. Only in real estate the name of the game is to leverage your equities, preferably without selling.

I mentioned cycles, so I must also point out the one cycle that HAS NOT TAKEN PLACE. And that is that during the bouncy 60's and 70's the value of real estate has done only one thing—and that has been to increase.

Keep in mind that people will always need a place to live . . . and the single-family home is and will probably always be the most desirable and sought-after living mode. Through this book I'll help you learn how to satisfy the public's demand for this and other types of rental housing and at the same time deservedly line your own pockets.

PART I
Raising Investment Money

*Only one out of ten new businesses survive
more than five years—yet it is almost
impossible to lose money in real estate.*
                        —*Modern Statistics*

1

YOU CAN BE A WINNER

Can I really get rich by buying real estate? Can I truly find financial independence someday through this investment?

The odds are against you. Probably you will buy just one or two properties, giving you a nice, comfortable investment.

Yet I believe that anyone who wants to badly enough *can* and *will be* highly successful in real estate. A million dollars or more can be made in just four or five years. In fact I am going to show you how to do that.

There is a prerequisite to this success, though. And that is *desire*. You must *want* to succeed so badly that you can put other pleasures and needs out of mind and out of sight for at least six or seven years. It can be done . . . but believe me, it's not that easy.

This book is like a roadmap . . . it'll show you how and where to make a lot of money. But it won't lift you up and then miraculously put you at your destination. *You* have to do that!

You can be a winner—no matter how much money you have now or how much you take home each month. Any man, woman, senior citizen, minority, blue collar worker or what-have-you can make a big financial killing in real estate. In fact I will even stick my neck out to say that a person who wants to badly enough can walk away from an unemployment line (right now, today) and end up with a million dollars in less than five years.

You most likely could not do that in the stock market . . . or the bond market . . . or the gold market. But in real estate—well, that's a different ball game, and anything goes.

Now so far I haven't said anything at all about how hard you will have to work to get all your desires. Egad, work you say. "But all the financial opportunity advertisements I read say that once I learn the secret all I do is start collecting my money."

The work—the long hours of looking for property, outfoxing tenants, etc.—is what separates the winners from the losers . . . the millionaires from those who are always getting clobbered by inflation.

I can point the way to a half million dollars in the next five years. That's right, a half million dollars to spend any way you would like. But if you want it you better be prepared to work between 20 and 30 hours a week during that time span. I can also tell you how to make $100,000 in the same five-year span. You might be more comfortable with the $100,000 because you won't have to put in more than a few hours each week.

How would you like to make a million dollars from scratch in five years or less? It can be done, too. But the price you'll probably have to pay is a 50-plus hour week. Of course, for a million dollars you may decide that after your first year or two of investing you can afford to chuck your regular job. I know of several people who have done that and I'll be telling you about them later.

If I have popped your bubble—then good. There is no easy way to make a lot of money in real estate. If you can believe that then maybe you're ready to roll up your sleeves and go to work.

THE FIVE SECRETS OF SUCCESS

Since I wrote *The Monopoly Game*, I have talked with hundreds of other investors. Some have been unbelievably successful . . . a few were merely progressing along . . . and some weren't even able to get started. WHY?

I discovered that the real winners had five basic things in common. The losers also had some common traits. For instance, the losers gave up easily, didn't really understand what they were supposed to do, and they didn't have the determination and self-discipline necessary to stick to a winning investment program.

The successful people . . . well, let me tell you about some of them. And please note: One thing they DIDN'T have in common was race, sex, age, occupation or income.

• One man started in 1970 with just $5,000 . . . and today he is worth almost two million dollars.

• An Arizona waitress has bought and sold over 30 inexpensive homes near a military base. The last I heard was that she owned 20 with a value (her net worth in the properties) of over $350,000.

• A Texas divorcee started from scratch (no money even for her initial down payment) five years ago and today she owns four homes which produce a spendable cash flow of $400 a month.

• A New York man, as well as countless others that I talked with, bought just enough property so that he doesn't pay any federal income taxes.

• In California, one man accelerated the property acquisition plan laid out in *The Monopoly Game* and is now worth one million dollars—and in less than 3 years.

• Many, many others I have talked with are pursuing a more modest program but still have dramatically increased their net worth in just a few years.

From many of these remarkable accounts, I began to see that all the successful people I had talked with (and there were many) had these five traits in common with one another. I call them the FIVE SECRETS OF SUCCESS.

1. BELIEVE IT WILL HAPPEN: Believe! Believe! Believe! First of all you must have confidence in yourself . . . and you must believe that you are capable of making more money than you are presently making. (As strange as it may sound, some people think that they go around with a little black cloud hanging over their head and are thus incapable of doing anything on a grand scale.)

You must also believe in continued inflation. Inflation has always been with us (even before the days of the 5-cent ice cream cone) and will continue to be with us. Ask Uncle Sam—he knows. Isn't he planning bigger and bigger yearly Social Security bites from your paychecks? The government is planning ahead for inflation—shouldn't we be doing the same?

You must be able to believe that today's $75,000 home will be worth $150,000 in the future—if not in 5 years then in 10 years. You don't have to worry about the percentages—only the fact that it is happening.

2. BUY! BUY! BUY! You must buy as much real estate as you can with the smallest down payment possible if you really want to make big money. True, we all have financial or income limitations—but those who can find ways to overcome those limitations (to buy more property) will make a lot of money in a short period of time. Soon I will show you where to get money when you have very little or none at all.

3. DON'T GET DISCOURAGED: There are two points to remember here: Property ownership and market conditions—you can't let either discourage you.

Property ownership brings problems, but the great majority of them will be small. The winning investor does not let himself become discouraged with nagging problems like leaky faucets and unpleasant tenants—but he learns from these situations and resolves to never let them happen again. If you can learn from your mistakes you will then be one step closer to success.

4. KEEP YOUR EQUITIES IN REAL ESTATE: The success of a good idea depends on knowing what to do with it! Haphazard investing will never make you any substantial amounts of money. SET A FINANCIAL

GOAL and then stick to it. After you buy your first property, keep your growing equities working for you. Whether you sell or refinance a property, keep your money working with bigger and better buys. To become rich you must pyramid. Taking money out of your portfolios for long vacations, new boats, etc. can be lots of fun but you will never make as much money as you could if you resist the temptations and leave your investments alone.

5. **LEARN EVERYTHING YOU CAN ABOUT INVESTING:** Learn from your experiences and from the experiences of others. But don't stop there—set aside just one hour each week and read everything about real estate that you can get your hands on. When you meet someone who is successfully investing in real estate (or in any field for that matter) pick his brains. Find out what other successful people are doing, because just one new idea could bring you a $10,000 profit someday.

SINGLE-FAMILY HOME PHENOMENON

You have probably noticed that in the few pages you've read so far I have mentioned the single-family home a lot. I plead guilty . . . and for good reason. Contrary to what some nationally known real estate experts write and say, I believe that the best investment (real estate or otherwise) for the average American is the single-family home (S.F.H.).

But regardless of how I feel about the S.F.H., most of the techniques in DOUBLE YOUR MONEY will apply to any type of real estate investing. I don't care if you are buying 100-unit apartment buildings or if you are simply trying to pick up tips which you can use to buy a personal residence . . . the tested ideas in this book will definitely help you.

And despite the comparisons I am about to make, I do believe that buying and owning apartment buildings (whether 6 or 60 units) is a sound program which cannot help but make you money. But I don't believe it is the *only way* to go nor do I believe it is the best way.

I like the small and individual units—the basic detached single-family home. It is the *number one* best buy because of the simple fact that there is an unparalleled demand in this country for this type of property and the living style it represents. You know—the summer BBQ in the privacy of your own backyard. Can't you just smell the hotdogs and steaks cooking?

The single-family home is *Americana*. It always has been and always will be—even if fewer people will be able to afford to buy one. Because if they can't afford to buy a home—they will still be able to rent one.

What's next in line? I like condominiums, townhouses, duets (two separate units with a common wall not unlike a duplex) and duplexes. Why? Because they are the next best thing to S.F.H.'s. They also afford the resident a great deal of privacy as compared to a big apartment complex.

Without a great deal of trouble, you should be able to agree that most Americans have a strong desire for the S.F.H. Now think about that famous

Will Rogers line that you've probably heard a thousand times: "Buy land, they ain't making it anymore." It's true! We've got to make do with the earth we have because we can't grow any more. That's one reason why all real estate appreciates (goes up) in value. But have you ever noticed that Will Rogers' statement can also be applied to the inexpensive single-family home? Why? Because they simply ain't building them any more!

If you don't believe me . . . check it out. In my Northern California community you can't find a S.F.H. for under $60,000 today, although there is still a good selection available from $70,000 to $90,000. But because of governmental red tape, scarcity of land, higher labor and material costs, etc. the builders in my area are *not building any new homes for under $100,000.*

This figure might be $75,000 in your community, as mine is very high priced. But the undeniable point is there is no way to build additional inexpensive homes. Those "cheapies" we have now are the same ones we'll be using for starter homes or rentals ten years from now. The only difference is that they will be selling for a lot more then.

Following are other key reasons I like the S.F.H. better than apartment buildings. Note that most of the reasons cited have to do with simplicity. When you keep things simple and easy you keep them manageable. Believe me, that can be important.

1. *Valuation:* A home increases in value because of the law of supply and demand. The more pressure for housing, the more the price or rents are apt to increase. Home values are also very sensitive to inflation. As goods and services increase in value, so will the value of your property.

The above is not necessarily true with apartments. Sure, the value of one's building will probably increase with inflation, but the main way an owner of this type of income property increases his value is to increase rents. And that is because this so-called income property is valuated differently from S.F.H.'s. Its value is based upon the income the units bring in and this worth is established by using a relatively complicated formula called the *capitalization rate.*

It's for this reason that thousands of graduates of some of the leading real estate seminars are turned loose looking for small apartment buildings with low rents. The idea is to buy these possibly run-down units, raise the rents and then trade up for a bigger unit which also has low rents.

Do you see what I mean yet by keeping it simple?

2. *Rent Control:* What happens to the buyer of apartment buildings when he gets caught with rent control so he can't raise his rents so he can't raise his value so he can't trade up for a yet bigger building? It happens! The S.F.H. is eliminated from most rent control ordinances.

3. *Tenants:* I would like to know when the last time an owner of an apartment building had a tenant who did work and performed maintenance in such a manner as to increase the value of the building? It happens to me . . . and other owners of S.F.H. . . . all the time. By carefully choosing my

tenants, I have as many as one out of every four actually increase the value of my property. And not by a few hundred dollars but by several thousand!

Why? Because you are usually able to get better and more responsible tenants to rent homes. And they will also stay longer—my tenants average over 2½ years in the property. (See THE MONOPOLY GAME for exact details on how to rent and maintain your property.)

The average S.F.H. tenant is so much easier to handle that I honestly believe it is simpler to manage ten scattered homes than one apartment with twenty tenants under one roof.

4. *All your eggs in one basket:* Is it wise to have all your money tied up in one building, in one neighborhood? I think not. I'll take my properties scattered over a two- or three-mile area. It's safer. That way no natural disaster (like an earthquake or hurricane) can wipe me out and I won't have to worry about a better building with a fancy swimming pool being built down the street which will "steal away" all my tenants.

Financially it is also a plus to have separate units (like the S.F.H.) because I can sell, refinance or encumber with a second mortgage any one, two or three properties that I want to. It gives me my greatest flexibility. And if you don't think flexibility is important, just try getting stuck with all your eggs in one basket (an older 25-unit apartment building, for instance) in the middle of a tight-money, high-interest rate recession, when you can't borrow, refinance or sell. But if you owned ten or more separate homes you would be able to pick one to either sell or borrow against (second mortgage) to temporarily solve your problems.

Well, it's no secret that I think the single-family home is the vehicle which can make you money. Now let's find out how to do it.

THE WAY REAL ESTATE WEALTH IS CREATED

Thousands upon thousands of people are making big money in real estate. These people believe in themselves; then they work hard at buying property; they don't get discouraged; they keep their money working until they reach their goal; and they never stop learning—just about the time you think you know it all you find out you really don't.

It's a lot easier to be a success—if you have a goal. Your goals should be attainable and realistic. They should be written out and a copy kept where you will see it every day. You need to be reminded so you can inspire yourself each day to follow the strategies that will help you attain your goals.

Let's say you have $10,000 that you want to put into a real estate program. (In many areas that's enough to buy two properties.) After talking it over with your family, you decide to go for an income of $50,000 a year and a net worth of one-half million dollars after 10 years.

Set up this 10-year goal in stages. The first stage is to buy just the initial homes. The second stage would be to expand your holdings from two to four or more properties. This would probably be after the second or third year. Also write down how you intend to reach the goal—what strategies or techniques you plan to implement. The final stage of your personalized goal would be the point—about 10 years hence—when you will be able to refinance, sell, etc. so that you can get your $50,000 a year income. Also be sure to list how much time you are willing to put into the program at each stage.

By doing this (keeping a written goal) you will have a much better chance of succeeding. And keep it handy so you'll see it every day—you'll need that constant reminder to keep you from swerving off the path to success.

You have heard the propaganda before about the importance of a positive attitude. Well, hear it out one more time—it is important. Having a written goal is the first step. A second *necessary* step to be a winner is to eliminate all negative thoughts and influences.

Negative thoughts can cloud our thinking. They're like a poison in our bodies. One pessimistic idea breeds others. And pretty soon you go around with a long, sad face, believing in nothing and nobody. You begin to look for the bad in everyone and everything. It's catching . . . and it's disastrous.

How are you *thinking* right now? Are you reading this material with an open mind—awaiting each chapter so you can learn ideas which will help you make money? Or are you mentally "putting down" everything you read because you feel it's a lousy idea and wouldn't work "even if I tried"?

Do you recognize yourself? Which one of the personalities do you think is going to be a winner?

NO EXCUSES ALLOWED

Excuses are not for winners. They are negative and can be destructive. So if you're harboring some, let's get rid of them once and for all.

- NOW IS NOT THE TIME TO INVEST BECAUSE WE'RE HEADING INTO A MAJOR RECESSION OR EVEN A DEPRESSION: Contrary to what most people think, bad times are the best times to get rock-bottom prices in real estate. Sellers will be willing to negotiate and you'll be the one to come up with the best deal.

- INTEREST RATES ARE TOO HIGH: Yes, they are high and it's a problem to consider. But home prices are still going up and I would rather pay a high interest rate than lose a $3,000 to $4,000 profit that would pass me by if I waited for rates to come down. And besides you can always refinance the property a year or two down the road when you can get better interest rates. There is no law, either, that says you must buy property with new financing. There are a multitude of other methods which you can use.

- I DON'T HAVE ANY MONEY: This is only a minor handicap. In forthcoming chapters I'll show you how to use options, partnerships, syndications and bird-dogs. Any one of these ideas can get you started without money.

- MY FIRM MAY BE TRANSFERRING ME: Fantastic—it will give you the opportunity to keep your present home and use it as a rental and buy another one with FHA terms in your new area. (No, this is not practical if you are talking $150,000 homes.) Also, don't be afraid of using professional management or even of doing it yourself—despite the long distance.

- I'M TOO OLD, TIRED, IN BAD HEALTH AND HAVE NO TIME: If you fit this category you're probably just reading this book for the fun of it, or maybe you're a broken-down old real estate salesman who forgot to buy investment properties when you were younger. I hate to disappoint you, but this excuse has an answer, too. Read the chapter on partnerships. Go into business with some energetic young soul who has plenty of time and energy to run around town all day looking for steals. You can make a lot of money this way—and without lifting one tired old finger to do so.

- THE ONLY MONEY I HAVE SAVED IS FOR TAXES AND I AM AFRAID I DON'T EVEN HAVE ENOUGH: Some bureaucrat shuffling papers for the Internal Revenue Service probably won't like my saying this (but then I seldom like anything they say), but don't pay your taxes this one time. File, of course. It's when you don't file that they throw you in jail. Instead, use the money to buy a home or two and then sell or refinance one the next year and pay both years' taxes at once. You'll come out with a free property—courtesy of Uncle Sam. And next year your taxes will be a lot less because you'll have additional tax shelter.

- I'M A SINGLE WOMAN—WHAT CAN I DO: Plenty! Put your boy friends to work helping you fix up dirty dogs. Or locate bargain property for other investors who will repay you with either a bird-dog fee or a percentage of the equity in the property. It might be only a 10 percent interest in a property which may only represent $500 initially. But in five years that 10 percent could mean as much as $5,000. And if you are able to do that three or four times a year . . . well!

- I CAN'T AFFORD THE HIGH NEGATIVE CASH FLOWS—IN FACT I NEED AN INCOME FROM MY INVESTMENT: You can beat the negative cash flow syndrome, but you won't always be able to enjoy the high leverage that some investors are getting. You can also get a positive cash flow from your properties if you are careful in selecting them. I'll tell you how later.

- THE TIME TO BUY REAL ESTATE WAS THREE YEARS AGO— BEFORE EVERYONE ELSE RUSHED INTO THE MARKET: Apparently most people agree with you. In 1975-76-77 literally thousands of speculators and investors rushed into the market as soon as they realized what was happening to real estate values—particularly the single family home. The speculators (short-term investors who want a quick profit without management problems) have already dropped out. And not too many new investors have jumped into the market recently because they believe either that it has topped (it hasn't) or they found it too difficult to get tenants without suffering big negative cash flows.

What we have today is another cycle, not much unlike the 1974-75 recession and the real estate boom which followed. So now is the time to get into the market, before the speculators come back in droves. If you check your newspaper's "for rent" column you'll most likely find that there are few homes for rent in relationship to what is for sale. And if you can get your hands on a newspaper which is two or three years old you will find that the ratio of homes for rent today is dangerously low compared to that period. That means two things: First of all, what you read in the newspapers about a housing shortage is true. And, secondly, as rental properties become scarce, rents will increase, thus eliminating more and more of that negative cash flow.

Enough excuses! It's time to be positive—to be a winner.

"Does it pay to borrow?

Very often it does. The logic is clear when you consider that the domestic buying power of the dollar has been halved in just 11 years. The term borrowing is synonymous with 'paying back in cheaper dollars.' "

—Associated Press article . . .

October 1979

2

MONEY . . . WHERE AND HOW TO GET IT

"Okay, I'm convinced," you say. "But I only make $1,500 a month and $300 of that goes to Uncle Sam. I've got just $500 in the bank, so how can I ever buy real estate with prices and interest rates so high?"

That's what *DOUBLE YOUR MONEY* is all about—showing the moderate income family with just $500 in the bank how they can join their more financially blessed neighbor in buying real estate and creating needed tax shelter. After all, if the federal government can pay some 1.5 million dollars to send New England households a packet of energy-conservation tips and plastic devices to reduce water flow from faucets and shower heads, then Mr. Average Family can certainly shield more of their needed income from the tax collector. By providing rental shelter to families who need a place to live, you are doing more good with the money than the bureaucrats would have ever done.

Here are some proven ways of getting beginning capital so you can start making some decent money for a change. I'll begin with methods which are best used by those without much to start with and finish with both common and unusual ideas that can be employed by the person who already has money, but would like more.

Bird-dog fees: From my real estate sales experience I learned the value of having friends or contacts send listing or sale clients to me. Each one put a lot ·of money in my pocket. A typical real estate agent gets a six percent commission which on a $60,000 sale is $3,600. Normally that amount is divided between two offices and then possibly between two more salesmen. So the commission does get smaller sometimes, but nevertheless your referral can be worth from $200 to $500 largely depending on how well you negotiated a deal for yourself and whether or not you are working with a broker or a salesman.

Some people call this a kick-back. That's what it is in insurance sales and it is illegal there. But in real estate it is a referral fee and is usually legal (check your own state laws) and accepted as long as the person receiving the fee has not done a selling job on the prospect, but has merely passed along his or her name to the real estate salesperson.

Finder's Fee: A finder's fee, for the purposes of this discussion, is a fee paid by a buyer to the person who located or discovered a property in the first place. For instance, you locate a slightly rundown six-unit apartment house that is for sale at a low price. You then contact an investor whom you know is in the market for such property. You have him agree, in writing, to pay you a finder's fee of XX amount of dollars if he decides to buy the property.

Believe me! You can be doing someone a great service (and yourself too) by helping them locate property. I can tell you that there are some really good buys out there. Not many, but perhaps ½ percent of what comes on the market is priced ridiculously low. They get gobbled up. And as you can imagine, they are hard to find, especially when a busy investor has a hundred other things on his mind.

Needless to say a typical investor would be happy to pay $1,000 if you could help him find a property that he could buy for $4,000 beneath market value; or even $2,000 for something priced $7,000 or $8,000 under true value. Or instead of accepting cash, why not ask for 1/10 interest in the property?

As I said earlier—if you want to make money in real estate you are going to have to get off your duff and go to work. Now what better way for a beginner to get started—especially one who is flat broke—than to start looking at every property he can get into. And while you are looking at property and learning, why not find a Realtor you can bird-dog for, or a couple of investors who will agree to pay for what you bring them. Most of the properties you will be seeing won't be listed. If you don't have a real estate license you can't get into listed homes. And you can't ask an agent to cart you around town so you can find property for investors. But keep in mind that "For Sale By Owner" properties often are real steals.

Relatives and Friends: If you are fortunate enough to have a rich father, uncle or spinster aunt, then you may have the number-one best source for borrowing money right at your fingertips. But do it right! Even understanding relatives will only "get taken once."

So impress your friends and relatives right from the start by insisting that you sign a note, pay top interest rates, repay in monthly installments and even offer collateral—even if it's your old jalopy or your wife's diamond wedding ring.

Here are some important points to remember when dealing with relatives. They want you to succeed so they will lean over backwards. But they won't be taken to the cleaners, either. So put their minds at ease by offering them very special collateral—a percentage of the investments. By taking title as a tenant in common you can divide the legal interest in the property and thus can give your benefactor a 1/5 interest in what you are doing. This might be acceptable to them in lieu of interest payments.

Another thing to strive for when borrowing is the right to repay the loan with interest-only payments. Here's why: If you borrowed $10,000 at 10 percent interest with fully amortized payments over a five-year period, you would be repaying this loan at $212.48 per month. Those kinds of repayments, plus any negative cash flows which your property might have, could be the way to fail at the one endeavor which is almost fail-proof. So to prevent yourself from being snowed under, borrow only when you can repay with interest-only payments. On the $10,000 that would be just $83.33 rather than $212.48. The length of the loan should be for at least five years, because after that time you can either sell or refinance and pay back the $10,000 with easy money—the profit you made from "leveraging appreciation."

Life Insurance: If you have a life insurance policy with a cash value then the money is yours for the asking. The interest will be low and there is no great pressure to pay it back. Typically, though, you may only have a few thousand dollars in cash value available. If that's the case you might keep this source available for emergencies.

Credit Union: Many credit unions are now making secondary real estate loans and if you are a member in good standing you can take advantage of this low-interest source.

Banks: Banks are not the first place you will want to look for a loan. They are usually impossible to deal with and are completely unimpressed with your plans to make a lot of money by buying real estate. All that impresses them is whatever security you can put up for the loan. And when money is tight, theirs will be the most expensive. As of this writing, the prime interest rate reached a record-breaking 20 points, which means if I borrow any unsecured money against my line of credit, I would pay well over 22 percent interest. So obviously banks aren't the place to get money when times are tough.

After establishing general credit with your bank, you should try to get a decent line of credit. It is unsecured money and it usually must be paid back in 90 days. I have known these lines of credit to run anywhere from $2,000 to $100,000. It's great money to have available when interest rates are relatively low. But keep in mind that it is interim money (for 90 days or occasionally 180 with approved extensions) and it isn't the answer to long-term financing problems. But you can use it for interim financing. You can buy and then have 90 days to arrange permanent long-term financing. For this reason it is very useful and worthwhile to expend some effort in cultivating a banker. By taking out small loans—either installment or collateral—you can begin to work toward a line of credit. But don't goof by missing any payments along the way or you may lose your chance.

You'll have much better success getting a decent line of credit if you also have a business account with the bank. If that is impossible they may want you to have what is called compensating balances. That means you can borrow any amount you want—if you have up to that same amount in a savings account with the bank. They don't want much, do they!

A good bank, however, will be more lenient than I just described. So shop around for one. With proven credit, at least one major checking account, a small savings account with at least $1,000, and some assurance of proper security for the loan, you should eventually be able to develop a line of credit to about $15,000. It would help if that security could be 200 shares of General Motors stock which could be assigned to the bank in the event you defaulted the loan. Thus stock, bonds or other liquid and assignable assets can be used for a compensating balance.

I know that all of the above sounds like a lot of hassle just so you can get a $15,000 line of credit—someday. But someday you'll find a picture-perfect property you will want to buy. The scenario could go like this: With $15,000 down, the owner will carry the balance with a low-interest purchase money loan. But you must make a decision today—it's a hot buy that isn't going to last on the market. And the seller wants a quick sale and settlement. You are pretty sure you can come up with the $15,000 in 90 days. You have relatives to borrow from and another rental which you might be able to refinance or place a second against. You don't want to lose this good deal, but you need more than just a few days to even know that you can come up with the $15,000. WITH A LINE OF CREDIT YOUR PROBLEM WILL BE SOLVED. You could say "It's in the bank!" You'll be surprised how many times the above-described situation takes place.

"Gene Whitman is not yet a millionaire . . .
but he will be within two years. He is only 33
years old and he works at his property invest-
ment syndication only about one and a half days
a week."   *—From Impact Report*
           WINNING METHODS

3

SYNDICATIONS

A syndication, for our purposes, is not an organization of gangsters but another form of property ownership.

A syndication is another tool which the ambitious investor can use to make a lot of money in real estate—even though he may not have much money himself at the start.

Most syndications are actually limited partnerships. And while they may appear to be terribly complicated at first, once you get down to the basics they really aren't that difficult to operate. The rewards can certainly be high. Here's what I mean:

In 1979 I wrote an Impact Report (a subscription service publication) about Gene Whitman, a rather remarkable young man who is currently making a lot of money with syndications. He is only 33 years old and he works at his property investment syndication only about one and a half days a week.

It all started for Gene in 1975 when he finally decided to do what he had always thought about doing since his college days—and that was to buy a single-family home for his first investment. Only one problem stood in his way—and it appeared to be a big one. He didn't have any money, but he did have a good job at a California University and a modest contemporary home in the hills.

Gene was motivated then because he really wasn't happy with his job which he felt was limiting his abilities and engulfing him in a work-life-style which boringly laid out in advance what he had to do until the day he would retire. The heck with that, he thought. So, with no money, Gene set out to find a better way of making a living.

Gene got together with his brother and borrowed $6,000 from understanding relatives — enough to buy his first rental home. They assumed an FHA loan and had the seller carry back a purchase money second deed of trust for $4,000.

So far so good! With that indescribably warm feeling you get as a new property owner, Gene became even more motivated to buy. For money he turned to the only other available source he had — his residence. He decided to refinance.

He bought three single-family homes next. He financed them with a conventional loan, a VA assumption and a contract of sale. For the time being this was as far as he could go with his investment plans — he was almost out of money and all of the properties he owned were leveraged to the hilt.

But what happened next is what made Gene Whitman successful. He took a course of action that was to separate him from the many thousands of investors who are content to sit back and wait for property equities to grow before they buy again.

Gene could not sit idly by and accept the answer that he was stopped — even temporarily. Remembering a friend who was into syndications, Gene decided to look into this alternative. First he read every book about syndications that he could get his hands on. The next thing he did was work out a unique and original syndication plan which he took to a prestigious and high-priced San Francisco law firm.

They told him his idea was workable and then proceeded to create the agreement which he would later use. The cost was $2,000. Gene admits that this action was the most risky thing he had ever done with money, but later it paid big dividends for him. To this day he feels that without this agreement prepared by a recognized group of attorneys, he never would have gotten his first group going. And there never would have been a second group if the first had failed.

Gene believed that his syndication agreement would be the key to his success or failure — and he was right. His first investors were properly impressed with it. So much, in fact, that he exceeded his wildest dreams when he signed up nine investors who put in a total of $80,000. He had only expected to get $20,000. After this happy beginning, things began to roll.

Gene's unique agreement was designed to appeal to the average person who wanted some tax shelter plus a good return on his dollar. It was not designed to appeal to the individual who wants to get rich overnight. The terms called for the investors (limited partners) to receive 13 percent annually, but payable on a regular quarterly basis. They would also get a lot of tax shelter — as much as a $2,500 write-off annually on each $5,000 invested. For the right person these terms represented quite a deal then because they sure as heck beat out whatever plans savings and loans could ever offer. And what was important to Gene was that his agreement would be acceptable to the IRS—if it had not been, it wouldn't be worth the paper it was written on.

What makes Gene's syndication different from others is that it offers investors no real growth potential, but a lot of security. For instance, the 13 percent is a share in the profits, but a limited share. Gene receives most of the capital gains. Payment of the quarterly returns was assured by reserving a small amount of the $80,000 (initial investments raised) for this purpose. After a few years, however, this would not be necessary as the 13 percent return would be met easily by either selling or refinancing a small part of the portfolio.

Here are some of the other key elements in Gene's syndication agreement:

- The partnership has no time limit. It could last for one year or 10 to 20 years. It's basically up to Gene. If the real estate market ever took a bad turn, he could then bring the syndication to an abrupt end. But any limited partner wanting out can have his share purchased within 90 days. Gene feels that this clause gives his people a lot of liquidity. A liquidity, he says, that is only possible because his investment portfolio consists entirely of single family homes which can be easily sold, refinanced or encumbered with a second mortgage. Gene says that a few investors have asked to get out of the agreement in the past, but it is never a problem as he has always had others who wanted to get in.

- The agreement allows Gene to buy out any limited partner with six months notice. He must also give a six-month notice if he decides to close up shop.

- By the terms of the agreement, Gene personally invests a portion of his own money in all of the partnership properties. And he cannot withdraw this money until the partnership is liquidated. This concept, according to Gene, instills a lot of confidence in the investors.

- Gene uses his name and good credit to buy each of the houses and to qualify for any loan which might be needed. In this way he acts as an agent for the syndication. After escrow is closed he gives the deed to an attorney who holds it on behalf of the limited partners. Gene says that it is much easier to buy property this way because most bankers just don't understand partnerships. They don't see the profit accumulating, but only the tax losses and then, of course, they can't justify lending money to a group which is "losing money."

Needless to say, Gene Whitman is making a lot of money with his unique syndication. The point I want to make with his story is that even though syndications can be complicated, the average investor can create his own (and have the proper clauses drawn by competent attorneys) or even go into the offices of attorneys who specialize in such agreements and have a workable one drawn up. They have all the parts, and all that must be done is to put together the ones that are right for you. But one word of warning—there are penalties for misuse of syndications, so you better be sure that you are fairly competent in real estate. You also must fully understand the syndication laws that apply in your state.

HOW A SYNDICATION WORKS

So that you can quickly decide whether or not a syndication might be for you . . . I am going to cover some of the things you should know.

Some of the basic advantages *for the syndicator* are that it is a way to obtain equity in a tax shelter investment with either little or no cash outlay. The syndicator's "investment" will be mostly one of time and knowledge. By forming a syndication, the syndicator can control greater purchasing power and can diversify the investments into various types of real estate, thus not putting all the eggs in one basket.

The financial rewards are usually very attractive. For instance, the syndicator can be paid for managing the portfolio as well as receive 25 percent of the equities as his fee for putting together and operating the group. These figures are not usually set by law, but negotiated by the syndicator.

Another advantage is derived from the fact that many large groups of investors, all with equal power, do not work out. For instance, ten equal partners can bring upon themselves a lot of trouble and confusion. Too many cooks simply spoil the broth. But with a ten-person syndicate in which one (the syndicator) is the general partner and the remaining nine are limited partners (investors) this problem is eliminated. Why? Because by the terms of the limited partnership the investors must refrain from participating in the day-to-day operations of the business. I'll tell you more about this shortly.

Although you can have a syndication that is not a limited partnership entity, most real estate syndications are this type; so I'll limit my discussions to them. Thus, as a limited partnership, an additional benefit is that the business enterprise may be treated as an ordinary partnership for income tax purposes. There is no tax at the partnership level, unlike the corporation which pays a corporate income tax.

The disadvantages of a limited partnership syndication are basically the many laws with which the syndicator must comply. Syndications are real estate security offerings; over 100 government agencies have jurisdiction! Also, the general partner assumes all liability beyond the capital contributions of the limited partners.

Let's take a closer look at the rights, duties and obligations of the partners:

The General Partner:

The general partner assumes all liability beyond the capital contributions of the limited partners. This includes losses, the obligation on Trust Deeds and other encumbrances and any other liability. The general partner has complete charge of the operation of the Partnership business, managing it in accordance with the Partnership Agreement and various regulatory laws. He must make full and complete disclosure of all aspects of the operation of the Partnership business through reports and meetings of the investors. The general partner has a right to share in the profits, but generally subordinates this right to the right of the limited partners to receive the first disbursement of profits. The general partner may be removed by the limited partners if he does not perform in a satisfactory manner.

The Limited Partners:

The limited partners must contribute the agreed amount of capital. Their liability is limited to the amount of agreed capital contribution. They must refrain from participating in the day-to-day operations of the business to maintain this exemption from liability. The limited partners have the right to vote on major issues affecting the conduct of the business. They have the right to have the Partnership run in strict accordance with the Partnership Agreement and applicable regulatory laws. They have the right to replace the general partner if he does not perform in a satisfactory manner. The limited partners have the right to inspect all books and records relative to the conduct of the Partnership business. Generally, the limited partners have the right to the disbursement of profits before participation in the profits by the general partner.

As I mentioned earlier, there are a lot of state and federal regulations that you will have to deal with, although there are "exemptions" which help make the syndicator's task a little easier than it might first appear.

Noncompliance with regulatory requirements can result in severe criminal, civil, and administrative actions. You must take time to learn what the basic laws and regulations are. One of the more ominous agencies that you will have to contend with is the Security and Exchange Commission (SEC). They come into the picture because of the federal Securities Act of 1933. Basically when an investment is sold on the basis of a continuing management involvement by either the sponsor or a third party, and when investors purchase property for a return rather than solely for their own personal use, the attributes of an investment contract are present. Thus the SEC has jurisdiction over most syndications.

But you can get out from under the wing of the SEC. For instance, you can apply for an exemption. If you can't get an exemption, you must register your offering with the SEC. The most common of the exemptions are the

INTRASTATE and the PRIVATE PLACEMENT.

The intrastate exemption applies where the sponsor, investors, all officers, and the business of the syndicate offering are all contained within the boundaries of a single state. To qualify, the offering must comply with the letter and not merely the spirit of this provision. The specific guidelines as to what is and what is not an intrastate offering are covered in Rule 147, a release by the SEC that interprets and clarifies the basic legislation.

The private placement exemption applies when a transaction is not a "public offering." In other words, what is significant is the relationships between those involved (did they know each other prior to the offering?), their level of sophistication, the manner of the offering, and the size and nature of the investment. So to qualify, the offering must meet this type of criteria, plus there must not be more than 35 investors and only 10 in some states.

HOW TO START YOUR OWN SYNDICATE

How easily can you get started making good profits with your own syndication? It isn't really that hard to do. First of all, you must make sure that you fully understand investment real estate. It would certainly help if you had some sort of track record with investments. Would you want to invest $5,000 or $10,000 with a syndicator who would be buying his very first rental home?

The next step is to read a good book or two about syndications. They are not hard to find as most large libraries will have a good selection. One I can recommend is *How to Invest in Real Estate Syndicates*, by Daniel A. Miller. Or you can write Impact Publishing Company, 1601 Oak Park Blvd., Pleasant Hill, CA 94523, and for $9 you may purchase the Impact Report *Syndications and Partnerships* by Tom Binford. It's an excellent 28-page Report which is good first reading for the beginning syndicator. This Report may be purchased for considerably less when subscribing to Impact Reports. See the special order coupon in the back of this book and find out how you can buy this Report at a discount.

After you have a better understanding of syndications, you'll want to devise a rough plan. For instance, what kind of property will you be buying and how much money will you be asking each of your limited partners to contribute? Then take your ideas to an attorney who either specializes in this type of real estate syndicate or who has drawn several such syndication agreements in the past. This is important. Your best friend may be a competent attorney—but if he does not understand this type of law you will probably pay the price later on. Get off on the right foot. You might also want to meet with a tax expert.

In addition to your partnership agreement, you'll need an *offering circular*. Again, your attorney will help you prepare one. Your offering circular will contain such things as an introductory statement, purpose of the partnership, plan of operation, etc. It is basically used to introduce the prospective limited partners to your syndication.

Your next step is to contact everyone you know who would be a candidate for your limited partnership. Be sure they can afford to invest the amount of money you will be asking from them.

The approach I like is to invite all those who are interested to a dinner (you should pick up the tab too; what's a couple hundred dollars when you stand to make several thousand). When inviting these friends and business acquaintances to this dinner, be sure to tell them to come prepared to make a significant decision that night. You want to make your presentation and then get commitments on the spot. If someone drags you on, you both run the risk of losing interest in the project. And needless to say, the more professional a job you do with your presentation, the better chance you will have of succeeding.

If this sounds like too much work, then you probably are not cut out for the life of a general partner. But keep one thing in mind. Almost every syndicator that I have ever talked with says that the first one is the hardest. After a year or two of success, you'll have people knocking on your door to get into your second syndication.

4

RICH MAN-POOR MAN PARTNERSHIPS

If you've got a good job that provides a lot of security and a big paycheck but is over-demanding on your personal time, then a partnership may be the way for you to invest in real estate. In a simple "rich man-poor man" partnership, you would simply get together with a skilled investor, advance all or most of the partnership cash, and participate in some important decisions.

However, if you don't have a big bank account but are loaded with investment skills and that important ingredient called "time," you too are a good candidate for a two-partner partnership.

This type of partnership should be a good "marriage" . . . and its success depends heavily on how well you put it together at the beginning.

Terms such as limited partnerships, syndications, and joint ventures have a mysterious ring about them which seems to be more than enough to scare away the casual investor. And that's too bad! Because you can be the loser. Real estate partnerships are not just for the "big boys" who throw around millions of dollars. A lot of average people are making a killing today in real estate because they have taken the time to learn about, and become involved in, small real estate partnerships. With this chapter I'll point you in a successful direction—but what you do is up to you.

These simple and small partnerships which I am about to tell you of are related to limited partnerships discussed in the last chapter. They are also akin to Real Estate Investment Trusts (REIT's), Corporations, and joint ventures. Why? One reason is because they are all legal ways of owning real estate. And they are all governed by a maze of state and federal laws.

Small general partnerships also come under the wings of the Security and Exchange Commission. Why? Because whenever two people get together to buy real estate (except husband and wife) a security may be involved. The California Supreme Court, for instance, has held that a security is involved if an offering is made to a single purchaser "selected at random from the public."

Even though any small partnership you may form will come under the auspices of both federal and state securities laws, you should not have to worry about it because of two things. First of all, exceptions are allowed. Thus if you have what is called a *private offering*, you will not have to register your partnership with the government agencies. A private offering, as the name implies, cannot be advertised to the general public. It also requires a limited number of investors and that all parties to the agreement have a similar or fairly substantial financial background.

The second reason why you shouldn't get overly concerned with the sometimes complicated maze of bureaucratic red tape, departmental rulings and stacks of precedent-setting court decisions is that you should never put together a partnership or syndication without hiring a competent attorney. He or she should be fully versed and experienced in such matters. THIS IS AN IMPORTANT TIP—DON'T FORGET IT. You don't want just an attorney—you need one who specializes in these partnership matters. While any attorney can, by law, put together a partnership, you will be much better off (legally and financially) if you go to a pro and tell him what aspects you want your agreement to contain. Having done this before he will be able to tell you exactly what state laws require and be able to draft an agreement incorporating your ideas together with other standard clauses which he knows are important. An attorney who specializes in nothing but divorces may take on this task, but he will have to put in a lot of extra research time; and there is a good chance he will make a mistake or two along the way.

The partnerships I speak of in this chapter are easy to set up—but only when you hire the right legal help. By the way, the fee for this should run between $250 and $1,000, depending somewhat on how many of your own unique ideas you may want put into the agreement.

ADVANTAGES AND PITFALLS

As I said before, there are few differences between the limited partnership which was discussed in the previous chapter, and the Rich Man-Poor Man Partnership, which for our discussion will be considered a general partnership and referred to as such throughout this chapter. The differences are subtle, but they can be important.

The most important of the differences has to do with liability. If a limited partner, for instance, does not allow his name to be used in the business and does not participate in management, then he is not responsible for firm debts beyond his investment. However, at least one partner must be a general partner and take on unlimited liability.

In a general partnership the liability extends to all partners. There is basically an agency relationship between the partners making each the agent of the other, insofar as partnership business is concerned. This means that there is an equal participation of members in management and a co-ownership of partnership assets. It does not matter that one partner is basically contributing the money to the partnership and that the other partner is doing the bulk of the work—what is important is that both partners have a decision in what is done. Thus the partner buying property should obtain the permission and signature of the other partner on the deposit receipt when purchasing an investment unit.

The pros and cons of these two approaches cannot be answered here but must be weighed against all given facts when you are putting together your own group. For instance, two well-financed partners who have known each other for several years should be able to live comfortably with the shared liability aspects of the general partnership.

But the guy who is approached by a slick stranger wearing suede shoes and a $300 suit will perhaps feel more secure in a limited partnership, where if something does go wrong he will be only out the money he personally invested.

Another advantage of the general partnership is that it is a more personal relationship. Both partners have a voice in running the partnership business, therefore it is both safer and possibly more profitable for the participants. This type of partnership is usually formed by people who know and trust each other. It is born out of a mutual desire to make money together.

Although not always true, many of the larger syndications (limited partnerships) are formed by the general partner(s) for one purpose only—and that is to make a profit. And many of these organizers (the general partner of the limited partnership) are looking for profits up front.

Both types of partnerships will be under the wings of federal and most state securities laws, but there is less concern when beginning and operating a typical small general partnership. This is partially because of the recruitment methods you have to implement with each type of partnership. It is one thing to locate an acquaintance with $40,000 to $50,000 to spend in a general partnership as compared to finding as many as ten limited partners to invest anywhere from $2,000 to $20,000 apiece. When going after the larger numbers, a promoter is more apt to cross over the accepted lines of recruitment, and thus bring down the many laws which govern his activities.

I often speak of the general partnership as though it is only between two parties. You can have as many as you want (depending upon which type of security offering you are willing to make, public or private) but I firmly believe that your most effective partnership will be with just two or three principals. One reason is that you must have a division of duties or else you run the risk of having all kinds of problems. When you start taking turns showing property to prospective tenants, that's when the trouble starts. I therefore strongly recommend the rich man-poor man style partnership where the duties are clearly defined in the partnership agreement.

TYPICAL GENERAL PARTNERSHIP STRUCTURE

Following are some of the more important aspects of a general partnership agreement. It is based upon the one I personally use. You may wish to use some of the concepts, or your attorney may recommend wording which is completely opposite to mine but proper for your state. Much of what is in the agreement is a matter of personal choice—for instance, how the profit is divided among the partners.

1. PURPOSE: It's a good idea to state the purpose of your partnership and to set the limits. For instance: "The partnership has been formed for the purpose of engaging in the business of investing in real property, particularly, single family residential rental property, for the production of income and long-term capital gain." This prevents a partner from getting off on a tangent like buying a series of coin-operated snow cone vending machines.

2. TERM: How long should the partnership last . . . 5 years, 10 years or until the death of either of the partners? Your agreement will probably not be valid without a termination date or a method which can be used to terminate the agreement, unless you are designing a partnership (a joint venture) for just one project. Give yourselves enough time to properly make money. And that time would be about ten years so you could buy, later sell or refinance, and then run that cycle over again. After the ten years you could either rewrite the partnership agreement or even just divide the properties—that way there will be no sale to trigger extra tax burdens.

3. INITIAL CAPITAL CONTRIBUTIONS AND OWNERSHIP INTERESTS: Needless to say this is a very important section. In a typical rich man-poor man partnership, one person is putting up all the cash and the other is doing all the work. (But remember, important decisions are to be shared.)

I can't tell you what would be fair. Each partnership can and probably will be distinctly different. For the sake of example, in my partnership my partner gets back his original investment plus 10 percent interest, which is compounded annually, and then he receives 50 percent of what is left and I get 50 percent. Thus if he invests $100,000 and after ten years the property is sold and $500,000 is realized, he will get back his $100,000 plus about

$130,000 in interest. The remaining $270,000 would be divided giving us each $135,000.

Not a bad return for either partner. One puts up the money and has relatively little worry. The other advances no cash but a lot of blood, sweat and tears.

4. ADDITIONAL CONTRIBUTIONS: In my agreement "The cash contributing partner is liable for the first $275 of negative cash flow (all property expenses) and any sums over that will be divided equally among the partners." This need not be part of your agreement, however, because you can structure your investments so as not to have a negative cash flow. Any unusual or unexpected expenses can be taken care of out of an emergency contingency account which could be set up, with say $2000, at the time the partnership begins its business.

5. DUTIES OF SERVICING CONTRIBUTING PARTNER: Obviously a good legal agreement will carefully spell out the duties of each participating partner. It is especially important when it comes to the partner who will be getting a "piece of the rock" for merely his labors throughout the years. As management duties are the crux of a real estate partnership, careful consideration must be given to this point, as well as penalties for failure to perform.

6. DISTRIBUTIONS OF NET PROCEEDS OF OWNERSHIP, SALE AND REFINANCING OF PARTNERSHIP PROPERTY: This section spells out the priority of equity and profit distribution. It also tells how to allocate any losses the partnership may incur and it goes into the all-important question of taxes.

If your agreement does not call for equal capital contributions and tax loss benefits, you will need to consult with a tax expert. This is because the government is suspicious of someone getting tax shelter when he does not contribute capital to the partnership. This is one of those grey areas where there never seems to be a right or a wrong—so get advice.

In my agreement, the tax liability and/or depreciation and other tax shelter benefits are to be allocated to and/or paid for "by the individual partners in the same manner and proportion as the distributions of profits."

7. SALARIES AND EXPENSES: You probably won't have a partner receiving a salary, but you will have to carefully say how a partner is to be reimbursed for out-of-pocket expenses. You'll probably also want to place a ceiling on the amount of money that can be reimbursed in any one month.

As I am a licensed real estate Broker, my agreement goes one step further than yours might. I have specified that I will not take or receive any commissions for my efforts with the partnership. This does not mean that I will not take a commission on behalf of the partnership but it does say that I won't personally pocket any such money.

Why limit myself? Because I believe that my partner must completely trust my ability and judgment and he should never, even for a moment, think that I might be buying property (any property) just to get a commission. And by the same token, I don't want to ever be tempted to forego searching for the best buys just so I can get the job over with and earn a commission. If my partner isn't going to personally inspect each property I select (he may or may not), then he must be assured that the package (property and financing) is the best one available.

8. **TRANSFER OF INTEREST:** Neither partner in my agreement is given the automatic right "to sell, assign, or otherwise transfer or encumber his partnership interest" without prior written consent of the other partner. But partners are given the right to withdraw from the partnership at the end of any calendar year, after the partnership has been in effect for two full years. The agreement is drawn, of course, so that the withdrawal of a partner shall have no long-term adverse effect on the continuance of the partnership. The remaining partner can either choose to buy out, replace with another partner, or liquidate the partnership.

9. **DEATH OR DISABILITY OF PARTNER:** Any partnership agreement must deal with the question of what to do in the event of a death or permanent disability of either partner. One answer to this problem is to have each partner hold a life insurance policy on the other. Thus in case of death, enough cash would be raised to allow the surviving partner to buy out the deceased partner's half.

Another way to handle this problem is to have each partner agree to sell and transfer to the surviving partner all of his rights, title and interest in the partnership as of the time of death. This empowers the executors, administrators or other legal representatives to cause this transfer upon payment in full of the purchase price. This does two things: First of all you won't get a third party, like a son, daughter or brother wiggling into your partnership. And secondly, this agreement will circumvent many of the problems which you would otherwise have during the probate period.

The purchase price referred to is also predetermined by the agreement. While it does not set out the exact dollar amounts, it does spell out a formula (i.e., the hiring of M.A.I. appraisers) for determining the values of the property and thus the partnership equity.

And don't worry about where such large amounts of money will come from. Except for the first few years of the partnership, there will be enough property and equity so that in all probability these assets can be divided rather than sold. This won't be possible, however, if the partnership holds just one 20-unit apartment building with a large equity. But if the partnership holds six single-family homes then a 60/40 property division, for example, with just a minor transference of cash to help balance the books can easily be accomplished.

11. **OTHER ITEMS:** Needless to say, a lot more goes into a partnership agreement. Your attorney will guide you and supply additional items he feels are necessary. One item in particular you might want to ask him about is a *CONSENT OF SPOUSE* form. Basically this says spouses are aware of the provisions of the partnership and that any assets transferred to the partnership shall be subject to its provisions and buy and sell clauses. Their signature affixed to this document says that they are aware and do consent to the agreement.

Another significant part of your agreement is how each partner will handle taxes and allowable write-offs. Don't overlook this aspect—and if your attorney cannot supply you with the answers then you should consult a qualified tax advisor.

HOW TO FIND YOUR PARTNER

You cannot put an ad in the newspaper to find a partner. I'll admit that would be the easy way, but "big brother is watching" and he says no. And there are substantial reasons for this. When you are investing a big portion of your net worth, you want to make sure that you are dealing with qualified people—not strangers.

So the best way to find a partner is to carefully go over lists of people you know like relatives, neighbors, friends, and co-workers. If you plan to contribute the cash, then you'll want to find someone with exceptional talent, integrity, and spare time. One possibility is your real estate agent, or if that is not feasible, perhaps another agent that you may meet. You might find this quality agent by looking for investment property with several salespeople. When you find one who particularly impresses you, then pop the question. He is in an excellent position to be your partner (if his company policy will allow it) and when an agent stops to think about it—a good partnership will mean more money in the long run than taking a commission in the short run.

I realize this is a big question to cover in such a short space. But keep your Realtor in mind. They have the time and the knowledge. But just like attorneys, they come in all stripes. Find one who is experienced (about 7 out of 10 new agents fail during their first year in the business), one who is totally familiar with the type of real estate investment you'll be looking for and one who won't try to bleed you for sixty percent of the equities, **plus** management fees, **plus** full commissions.

On the other side of the coin is the person with the talent and time who is seeking Mr. Moneybags. Again, go through the same source of people, but this time try to think of someone who has money, investment knowledge, and job security, but may be short on time. There are literally hundreds of thousands of people who need tax shelter, who need to supplement their future retirement income, but who do not have the time or the experience to do it themselves. Some of the people who do have the time cannot invest in a practical manner because they live in very high cost areas where they would have to buy $125,000 houses which would bring large negative cash flows. Now if you happen to live in a good investment area where you can buy homes for $75,000 or so and rent them out at almost break-even, you are in an excellent position to convince friends from high cost areas.

There is probably no better way today for an eager young investor who has very little money of his own to make it, than through the partnership vehicle.

YOU SHOULD KNOW YOUR PARTNER

It's obvious that you will want to know everything you can about your partner's experience and ability. But don't just concentrate on the obvious. Find out all you can about the person's financial history, his (or her) available cash and net worth.

Now this isn't so important when you are considering the qualifications of Mr. Moneybags. He'll put up an amount of cash and for the most part that should be that. But this can be vital when considering the "worker." Even though the service-contributing partner may not be required to put any or very much cash into the partnership, you must be assured that he has substantial enough means so he won't eventually leave behind a trail of creditors who'll be slapping judgments and liens against your properties. Therein lies the risk to the general partnership, so select carefully. The rewards for this kind of investing can be great, so lay your groundwork with proper diligence. The sky is your limit!

"Left breathless by the dizzying rise in value of the house they live in, more and more Americans have come to see real estate as the one investment that offers protection against inflation." —Money Magazine, March 1979

5

CASH FROM YOUR HOME

Your investment decisions would be so easy . . . if only everything remained constant; if the cost of living increased by exactly 10 percent each year; and if you had a lifetime guarantee of an excellent job with fat annual raises.

Your money put into investments—any investment—would be predictably safe if you could chart the future. But predictability isn't what life has in store for us. You've got to stick your neck out and do what you think is the best thing.

Real estate—especially single-family home investments—has been a tremendously good investment over the past ten years and all indications are strong that it will continue to be in the next ten. But even so it takes some good old fashioned "guts" to pull money out of your personal residence and invest it in other properties. The future is uncertain. There are stumbling blocks. And these things must be reckoned with before you mortgage your "castle" to the hilt.

If you are like most people who are reading this book, you probably own your home or condominium. And you probably have more equity in this property than in all of your other assets combined. The temptation will be great to take a significant portion of your equity and buy two or three rental properties. It's obvious you'll be able to make a lot more money—and much faster too—than you would if you merely saved until you could buy just one. In the past it has worked out that way for a lot of investors I know. By starting with $30,000 or so retrieved from their residence in '76 and '77, many of them today have close to one-half million dollars in equity.

But this book is about today—and the future—and as I indicated before, we can get a blurred vision of the future but we can't accurately predict it. So before I tell you how you can get money out of your residence, let's first see if it makes sense for you to do so.

It's a very personal decision, whether or not to pull equity out of your home. This decision should be based largely upon the stability of your present job; your income level; your age; the particular investment opportunity; and the economic conditions at the time.

Your job obviously is important. Without one how would you be able to make the higher payments that will come with either a second mortgage or refinancing. Be totally honest with yourself. Will you still have your job five years down the road? If you are self employed, ask yourself whether you will be making more money in five years . . . or could you possibly be out of business?

Age, of course, is a state of mind. But you must ask yourself whether or not you are physically up to taking a loss. If you are 35 years old and your investment goes sour then you are still young enough (and hopefully have the energy it takes) to rebound and start building over again. But if you are 63 and looking forward to retirement a few years hence, maybe a loss would be a very serious matter for you. Sure, you will have a hard time losing money in real estate . . . but you can get in over your head. So you had better ask yourself this question: If I add $300 to my monthly home mortgage, and buy two rental properties which will cost me another $200 a month, what if everything goes sour and I end up with two vacant rental homes; will I be able to carry this burden?

As I say, this may never happen, but if it would mentally or physically destroy you if it did, perhaps you had better be conservative and leave the equity in your home. There will be other good ways to invest so that you don't have to bury yourself in debt. I'll tell you about those shortly.

You must also analyze the particular investment opportunities. If you would merely be buying two average properties with normal terms at market value prices, then you might want to give a lot of thought to taking money out of your residence. But if you are faced with the buy of a lifetime—a chance to buy a $75,000 home for just $60,000 because the seller is only days away from losing the property through foreclosure—then you may not want to think twice about further encumbering (borrowing against) your residence.

You must also consider the economic conditions that may or may not affect your investment plans. In tough times and steep recessions you will find a lot of good buys similar to the one I just described. But also keep in mind that during bad times some of your tenants may not pay their rent too regularly—or perhaps not pay at all.

Don't just leap without considering all of the factors. Your home is precious. It's a good source for investment cash . . . but only when you fully understand and can balance the pitfalls against the benefits. If the benefits win out, then take your cash and invest it wisely.

Here are the three main ways of getting money from your residence: selling, refinancing and encumbering with a junior mortgage.

SELLING

While selling your home to raise investment cash will probably be your last choice (it would be mine), it does deserve mention here because in some states (Texas, for instance) there is a law which effectively prohibits an investor from refinancing or second mortgaging to get investment cash. Thus, the only real answer is to sell—especially if your home is worth $100,000 and if the first mortgage is only $20,000. But if you really like your home and neighborhood, selling would not be a viable alternative.

One advantage of selling is that you can raise extra investment cash without necessarily putting yourself into debt with higher mortgage payments.

For the right person, an annual ritual of buying and selling a personal residence can be very rewarding. For instance, the best terms are always given to *owner-occupants*. They usually pay less down and get lower interest rates for new conventional loans than would an investor. They can also buy homes with low down FHA terms. Thus, for the right person—a single man or woman, or perhaps someone whose company is moving him every few years—buying a home with low down terms every year or so can be quite rewarding. In this way a person could buy a home a year (keep it) and after ten years would have a string of rentals—all bought with the most favorable financing available.

The cash for the downpayments would come from a combination of savings and that money raised by refinancing existing homes.

Granted, this method would take a lot of work. Be assured that there are easier ways of making money in real estate.

REFINANCING

If you've got the itch to get into real estate investments but are short on funds, you might want to seriously look into refinancing your residence. If you can pull enough money out of your home the higher costs may be worth it—if you don't squander the money on vacations, new furniture, new clothes and other fun things.

The only truly acceptable diversion for the serious investor would be debt consolidation. For instance, refinancing will raise your monthly payments. But if you can find a way to either soften the blow, or at least on paper eliminate the additional expense, then refinancing can make a lot of sense for you.

Here is what I mean: Suppose your current monthly house payment is

$300 but after refinancing it will jump to $600. Sure, you pull $30,000 cash out of your home, but is the price (additional $300 a month) worth it? Well, if you owe the department store $1,500 ($75 monthly); the bank $1,200 ($110 monthly) for your '77 car; and the finance company $2,300 ($125 monthly) for a new boat, you are a good candidate for refinancing. By paying off these debts you will only spend $5,000 of the $30,000 and you will eliminate $310 of your new payment, slightly more than the increase you will face by refinancing.

Of course not everyone will be able to do what I just described. And even if you can, it really isn't a way of getting $25,000 for free . . . it just seems like it. It's a psychological advantage. But don't discount matters of the mind. Negative attitudes or pessimistic outlooks are what keep most people from making money in real estate.

If and when you decide to refinance, you must carefully weigh all the facts involved. Here are four factors which you must consider.

1. **YOUR REASON FOR REFINANCING:** As I said earlier—you better have a good reason for the extra cash or else you are just putting yourself deeper in debt. A good reason, of course, would be to buy one or two rental properties with the money you get. The better the buy (say $5,000 under true market price) the more sense it makes to refinance.

2. **THE COSTS INVOLVED:** Here's the bad news. It costs a lot of money to refinance. You might be hit with a prepayment penalty on your current loan, you certainly will have to pay new loan fees and escrow and settlement charges, plus you will almost certainly be paying a higher interest rate.

Today's interest rates are extremely high—and what these higher rates are doing to your payments is almost criminal. For instance if you borrowed $60,000 at 7 percent for a 30-year term you would repay principal and interest at $399 a month. But if you are forced to pay 12 percent interest this same $60,000 will cost you $617 for P&I. If, by some miracle, interest rates were still at 7 percent, you could buy a home with a $90,000 mortgage and pay only about $617.

The point of this exercise in high interest rates is this: At this writing interest rates exceed 12 percent in most parts of the country. A lot of people have quit buying property at these high rates. They are waiting to sell or refinance when rates are lower—say 10 percent. But here is what will happen. When rates start to come down a little—just one or two percentage points less—buyers will start to rush back into the market and loan funds will again get scarce. So this demand will again push interest rates up. It's a cycle that has happened before and will happen over and over again.

Be aware of cycles—it will cost you a lot less to refinance when rates are lower, but don't get caught by waiting too long. You will probably never see normal interest rates drop by more than 2 percent in a six-month period.

Thus the most expensive portion of a refinance is the higher interest rates. Your other costs, although high, should not usually exceed four percent of the total loan amount. You should shop around too for the best lender. All lending institutions have different policies and varying costs. A few phone calls might just save you $500.

3. **YOUR TAX POSITION**: With all other criteria equal—it makes a lot more sense for the person in a higher tax bracket to refinance than it does the fellow in a lower bracket. Your added costs—like the $300 in the example I just gave—is mostly interest and that is tax deductible. So if you are in a 50 percent tax bracket, half of the $300 per month will be saved from the clutches of the tax collector.

But if you are a poor soul like me and pay no taxes because of the tax shelter provided from real estate investments, then there will be no additional tax benefits to be gained from the extra $300 in monthly mortgage payments. So obviously, I am going to think a lot harder about the merits of refinancing than someone who is making $100,000 a year and has very little tax shelter.

4. **LENDER AVAILABILITY**: This factor also has something to do with costs. If you have a conventional loan on your property with XYZ Savings & Loan, odds are that you will also have a prepayment penalty. Often these penalties can be as high as six months interest—which will translate into several hundred dollars. If you go to lender ABC and set up a refinance, you will find that ungrateful XYZ will zap you with the prepayment penalty. You would think they would be happy to have a 7 or 9 percent loan turned in so they could put out the funds again at 11 or 12 percent. But it doesn't work that way unless you let XYZ do the refinancing.

As each bank or savings and loan has its own peculiar policies, you'll run into different situations all the time. But usually you can negotiate a good deal for yourself which could include a full elimination of the prepayment fee. And don't forget that you'll have to qualify for the higher loan payments— and again some lenders have very restrictive qualifications.

If you have an FHA or VA loan you don't have to worry about a prepayment penalty because you don't have one. However, if you are refinancing with a new conventional loan consider finding a company with not only the lowest interest rates and fees going in, but one with a decent policy on prepayment penalties.

Some of the new conventional loans, like the variable rate mortgage pioneered in California, contain prepayment penalties. If and when, though, the lender raises the interest rate (they are allowed to do this but never in more than ¼ percent increments to a maximum of 2 percent) the borrower has a period of time in which he can sell or refinance without paying the penalty. I am currently in one of those periods now and will be taking advantage of it by selling one of my properties.

As you can see, a lot of the high costs of refinancing can be beaten with careful planning. And everything can be justified if you get a good buy.

SECONDARY FINANCING

Secondary financing is simply a loan secured by a second mortgage or deed of trust on real property. These junior or subordinate loans are called *seconds* because they are second in priority to first loans with respect to claims upon the proceeds in the event of foreclosure. It is also possible to have *third* and *fourth* loans and the only difference between them and the second one is a matter of priority in foreclosure.

Secondary loans are an excellent tool for borrowing money against your home. You can borrow as little or as much as you need as long as you do not exceed about 80 percent of the value of your home. For instance, if your home is worth $80,000 and you have a first mortgage of $30,000 you will normally be able to borrow the difference between $30,000 and $64,000 (80% of $80,000).

The best thing about seconds is that they are extremely flexible. You can pay any amount of interest agreed to up to the maximum rate allowed in your state. In many states restrictive usury rates have been raised or discarded so that these secondary loans can carry rates up to 14 and 15 percent. While you may not be excited about the prospects of paying higher interest rates, these higher figures do bring more money into play and thus increase your chances of obtaining secondary financing.

The length of the loan can also vary—usually between two and five years. The payback is also flexible—you can repay literally anything you want. This could be interest-only payments, or 2 percent a month, fully amortized or even no payments at all—just one heck of a balloon payment at the conclusion of the note. Junior liens are one of the most exciting tools you'll have at your disposal when buying and selling property. I am going to short-change this topic a little at this point but I'll refer you to chapter 15 for a more complete discussion. You may also want to read my book *How to Grow a Moneytree* which goes into the workings of these junior mortgages and trust deeds.

For the moment I want to cover just three basic sources for secondary financing should you decide to go this direction rather than sell or refinance when taking cash from your home. These sources are banks, mortgage brokers and private parties.

1. **BANKS:** While I realize that banks in some states either are not allowed to or just don't care to make secondary loans secured by real property, I feel this source is important enough to cover.

In the mid-seventies California allowed banks to make what is commonly known as equity loans. Although these loans are not governed by the same laws which rule secondary loans handled by real estate licensees, they serve the same purpose.

The home securing the loan must be owner-occupied. Thus you cannot borrow against a rental property. On the plus side is the fact that the interest rate may be slightly lower than what you would pay with a mortgage broker and the closing costs are considerably lower. You will pay no points, only a small overall charge which basically covers appraisal. The one hitch in California is that the funds are not supposed to be used for speculative purposes—and some people think that buying real estate is speculative. (I really have to appreciate Big Brother always looking out for my best interests.) You may not find this requirement too hard to get around.

2. MORTGAGE BROKERS: State licensed mortgage loan brokers are always available to give you the money, for a fee, if the equity in your home is sufficient to meet the security standards that the broker sets to protect his investors. He will often require that you have a minimum of 20 percent equity in your property. Some brokers will accept a minimum of only 15 percent equity. This means that if you have a property valued at $80,000, the broker who requires 15 percent equity in the property will not make a loan for more than $68,000.

Always keep an open mind when considering mortgage brokers as a source of borrowed money. Sure, the expenses can be high; perhaps as much as $1,800 on $10,000 borrowed. But there comes a time and place where this hard money source can be invaluable. For instance, you might stumble across a classic "steal" in which you can buy a home or property for $6,000 or more beneath market value, but only if you act today. So what really is $1,800 compared to making a quick $6,000?

3. PRIVATE SOURCES: Your best bet for secondary money is from private sources—aunts, uncles, fathers, mothers, friends, neighbors, co-workers, etc. Why? Because you can usually arrange your best terms and the costs for putting the loan together will be minimal. I'll have a lot more to say about this source later. For now let it suffice to say you should always be looking for people who are willing to lend you money—it will really pay off in the long run.

"There is an instrument which will permit the highest degree of leverage with only minimum risk! An investment vehicle which will capture all the growth in a property for the benefit of the investor! An investment which does not require any management effort at all! THIS INSTRUMENT IS THE OPTION!"

Jack Miller, from
Impact Report OPTIONS

6

OPTIONS

Options are an excellent means for an investor to control property without using a great deal of cash.

An option is basically a contract by which the owner of a property (the *optionor*), gives the right to purchase, or not to purchase, to another party called the *optionee*. The *optionee* must act within a set period of time and must give the *optionor* an agreed upon amount of cash (a consideration which can be as little as $1).

Why, you may ask, would anybody want to give an option on their property when they could sell it outright and get all their cash out . . . and get it out now, without waiting around six months to a year?

A good point! Most sellers won't even talk to you about an option. But many will . . . and when money is tight, or interest rates push 14 to 17 percent as they did in early '80, options begin to make sense.

When you learn how to effectively use options, you will be able to "control" property, often for as little as $200, and you will be able to sell your option (without ever taking title to the property) for maybe $2,000 or $5,000 or even $10,000.

Thus options are an exciting tool whereby a person of meager means can participate in the great economic adventure we call real estate investing. For the investor light on cash, an option is a temporary way of eliminating the need for a loan, yet during this period gaining control over all future appreciation of a property. After a year or two he can sell the option for a profit or exercise it, buy the property, and set up financing.

The successful investor will always carry with him a "mental bag" of solutions to as many buying and financing problems as possible. The option is one of those solutions. Here's how a friend of mine used an option:

A few years ago a friend, whom I'll call Bob, was looking for a basic home with a high balance FHA or VA loan he could assume. Every day he looked at two or three properties and would additionally talk with three or four people he came in contact with. He always asked whether they had heard of anyone who might be selling their home. In many ways he was doing the same thing a lot of real estate people do when looking for listings, only Bob was an investor looking for a good buy.

One day he posed his usual question to a waitress in a coffee shop. She said she didn't know of anyone in particular, but then after some hesitation she volunteered that a neighbor of hers seemed like a good candidate. Both the husband and wife, she pointed out, were in their seventies and the wife had recently been in the hospital. "And that old home of theirs," she told my friend, "is awful big and needs a lot of work. They must have over an acre."

Bob wasn't overwhelmed by this tip. He was looking for a simple rental home—preferably one that didn't require too much work. But to be polite, more than anything, he jotted down the address and thanked the waitress for the information.

He didn't pursue this lead until more than two weeks had passed. And then it was only an accident. He happened to be driving through the neighborhood, which was an older section of town containing a mixture of both new homes and older ones which were about fifty years old. The address matched one of the older homes, a nondescript two-story which was badly in need of paint. But what was most noticeable was the fruit orchard which graced the right-hand side of the property. It was a gorgeous piece of land! Gorgeous enough to prompt Bob to go ring the doorbell.

To make a long story short, my friend found that the elderly couple had been thinking about selling. They weren't overly anxious to part with what had been their home for over twenty years, but they wanted to move closer to a son who lived in Los Angeles.

Bob, who was also one of my clients, came by my office one day to "pick my brain" and have me go by and see the property with him. We toured the property and I gave him my professional opinion: If two building lots could be spun off the property, its market value, I felt, would be approximately $100,000. If for some reason the lots could not be built on, I felt the property would only be worth about $70,000. And if the property *could* be subdivided, then it would be possible for my friend to make a substantial profit.

Here's what was decided upon: Bob submitted an offer to the couple which was for a $500 option to buy the property at $72,000. The term of the option contract was rather short—six months. Bob could have offered less option money (say $100) but he wanted to come in with as strong an offer as possible so there would be no price haggling. As it turned out, his strategy failed, and he had to up the price to $79,000.

Bob went ahead with the contract and allowed the $500 option money to be kept by the sellers regardless of whether the option was later exercised or not. Bob could have negotiated in such a way that the option would apply towards the down payment at the time the option was exercised and an escrow was opened. Normally option money is kept by the optionor.

The price wasn't really too important—what was important was approval from the city of Walnut Creek to subdivide the lot, which turned out to be just short of an acre and a half, into two additional 20,000-square-foot parcels. So at his own expense, Bob pursued this course until he got city approval for the lot split, which under California law was a minor subdivision. Not only did Bob get approval but he also lined up a builder-buyer who would take the two parcels for $32,000 ($16,000 each). Obviously, Bob exercised his option at $79,000 with the help of a temporary bank loan, and then sold the two lots to the builder.

Bob was then able to get a new 25-year bank loan on the older home for $45,000. Considering the $32,000 he got from the builder, he was only out of pocket $2,000 on the sale plus subdivision costs. The story became even sweeter for Bob when he decided to sell the older home rather than try to fix it up. I listed the property for him and three weeks later my office had it sold for $67,000, thus helping Bob to pocket a before-tax profit of close to $15,000 after all expenses had been deducted.

Bob used the option approach to hold property while he further investigated its worth. One of my favorite ways of using the option is to *surprise* those people who casually remark that they will be selling their home in a year when their daughter graduates from high school, or for whatever reason. Maybe they are just teasing; but the quickest way to find out is to whip out an option contract and say: "I'll give you $100 right now for an option to buy your home for $70,000 in one year, with the escrow to close just after your daughter graduates."

Most people will back off, but a percentage will say okay. And why not? If they are serious about selling, why not get a buyer now and not have to worry about fixing up, planting, painting and finding a suitable real estate company? The only thing you'll probably have problems with is the price. For an option to work effectively, you'll want to pay what is approximately today's value—the $70,000 in this example. If by the end of the year the home goes up in value to $80,000, then you will certainly want to exercise your option. And it's still not a bad deal for the sellers because they will be saving a real estate commission (very possibly 6 percent, or $4,800) and unless otherwise agreed to will be spared the expenses of preparing the home for sale.

But keep in mind that if you agree to pay tomorrow's price you are defeating the greatest benefit of the option — the opportunity to gain control over future appreciation.

An option to purchase is easy to use. It's a good idea to always have these forms available. Following is an example of an excellent option contract which I personally use. It can be purchased from *Professional Publishing Corporation, 122 Paul Drive, San Rafael, Calif. 94903. The cost is $2.65 for a pad of 50 plus $1.50 shipping for each $15 worth of forms ordered.*

THE LEASE OPTION

There are two basic types of options which I am discussing in this chapter. One is the basic *option to purchase*, which I just covered. The other is the *lease with option to purchase*. The latter type, which for brevity I'll call the *lease option*, is truly a remarkable tool to have in your hands when you use it creatively and properly.

For instance, I have found that many so-called landlords are not true investors, or they are tired of performing the required management chores. The first group includes the many people who either kept their first home when they moved to another city or a larger home, or perhaps they inherited a home from a parent, aunt, uncle, or whomever. The second group includes the investor whom you might describe as being at the "end of the trail." After 10 or 15 years of chasing tenants around, one is apt to get a little tired of it — regardless of how much money is being made. I refer to this person as the *tired landlord.*

In any given community there are hundreds of people who fit the above categories. And the best place to find them is to call every "For Rent'by Owner" ad in your local newspaper. It may take nine or ten actual conversations before you find an owner who would consider selling or lease-optioning his property. But they're there, believe me. I used to call these people for listing leads and this little known source was a virtual goldmine. And you should do much better when you are offering to purchase rather than to list.

Now you know *who* the sources for lease options are, and you know where the best place is to find them. Next is the all-important *what do I do?* Unless you've got a lot of cash and you are offered too good a deal to pass up, you'll want to lease option the home rather than buy it outright.

Most owners will be thrown off guard when you tell them that you want to buy their property rather than lease it. They were expecting another call from a prospective tenant, not a purchaser. Take advantage of their being off guard and in rapid succession ask these questions: Would you be interested in selling your home rather than renting it? Would you let me take over the management of your home for the next year? (Explain that he would still

OPTION TO PURCHASE

In consideration of the payment by ....

...., hereinafter referred to as Optionee, in the amount of

$.............................. (..DOLLARS),

receipt of which is hereby acknowledged, ...

...., hereinafter referred to as Optionor, grants to Optionee an option to purchase the real property situated in the

City of ...., County of ...., State of ....,

described as ....

for a PURCHASE PRICE OF $.............................. (..DOLLARS),

upon the following TERMS and CONDITIONS:

ENCUMBRANCES: In addition to any encumbrances referred to above, Optionee shall take title to the property subject to: 1) Real Estate Taxes not yet due and 2) Covenants, conditions, restrictions, reservations, rights, rights of way and easements of record, if any, which do not materially affect the value or intended use of the property.

The amount of any bond or assessment which is a lien shall be ☐ paid, ☐ assumed by ....

EXAMINATION OF TITLE: Fifteen (15) days from date of exercise hereof are allowed the Optionee to examine the title to the property and to report in writing any valid objections thereto. Any exceptions to the title which would be disclosed by examination of the records shall be deemed to have been accepted unless reported in writing within said 15 days. If Optionee objects to any exceptions to the title, Optionor shall use all due diligence to remove such exceptions at his own expense within 60 days thereafter. But if such exceptions cannot be removed within the 60 days allowed, all rights and obligations hereunder may, at the election of the Optionee, terminate and end, and the option payment shall be returned to Optionee, unless he elects to purchase the property subject to such exceptions.

EVIDENCE OF TITLE. Evidence of Title shall be in the form of ☐ a policy of title insurance, ☐ other: .... to be paid for by ....

CLOSE OF ESCROW: Within .... days from exercise of the option, or upon removal of any exceptions to the title by the Optionor, as provided above, whichever is later, both parties shall deposit with an authorized escrow holder, to be selected by the Optionee, all funds and instruments necessary to complete the sale in accordance with the terms and conditions hereof.

POSSESSION: Possession shall be delivered to Optionee: ☐ Upon recordation of the deed. ☐ After recordation, but not later than .... Unless Optionor has vacated the premises prior to recordation of the deed, Optionor agrees to pay Optionee $............ per day from recordation to date possession is delivered and to leave this sum in escrow, to be disbursed to the persons entitled thereto on the date possession is delivered.

PRORATIONS: Rents, taxes, premiums on insurance acceptable to Optionee, interest and other expenses of the property to be prorated as of recordation of deed. Security deposits, advance rentals or considerations involving future lease credits shall be credited to Optionee.

MAINTENANCE: Until possession is delivered Optionor agrees to maintain heating, sewer, plumbing and electrical systems and any built-in appliances and equipment in normal working order, to keep the roof watertight and to maintain the grounds.

NOTICES: By acceptance hereof, Optionor warrants that he has no notice of violations relating to the property from City, County or State agencies.

TIME: Time is of the essence of this agreement.

EXPIRATION OF OPTION: If not exercised, this option shall expire .... days from date and Optionor shall be released from all obligations hereunder and all of Optionee's rights hereunder. legal or equitable. shall cease and the consideration hereinabove receipted for by Optionor shall be retained by Optionor.

EXERCISE OF OPTION: The option shall be exercised by mailing or delivering written notice to the Optionor prior to the expiration of this option and by an additional payment, on account of the purchase price, in the amount of .... DOLLARS)
$............ (............
for account of Optionor to the authorized escrow holder referred to above, prior to the expiration of this option.

Notice, if mailed, shall be by certified mail, postage prepaid. to the Optionor at the address set forth below, and shall be deemed to have been given upon the day following the day shown on the postmark of the envelope in which such notice is mailed.

In the event the option is exercised, the consideration hereinabove receipted for by Optionor ☐ shall ☐ shall not be credited upon the purchase price.

BROKERAGE FEE: Upon execution of this option the Optionor agrees to pay to ....
............, the Agent in this transaction, the sum of $............ (............
DOLLARS) and in the event the option is exercised, Optionor
agrees to pay Agent the additional sum of $............ (............ DOLLARS)
for services rendered. This agreement shall not limit the rights of Agent provided for in any listing or other agreement which may be in effect between Owner and Agent. In the event legal action is instituted to collect this fee, or any portion thereof, the Optionor agrees to pay the Agent a reasonable attorney's fee and all costs in connection with such action.

DATED............

.... Optionor .... Optionee

.... Optionor .... Optionee

.... Address .... Address

.... Phone .... Phone

.... Agent .... Agent's Address

By............ Agent's Phone

FORM 10U (5-14-74) (COPYRIGHT 1970. BY PROFESSIONAL PUBLISHING CORP., 122 PAUL DRIVE, SAN RAFAEL, CALIFORNIA 94903

OPTIONS

receive all the tax shelter benefits while you are managing the home.)

After one year, explain to him: "I'll buy your property. If this sounds interesting may I make an appointment to meet with you at the rental property? Would this afternoon at 4 p.m. be okay or would tonight at 8 p.m. be better?"

If the owner is not interested in your proposal he will tell you so—and as I said most (maybe even 4 of every 5) will not be. But some will. These people will not be able to make a decision over the telephone, but at least you have caused them to think. And one thing they are most likely thinking about before meeting you is *how nice it would be not to have any more tenant problems and where and how they would spend all that money.*

If you have not used the word *lease option* over the telephone then the owner is probably thinking more about an outright sale than he is the option. He may be slightly disappointed when you offer your proposal. But at least he is now prepared to consider a sale of some type—and this is something he probably wasn't thinking about until you came along.

Your actual lease option offer should be something along this line: 1) You will agree to lease the property for XXX amount of dollars each month. (This amount should be about what he was asking in his rental ad.) 2) You insist that he give you the unrestricted right to sublease the home without written consent. (This means that section in most lease option contracts which requires prior written consent of the owner before subleasing must be stricken from the contract and initialed by all parties involved.) 3) That after one year (or whatever date agreed upon) you will buy the property for XXX amount of dollars.

The above stipulation number three is the tough one to negotiate. You, of course, want today's value or even lower. The seller, on the other hand, will want tomorrow's value. But it should be obvious that this lease option concept has little value if you are going to pay tomorrow's price. That is what you are gambling upon—tomorrow's value. And if you can't get it, walk away and go after a different property.

There is another critical factor which you must negotiate. And that is how much of your monthly rent will apply towards the down payment and closing costs. Traditionally in a down real estate market, many sellers with a lease option contract will allow a hefty portion of the monthly rent to apply toward those costs. However, in an up (seller's) market this amount might be anywhere from zero to just $100 from each accumulated month's rent.

The amount of money which applies to the sale, therefore, is something which you will have to negotiate. If, for instance, the seller insists on getting $1,000 more than what you estimate the current property value to be, then you might say that's okay if he will allow $250 of each month's rent to apply to your purchase costs.

You should be able to recognize the advantage of this type of contract. You will be able to buy a home for say $75,000 when its real value may be

$85,000. And, to boot, you may be given $3,000 ($250 per month) to help buy it. And as icing on the cake—you'll be able to borrow money easier against the property because of the larger equity.

See page 60 for a look at Professional Publishing Company's *Residential Lease with Option to Purchase*.

Many variations of the above described lease option are possible. All you have to do is use your imagination. To get you started, here is one variation which is useful when interest rates are high and money is tight.

For this example, let's assume that you have located a potentially nice home. The only problem is that it is vacant and needs about $2,000 worth of refurbishing—mostly painting, fence repairs and yard maintenance. You estimate its value at about $60,000 when the repairs are completed.

You offer the owner a six-month lease option agreement in which you agree to buy the home for $58,000 in six months time. You also agree, in the contract, to perform certain basic repairs to the property during the six months, whether you elect to buy it or not. You agree to this to give something to the seller—primarily a sense of security. You could have paid the seller $1,000 option money—but the money is better used fixing up the property rather than putting it into the seller's pocket. So your option cost is just $1.00.

What you now have is a contract on a home which could be worth $64,000 after you fix it up and after six months of inflation boosts its value. And in six months you might be able to get a new first mortgage for 11 to 12 percent, rather than perhaps a higher current rate. What you are doing with this lease option is using a little time and effort to "put away" equities and properties which you can finance when conditions are more favorable.

Before you run out and put together an option . . . a word of warning is in order. BE SURE TO RECORD YOUR OPTION CONTRACT WITH YOUR APPROPRIATE LOCAL GOVERNMENTAL AGENCY. In most cases this will be the county recorder. And you don't necessarily have to do it in person. A friendly title company will have this done for you for a small fee. But if you don't record your interest in the property, you'll deserve to have the optionor sell the property out from underneath you.

RESIDENTIAL LEASE WITH OPTION TO PURCHASE

RECEIVED FROM.. .... hereinafter referred to as Tenant,

the sum of $ .... (.. DOLLARS),

evidenced by .... as a deposit which, upon acceptance of this Lease, the Owner

of the premises, hereinafter referred to as Owner, shall apply said deposit as follows:

	RECEIVED	PAYABLE PRIOR TO OCCUPANCY
Rent for the period from. .... to	$	$
Last. ....month's rent	$	$
Security Deposit	$	$
Key Deposit.	$	$
Cleaning charge	$	$
Other	$	$
TOTAL	$	$

In the event that this agreement is not accepted by the Owner or his authorized agent, within .... days, the total deposit received shall be refunded.

Tenant hereby offers to lease from the Owner the premises situated in the City of ...., County of ...., State of ....,

described as ....

and consisting of ....
upon the following TERMS and CONDITIONS:

TERM: The term hereof shall commence on. ...., 19.... , and continue for a period of ...., months thereafter.

RENT: Rent shall be $ .... per month, payable in advance, upon the................... day of each calendar month to Owner or

his authorized agent, at the following address: ....
or at such other places as may be designated by Owner from time to time. In the event rent is not paid within five (5) days after due date, Tenant agrees to pay a late charge
of $10.00 per annum on the delinquent amount. Tenant agrees further to pay $5.00 for each dishonored bank check.

UTILITIES: Tenant shall be responsible for the payment of all utilities and services, except: .... ;
which shall be paid by Owner.

USE: The premises shall be used as a residence with no more than................... adults and .... children, and for no other
purpose, without the prior written consent of the Owner.

PETS: No pets shall be brought on the premises without the prior consent of the Owner.

ORDINANCES AND STATUTES: Tenant shall comply with all statutes, ordinances and requirements of all municipal, state and federal authorities now in force, or
which may hereafter be in force, pertaining to the use of the premises.

ASSIGNMENT AND SUBLETTING: Tenant shall not assign this agreement or sublet any portion of the premises without prior written consent of the Owner which may
not be unreasonably withheld.

MAINTENANCE, REPAIRS OR ALTERATIONS: Tenant acknowledges that the premises are in good order and repair, unless otherwise indicated herein. Owner may
at any time give Tenant a written inventory of furniture and furnishings on the premises and Tenant shall be deemed to have possession of all said furniture and furnishings in good condition and repair, unless he objects thereto in writing within five days after receipt of such inventory. Tenant shall, at his own expense, and at all times,
maintain the premises in a clean and sanitary manner including all equipment, appliances, furniture and furnishings therein and shall surrender the same, at termination
hereof, in as good condition as received, normal wear and tear excepted. Tenant shall be responsible for damages caused by his negligence and that of his family or
invitees and guests. Tenant shall not paint, paper or otherwise redecorate or make alterations to the premises without the prior written consent of the Owner. Tenant shall
irrigate and maintain any surrounding grounds, including lawns and shrubbery, and keep the same clear of rubbish or weeds, if such grounds are a part of the premises
and are exclusively for the use of the Tenant.

ENTRY AND INSPECTION: Tenant shall permit Owner or Owner's agents to enter the premises at reasonable times and upon reasonable notice for the purpose of making necessary or convenient repairs, or to show the premises to prospective tenants, purchasers, or mortgagees.

INDEMNIFICATION: Owner shall not be liable for: any damage or injury to Tenant, or any other person, or to any property, occurring on the premises, or any part thereof, or in common areas thereof, unless such damage is the proximate result of the negligence or unlawful act of Owner, his agents, or his employees. Tenant agrees to hold Owner harmless from any claims for damages no matter how caused, except for injury or damages for which Owner is legally responsible.

POSSESSION: If Owner is unable to deliver possession of the premises at the commencement hereof, Owner shall not be liable for any damage caused thereby, nor shall this agreement be void or voidable, but Tenant shall not be liable for any rent until possession is delivered. Tenant may terminate this agreement if possession is not delivered within . . . . days of the commencement of the term hereof.

DEFAULT: If Tenant shall fail to pay rent when due, or perform any term hereof, after not less than three (3) days written notice of such default given in the manner required by law, the Owner, at his option, may terminate all rights of Tenant hereunder, unless Tenant, within said time, shall cure such default. If Tenant abandons or vacates the property, while in default of the payment of rent, Owner may consider any property left on the premises to be abandoned and may dispose of the same in any manner allowed by law. In the event the Owner reasonably believes that such abandoned property has no value, it may be discarded. All property on the premises is hereby subject to a lien in favor of Owner for the payment of all sums due hereunder, to the maximum extent allowed by law.

In the event of a default by Tenant, Owner may elect to (a) continue the lease in effect and enforce all his rights and remedies hereunder, including the right to recover the rent as it becomes due, or (b) at any time, terminate all of Tenant's rights hereunder and recover from Tenant all damages he may incur by reason of the breach of the lease, including the cost of recovering the premises, and including the worth at the time of such termination, or at the time of an award if suit be instituted to enforce this provision, of the amount by which the unpaid rent for the balance of the term exceeds the amount of such rental loss which the tenant proves could be reasonably avoided.

SECURITY: The security deposit set forth above, if any, shall secure the performance of Tenant's obligations hereunder. Owner may, but shall not be obligated to, apply all or portions of said deposit on account of Tenant's obligations hereunder. Any balance remaining upon termination shall be returned to Tenant.

DEPOSIT REFUNDS: The balance of all deposits shall be refunded within two weeks from date possession is delivered to Owner or his Authorized Agent, together with a statement showing any charges made against such deposits by Owner.

ATTORNEYS FEES: In any legal action brought by either party to enforce the terms hereof or relating to the demised premises, the prevailing party shall be entitled to all costs incurred in connection with such action, including a reasonable attorney's fee.

WAIVER: No failure of Owner to enforce any term hereof shall be deemed a waiver, nor shall any acceptance of a partial payment of rent be deemed a waiver of Owner's right to the full amount thereof.

NOTICES: Any notice which either party may or is required to give, may be given by mailing the same, postage prepaid, to Tenant at the premises or to Owner at the address shown below or at such other places as may be designated by the parties from time to time.

HEIRS, ASSIGNS, SUCCESSORS: This lease is binding upon and inures to the benefit of the heirs, assigns and successors in interest to the parties.

TIME: Time is of the essence of this agreement.

HOLDING OVER: Any holding over after expiration hereof, with the consent of Owner, shall be construed as a month-to-month tenancy in accordance with the terms hereof, as applicable. No such holding over or extension of this lease shall extend the time for the exercise of the option unless agreed upon in writing by Owner.

CONTINUED ON REVERSE SIDE

FORM 106   (7-18-78)   © COPYRIGHT, 1970, BY PROFESSIONAL PUBLISHING CORP., 122 PAUL DRIVE, SAN RAFAEL, CA 94903. ALL RIGHTS RESERVED

PROFESSIONAL PUBLISHING CORPORATION

OPTIONS

61

OPTION: So long as tenant is not in substantial default in the performance of any term of this lease, Tenant shall have the option to purchase the real property described herein for a PURCHASE PRICE OF $................................. (.. DOLLARS), upon the following TERMS and CONDITIONS:

ENCUMBRANCES: In addition to any encumbrances referred to above, Tenant shall take title to the property subject to: 1) Real Estate Taxes not yet due and 2) Covenants, conditions, restrictions, reservations, rights, rights of way and easements of record, if any, which do not materially affect the value or intended use of the property.

The amount of any bond or assessment which is a lien shall be ☐ paid, ☐ assumed by ....

EXAMINATION OF TITLE: Fifteen (15) days from date of exercise of this option are allowed the Tenant to examine the title to the property and to report in writing any valid objections thereto. Any exceptions to the title which would be disclosed by examination of the records shall be deemed to have been accepted unless reported in writing within said 15 days. If Tenant objects to any exceptions to the title, Owner shall use all due diligence to remove such exceptions at his own expense within 60 days thereafter. But if such exceptions cannot be removed within the 60 days allowed, all rights and obligations hereunder may, at the election of the Tenant, terminate and end, unless he elects to purchase the property subject to such exceptions.

EVIDENCE OF TITLE: Evidence of Title shall be in the form of ☐ a policy of title insurance, ☐ other:............................ to be paid for by............

CLOSE OF ESCROW: Within .... days from exercise of the option, or upon removal of any exceptions to the title by the Owner, as provided above, whichever is later, both parties shall deposit with an authorized escrow holder, to be selected by the Tenant, all funds and instruments necessary to complete the sale in accordance with the terms and conditions hereof.

PRORATIONS: Rents, taxes, premiums on insurance acceptable to Tenant, interest and other expenses of the property to be prorated as of recordation of deed. Security deposits, advance rentals or considerations involving future lease credits shall be credited to Tenant.

EXPIRATION OF OPTION: This option may be exercised at any time after............ 19........ and shall expire at midnight............ 19........ unless exercised prior thereto. Upon expiration Owner shall be released from all obligations hereunder and all of Tenants rights hereunder, legal or equitable, shall cease.

EXERCISE OF OPTION: The option shall be exercised by mailing or delivering written notice to the Owner prior to the expiration of this option and by an additional payment, on account of the purchase price, in the amount of

$............ (..DOLLARS)
for account of Owner to the authorized escrow holder referred to above, prior to the expiration of this option.

Notice, if mailed, shall be by certified mail, postage prepaid, to the Owner at the address set forth below, and shall be deemed to have been given upon the day following the day shown on the postmark of the envelope in which such notice is mailed.

In the event the option is exercised,............ percent from the rent paid hereunder prior to the exercise of the option shall be credited upon the purchase price.

The undersigned Tenant hereby acknowledges receipt of a copy hereof.

............................Agent   DATED............

....Tenant

By:.. ....Tenant

Broker:.. ....Address

....Phone

ACCEPTANCE

The undersigned Owner accepts the foregoing offer.

BROKERAGE FEE: Upon execution hereof the Owner agrees to pay to .... the Agent in this transaction, the sum of $............ (..DOLLARS)
for leasing services rendered and authorizes Agent to deduct said sum from the deposit received from Tenant. In the event the option is exercised, the Owner agrees to pay Agent the additional sum of $............ (..DOLLARS).
This agreement shall not limit the rights of Agent provided for in any listing or other agreement which may be in effect between Owner and Agent. In the event legal action is instituted to collect this fee, or any portion thereof, the Owner agrees to pay the Agent a reasonable attorney's fee and all costs in connection with such action.

The undersigned Owner hereby acknowledges receipt of a copy hereof.

Dated............

....Owner

............................Address

............................Phone ....Owner

(8-6-79)

OPTIONS

PART II
Finding and Controlling
the Property

"Real property has significance only as it satisfies man's needs and desires. Man's utilization of real property gives it character. Man's collective desire for real property gives it value."

—*From* The Appraisal of Real Estate

7

KNOW THE PROPERTY— INSIDE AND OUTSIDE

You can't underestimate the value and importance of *THE PROPERTY* and have a good or even successful real estate investment program. It is the cornerstone! Your portfolio is only as good as your property.

Your property secures your investment . . . if it ever became worthless, your financial interests in the property would have no value. Your property is what attracts tenants . . . and the better it is, the better your tenants.

In this chapter I am going to give you some tips that will help you do a better job of selecting investment property. I'll show you how to look at property and how to evaluate it. After understanding how the game is played you'll have a much better chance of success in real estate. And you won't be at the mercy of a fast-talking real estate agent who might otherwise try to persuade you to buy a white elephant for $10,000 over market. And even more importantly, you won't be at the mercy of your own emotional whims.

It will do you absolutely no good to start off your investment program by buying a 35-year-old home which, as you later find out, you paid $4,000 too much for; needs a new $3,000 roof; and is in the wrong school district, so will bring only $300 a month in rent (not the $375 that everyone said it could). "After all," you remember the owner saying when you were going through the property for the first time, "the house down the street rents for $380 and it isn't half as good as mine."

HOW TO LOOK AT PROPERTY

This may come as a surprise . . . maybe even a shock to most people, but the way to look at prospective investment property is TO DO IT FAST. Note that I didn't say *buy* it fast . . . I said *look* at the property as fast as you can.

Now pick yourself up off the floor and I'll explain what I mean. In my opinion there are three factors which are important—even critical—when inspecting property. They are: 1) Your first impressions are reliable; 2) The more property you see the more qualified you are; and 3) Time is money.

You should know what you are basically looking for, what you can afford, and what type of financing you want *before* you even inspect the first property. One reason for looking at a lot of property is to get a feel for values. Another reason for looking at numerous homes (say 30 instead of 5) is to come up with the best buy. Now here is my point—the more property one sees the more confusing the issues become. After looking carefully at a dozen homes it seems like your brain becomes mush—you cannot remember which one had the pink bathroom and which one had the green kitchen appliances.

So by seeing too much property, and by spending too much time at each home, you begin to confuse the unimportant factors. What you want to do is to see as many homes as you can in the shortest period of time. And while you are at those properties you should strive to make a mental picture of the key features of each one.

Those key features include: The outside approach to the home and the immediate neighborhood; the basic floor plan, especially as it develops from the entry into the living areas of the home; the general condition of the home; and the price and the basic terms available. Save the finer points like missing molding, odd bedroom paint colors and chips in the appliances for the next visit—if there is to be a next visit.

You should be able to tour a 1400-square-foot home in less than four minutes and at the same time "print" a fairly accurate picture in your head. Then move on to the next one—regardless of how much you may have liked the home you just left. After seeing all the possible properties in the areas or price range you're considering, make a list of the two or three you want to go back and see. With your second visit you can start to make detailed lists of things to do, etc. But now it's easy because you'll only be comparing two or three properties, not 10 to 20.

There are exceptions, of course, to what I have just said. After you become completely familiar with a particular neighborhood you'll probably be able to make a yes or no decision within a matter of minutes—and without seeing numerous homes.

But until you reach that experience level, the more homes you see the better it is. And besides, it's nice to be able to tour 10 or so properties in a couple of hours rather than make it an all-day affair. After all, time *is* money.

AVOIDING PITFALLS

There are a lot of pros and cons to consider when looking at property. Following are several areas of consideration. Keep in mind that when you learn what to avoid in a property, you also learn what to look for. Much of the following is my personal opinion, based on my experiences in Northern California; thus in some instances the facts could be slightly different for your area.

AGE: Age by itself is not an important consideration. If to the best of my ability I could not determine any difference between a 5-year-old home and a 35-year-old home, I would opt for the younger of the two. Why? Because odds are I would have more maintenance costs with the older home. The two main attractions that most older homes might have over newer ones are 1) better construction and 2) the possibility of its being in a prestigious neighborhood which is in great demand.

Most of my rental homes are in a 28-year-old subdivision. And I find that they rent better than some newer homes just five miles away. That's because there are a lot of other factors more important than age.

AMENITIES: These are all the extra features that can come with a property. They include panoramic views, custom draperies, built-in range and ovens, self-cleaning ovens, air conditioning and other goodies that almost anyone can appreciate. They are nice to have and may enter into your decision to buy or not to buy a particular home. But keep this in mind—YOU'RE BUYING A HOME FOR INVESTMENT PURPOSES AND NOT TO LIVE IN. Take the emotion out of your decision.

While you might not consider living in a home that didn't have a garbage compactor or a built-in intercom, the absence of these things will not bother your tenant nor will they greatly affect your eventual resale price. Keep in mind that the more workable parts you have in a property, the more repair expenses you'll have in the future.

Some of these extra features, however, might be necessary. It depends upon what is expected in your community. If, for instance, most homes in your community valued over $60,000 have wall-to-wall carpeting, central air conditioning and hummingbird feeders, then yours had better have the same. Don't buck obvious trends or else it'll be your home that goes vacant for three months.

CONSTRUCTION QUALITY: I don't like to have an owner follow me around when I am inspecting a property, because I find it embarrassing when I pound their walls with my fist and jump up and down on their floors. My method may not be the most scientific, but at least it gives me a quick idea of construction quality without having to hire a professional to come in and make a formal report.

I get very upset with squeaky or soft floors. I once lived in a home where you could hear someone walking in the opposite end of the house. These conditions may not indicate that the place is falling apart, but I do appreciate the fact that all my rentals are well-built homes. And I have to believe that some of my tenants (or a prospective buyer in the future) may also appreciate the fact that when they are walking around the house they won't be heard by everyone else.

The moral of this segment is that when you pound on the floors and walls and you get a solid *thump* in return, you can probably be assured that the home is at least in average condition. However, if this action brings on a minor earthquake, I suggest that you hire a professional to dig a little deeper into the current condition of the property. I'll tell you more about these inspections a little later in this chapter.

In addition to pounding walls, keep your eyes open for doors and windows that don't close properly, a sagging roof line, or excessive cracks in walls and/or the foundation. They are all signs that everything may not be okay and that further inspection would be wise.

CORNER LOT INFLUENCE: I bring this up because I have had several people in the past ask me whether a home is more valuable because it is on a corner lot. The answer is no. A corner lot is definitely more valuable when you are considering commercial property, because it gives a store two sets of windows facing traffic instead of one. But when it comes to residential property, the opposite is true. Those dwelling in a single-family home would rather have more yard and privacy in the back than a lot of front yard which would need constant care. Corner lots are also good places for school-age children to take short-cuts through.

ENERGY: It goes without saying, with the high energy costs of today you owe it to yourself and your future tenants to make sure the property you buy is well insulated. And if it is not, then you may want to consider getting a bid (preferably before you're locked into a contract) to find out how much it may cost to have the job done.

There is a lot more to be concerned with than just insulation. You'll also want to consider the degree of energy loss. Rather than hire experts to inspect the property, why not ask the seller to see all his gas and electric bills for the past year? By doing this often, you'll soon be able to spot a property with extraordinary utility bills. This can be especially important in the colder northeast. You can be sure that if a tenant of yours is paying 50 percent more in heating costs than his neighbors, he'll soon be giving you notice to move.

EYE APPEAL: Believe it or not . . . eye appeal is probably the most important consideration of all when buying a rental property. Sure, you are not going to live in a property. But consider the fact that almost everyone is tainted by some degree of snob appeal. After 12-plus years of showing property to both buyers and renters, I couldn't help but notice that almost all my clients made their yes or no decision about a house at the very moment we drove up in front of it. Some, of course, after liking the outside would change their minds after inspecting the inside. But the important point is that I can't remember anyone changing their mind after deciding they didn't like the outside appearance.

By outside appearance I am referring to the exterior appeal of the home, including lawn, landscaping, trees and the immediate neighborhood.

You can change, to a small degree, the outside appearance of a property. You can paint the house, trim the shrubberies, cut the grass, plant a lawn, add shutters or put in a winding cobblestone walkway. But truly, there is not a lot you can effectively do to the exterior appearance of a home. Some just don't have it—the original builder may have had the "taste" of a Neanderthal man, and there will be nothing you can do to liven up the appearance short of spending $10,000.

While there is little you can do to change the outside appearance of a "turkey," there is absolutely nothing you can do to change the appearance of the neighborhood. If homes are rundown, lawns are uncut or even nonexistent, jacked-up cars are in driveways, paint is flaking off exteriors, etc., then forget it. You can't change the neighborhood. But don't be too harsh on a neighborhood or street where just a single property looks like a disaster area. There will always be one bad apple in a bunch. But when most of the barrel is bad, throw them out.

How do you protect yourself? I can't give you any clearcut answer, because while I may hate two-story, Arabic colonials, you may think they're out of this world. Just don't go for anything that is too unusual—stay with the style that is most popular in your area.

EXTERIOR CONDITION: I am not speaking of eye appeal here but about the hard dollar & cents facts in relation to the exterior condition of the property. The key factors here are the roof, the rain gutters, the garage door and the condition of the paint.

If the roof is new, or relatively new, that's one worry out of the way. But if you have any suspicions, or if it is getting a little frayed on the rooftop ridges, you had better call in an expert to take a closer look. The roof is vitally important because it costs a small fortune today to repair or replace them. So why buy a property that is going to need a new $4,000 roof within two years when you can buy a similar home down the street (for maybe just $1,000 more in price) that has just had a new roof installed? Here is a general guideline that may be of some help:

Minimum Life Expectancy of Different Types of Roofs

Asphalt shingles	15 to 25 years
Tar and gravel	12 to 15 years
Lightweight cedar shingle	17 to 20 years
Heavy cedar shake	18 to 24 years
Red clay tile	24 to 35 years

The above lifetime estimates depend on several factors including the original grade of materials, the competence of the installers, and wind and storm conditions affecting the particular property. Clay tiles are particularly affected by this, as an inferior membrane—the felting below the tiles—may sag and start to leak in only 5 years. And the only way to really fix it is to remove all the tiles and start over—a big, *expensive* job!

The value of a home is enhanced when rain gutters and an appropriate number of downspouts entirely circle the property. At a very minimum there should be gutters over every doorway to the property. Like everything else, these rain gutters have a life expectancy. They frequently rust out or separate from the edge of the roof. When inspecting property take a close look at them, realizing that this is another possible cost if they need repairing or replacement.

Don't overlook the garage door. Get out there and open and shut it a few times. With homes over ten years old, many of the garage doors either stick, bulge, won't close tight, won't stay open by themselves, or just don't work. If you overlook this, I can assure you that your tenant won't—and he'll bug you until you make the repairs. And you really can't blame him. So be smart and check out the garage door; then if it needs fixing or replacing, you can have the seller pay for it.

The condition of the exterior paint is doubly important because not only is it a factor in the eye appeal of the home, but it also offers your home (especially with wood exteriors) a degree of protection from the elements. It costs a lot to have a home painted these days and if you do it yourself, you may be spending a lot more time than you originally expected to. This is especially true when chipped paint must be sanded off wood exteriors. When making an offer or deciding between two homes, keep the potential costs of an exterior paint job in mind.

FLOOR PLAN: When it comes to floor plans, keep this in mind—with inexpensive homes, like the ones you'll be looking at for your portfolio, *different* is bad. When considering expensive homes (like $200,000 and more), different can be good.

So don't get carried away with an unusual floor plan. Most buyers and tenants won't want the master bedroom off the kitchen, or the family room practically on top of the bedrooms.

When considering floor plans, also look for as much storage space as you can get—it's a plus. Also keep noise levels in mind. Most likely you'll be renting your property to a family with children, and from experience I know how noisy the little rascals can get. So the best home is one in which there can be some separation of children and adults. For instance, are the bedrooms big enough for play? Or is there a separate rumpus room or basement area where the children can stretch out their legs . . . and lungs? The home that has these features will definitely be a plus over one that does not have them.

NEIGHBORHOOD: I am not talking about the immediate street in your neighborhood (see *EYE APPEAL* above), but the more general and larger neighborhood concept which includes the schools, surrounding subdivisions, shopping facilities, transportation depots, and zoning laws.

It is this general neighborhood factor that has a big influence on how much you'll pay for your home and for how much (and how fast) you'll be able to rent it. It's a big part of the *LOCATION, LOCATION, LOCATION* factor which is given so much attention in the appraisal of real estate. Call it snob appeal or whatever, but in each city there are neighborhoods which are more prestigious than others. It may have something to do with a good school district (perhaps one in which there is no forced busing), or it may be that the area is newer, or that it consists of older but elegant homes, or that it is far away from troubled slum areas of the city.

As an investor you must understand this factor and give it serious consideration when buying property. Now it's quite possible that the homes in your community's prestigious area cost well over $100,000 and are thus not suitable for rentals. But in all likelihood you'll find strata of prestige, so you can look in the second or perhaps the third level.

But don't underestimate the importance of the general neighborhood. I did once—and the home I owned in that marginal neighborhood, and the tenants I had, practically drove me crazy. In an area besieged by crime, poor schools, etc., you are not going to find many good and steady-paying tenants. So there will be some bargain-priced properties that you won't want to get involved with; that is, unless you fully understand the risks and are willing to work with low income tenants.

Most cities and counties have rather strict zoning requirements which limit or even prohibit certain types of structures in the wrong zone. For instance, single-family residences built on basic quarter-acre lots may be designated as R-10. Strict compliance to the zoning laws means that no other type of structure may be built (sometimes churches or schools are an exception) in those blocks that are designated R-10. Thus, condominiums must be built in another area, where the zoning may be designated Planned Unit Development (PUD). Apartments and commercial buildings must be built in yet another area.

This type of planned development is basically a good thing for the homeowner and rental property owner. You know where you stand. But there is one problem with this—you cannot completely rely upon what the stated zoning is because these laws and requirements change. If, for instance, there is a parcel of vacant land backing your home on two sides, don't assume that other homes will be built there just because the land is zoned for single-family. Cost conscious builders are constantly at war with city halls to increase density requirements. And if one should win the battle, that vacant land could be turned into a three-story, 150-unit apartment building. That would not be a good thing for you.

Residential property holds and increases its value most when it's not crowded by commercial and high-density multiple properties. So check with city hall to make sure that current zoning laws are not being too easily broken down by developers.

OVER-IMPROVED PROPERTY: Imagine a subdivision of homes, all with three bedrooms, 2 baths, a small family room, a double car garage and about 1400 square feet of living space. Let's assume these homes are selling for $65,000. Now along comes Mr. and Mrs. Pretentious and their nine children. They buy one of the homes, but naturally it isn't big enough or nice enough for them. So Mr. Pretentious hires a remodeling contractor who during a three-month period tears up the home and rebuilds it again. When they are finished, Mr. and Mrs. Pretentious have a 2400-square-foot home with four bedrooms, including an enlarged master bedroom, a family room which has been turned into a formal dining room, and a garage which is made into a deluxe family room complete with a second fireplace. And next to the garage is a new carport just big enough for the Pretentious's two big cars. All this they get for just $40,000.

There is a name for what the Pretentiouses did. No, it's not called being "the big frog in a small pond." It's called over-building, or over-improvement. The neighborhood of $65,000 homes did not justify such major improvements!

Now here is the rub. A year after the addition is completed, Mr. Pretentious's company transfers him across the country. They even agree to pay for his moving costs; and if he can't sell his home in two months, they will buy it for the appraised value. So Mr. Pretentious puts a sign on the lawn and an ad in his local newspaper. He is now a "For Sale by Owner" (FISBO). His price is $125,000. Mr. Pretentious based his asking price on the reasoning that he paid $65,000 for the home and then spent another $40,000 on those wonderful improvements that everyone raves about. He then threw in another $20,000 for appreciation.

After several weeks passed, Mr. Pretentious finally began to listen to some of the real estate agents who had been practically camping at his front door step. He even agreed to pay $75 for a formal appraisal. But what he wasn't prepared for were the results . . . a value of $90,000.

The "why" is basic and simple. While many people might like his gorgeous home, they are not willing to spend $125,000 for a home in a (now) $75,000 neighborhood. If the typical buyer wants to spend $125,000 he'll buy a home in a $125,000 neighborhood. Unless housing is very, very scarce, the most an owner-remodeler should ever expect to get back is about 50 percent of his original costs. The only exception would be in an expensive custom-home neighborhood where closer to the full remodeling costs could be recouped.

One reason the full remodeling costs are seldom recovered is that additions almost always cost more per square foot than complete houses built by the original contractor.

While the original owner-remodeler usually takes a financial bath when selling his over-improved property, the buyer usually comes out of the deal "smelling like a rose."

I own two greatly over-improved homes and I was able to buy each one for just $3,000 to $4,000 over the cost of standard homes in the subdivision. But even better is the fact that I can get up to $50 more in rent for these homes than I can for the standard models. So while I caution you against over-improving your properties, I also urge you to look for over-improved property when buying.

One caution, though, when buying this type of property. Learn who did the remodeling and find out whether a building permit was issued. Ask to see it. This can be important if you want to avoid future problems. Some lenders, including FHA, will not consider a property for a loan unless the appraiser sees a building permit. If there is no permit you'll have to call in the city or county inspector. And the odds are against that inspector passing this work which may have been completed 10 years earlier. So to avoid trouble down the road, make sure a permit was properly issued at the time the work was done. And if not, then make the seller procure one from the proper government agency before you close the sale.

In the above example, Mr. Pretentious turned his garage into a family room and added a carport. This is often a bad thing to do. Most men want the storage space and the workbench area that comes with garages. Thus you limit the number of prospects for the home. And the carport is little help. I have seen actual examples of homes with converted garages selling for less money than similar homes with the garage intact.

PRICE: The price you pay for your rental property is relative to many things. Thus I cannot give you any specific advice here, but just a few general guidelines you may want to follow.

In a typical community where prices range from a low of $25,000 to a high of $150,000, you'll probably be best off looking for homes priced between $40,000 and $80,000. The reasons are that this is the range in which the most people will be looking for a rental unit; and it is also an active price range which shows the greatest potential for continued appreciation. Currently in many parts of the United States the sales of homes from $100,000 plus are a little sluggish.

The problem with the low price ranges, from $25,000 to about $40,000, is that the properties (and neighborhoods) are probably very old and the quality of tenant you'll get for those homes will be very low. If you want to take a gun with you when you go to collect your rents, then you're welcome to do so. Personally I like (and expect) my tenants to mail or deliver their rent checks to me each month.

You're familiar with the phrase "You get what you pay for." This phrase also applies well to real estate. For instance, many homes have obviously bad problems—perhaps they back up to a busy, noisy freeway, or they're next to a school or playground where noisy softball games are played nightly from April through October. I personally don't own any such property. But if I did, I would make darn sure that the price I paid was well below what the market value might be if these homes did not have their drawbacks.

In my town, for instance, there is a street in which the even-numbered homes back up to a very congested freeway. But the odd-numbered homes on the other side of the street seem to exist in a different—and quieter—world. The odd-numbered homes sell for $5,000 to $6,000 more than the even-numbered ones. This has always been the story for as long as I can remember. Even though I prefer not to own one of the freeway-side homes, it would not be a disaster for my portfolio, as long as I paid the lower price. As you can see, many things are relative to price. And in the long run the price you pay is not as important as what financing is available, what you are getting for the price, what your payments will be, etc.

SIZE: The size of a home or even its yard is also relative to many other factors. I always like to get the most home for the money but still keep all my figures in sight of what the negative cash flow might be. Thus if I feel $80,000 is as much as I want to spend, I'll try to find the most for my money up to that price. I may arbitrarily pick the $80,000 price because any higher figure might mean more negative cash flow than I want to deal with. (Later on I'll tell you how you can minimize negative cash flow.)

Let's talk about bedrooms. I will buy either a two-, three- or four-bedroom home. I have had excellent results with two-bedroom properties. The tenants in these smaller homes usually don't have children and there seems to be a lot of demand for such rentals. One reason, of course, is that family sizes are smaller these days. Three-bedroom homes are the most popular because they have the widest resale possibilities. Four-bedroom properties have their selling points too, because they attract families with children. While your first inclination might be to reject children from your units, let me remind you that one of the major reasons for the popularity of the single-family home as a rental entity is that it is the proper place for children. They certainly don't do very well in large apartment complexes.

When it comes to yard sizes, you might as well flip a coin. I have sold and rented as many homes with large yards to people who wanted the space, as I have those with small yards to families who wanted an easy-care yard.

THE WORKING PARTS OF THE HOME: Closely inspect those parts of the home that perform vital functions. This would include any built-in kitchen appliances as well as the heating, cooling, plumbing and electrical systems. A lot of potential repair costs are involved here—so check out each item carefully.

Much of the testing can be done simply. For instance, flush each toilet and turn on every faucet. You'll be able to find out easily whether there is a problem or a nagging leak.

Turn on each electrical switch and try out the wall outlets. Odds are you won't have any electrical problem if the home was not altered or remodeled. However, check the amp service. If this is too low, say under 100 amps, you might want to consider increasing the service, or your tenant may constantly complain about blow-outs.

Check the age of the hot-water heater. Many have only a ten-year life expectancy. Look for leaks or other telltale signs that indicate it may be nearing the end of its useful life.

The most important inspection—and one you will most likely need professional help with—is the heating and cooling system, especially if it's centralized. If the system is less than ten years old and if the owner can assure you that it's working properly, you may elect to forego spending money on an inspection.

Also give all kitchen appliances the use test. Be sure that each range burner works, and don't forget to test the garbage disposal, if the home has one. (By the way, a recent survey of home owners found that the number-one desire was for a garbage disposal.)

WARRANTIES AND INSPECTIONS

It is possible that the home and its working parts may be covered by a home protection warranty the seller may have purchased. Some warranties cover the property for two years; many have deductibles (some as high as $100) and most have exclusions (occasionally homes which are rented are dropped from coverage), so don't expect any miracles. The truth is that many real estate companies use these warranties as tools for getting listings. They're designed to impress buyers and sellers and not much more. But as they vary greatly from company to company be sure and shop carefully when you have that choice.

You will probably be just as well off inserting the following clause in your purchase agreement: "*Seller warrants that grounds and improvements will be maintained, that roof is watertight, and that all appliances and heating, plumbing, sewer, and electrical systems shall be in working order at close of escrow. Seller agrees to permit inspection thereof prior to close of escrow and pay for any necessary repairs.*"

The last part of the above warranty clause is very important. If you enter into a contract today that is to close or settle two months from now, a lot of things can go wrong with the appliances and other working parts in that lengthy period. Thus a last-minute inspection a day or two before escrow is to close is very important. If you find at that time that a range burner element is out, you can direct escrow to set aside a small amount of cash to pay for the correction. A word of warning—don't wait until after you close escrow, because it's too late then. Do it before.

If you aren't getting a warranty with the property and don't want to rely upon your own inspection, you can hire one or more professionals to come in and make an inspection. You can even go one step further and make the purchase contingent upon the favorable results of the inspection. Just insert into your purchase agreement (before it is presented to the owner) a clause similar to the following: *This sale is subject to the buyer receiving and approving a roofing report to be issued by a licensed roofing contractor.*

Note that the above clause will allow the buyer to *escape* from the contract if he does not like or approve of the report. Thus this open-end-type clause can be used (with discretion) to actually back out of a sale without forfeiture of deposit. This clause also does not say who is paying for the repairs or possible new roof, but indicates it will be the buyer. The buyer can either "take it or leave it." Sometimes this is necessary when you're considering an older home with a suspect roof and the seller insists that he will not spend one penny on it.

Here is another way to write your clause—a way that puts the seller's money on the line. *This sale is subject to an inspection, at the buyer's expense, of the roof and gutters by a licensed roofing contractor to be named by the buyer. Any corrections, alterations or new roof costs recommended in the report are to be paid for by seller prior to close of escrow.*

This "blank check" second method is better for the buyer. But sometimes you just won't be able to win the negotiations and will only be allowed to have a delayed "yes" or "no" choice. But that is better than being stuck with both a high price for the property and new roof expenses . . . or the cost of a new central heating system. Keep in mind too that these clauses are flexible. They are designed to do almost anything you want them to. I'll be telling you more about them in later chapters.

CONDOMINIUM CONSIDERATIONS

Almost everything written in this chapter applies to whatever type property the investor is buying—single family, small three- and four-unit multiples and condominiums. However, when considering a condominium for your portfolio, some new wrinkles come into play.

Condominium living is rapidly gaining in popularity and, as land costs increase, it is destined to become even more popular in the future. In fact, many housing economists predict that 50 percent of the United States population will live in some form of condominium housing within 20 years. Statistical trends support that prediction.

Condiminiums come in many forms, from towering inner-city structures to suburban townhouses with beautiful, environmentally designed surroundings. Some are conversions of luxurious old rental structures which have been "converted" and modernized into highly desirable dwellings. Some, however, are merely old, exhausted rental properties which have been painted, carpeted, given new kitchen equipment and cast into the condominium market.

In many ways condos are just like single-family homes and much of the same criteria will apply when considering a purchase. But with condos there is another whole set of questions you must get answered. For instance, before you sign any purchase agreement you should have received and read a copy of the Declaration, Bylaws, Operating Budget, Management Agreement and any Regulatory Agreement.

With condominiums you own your unit, but all common walls, walkways, grounds and recreational facilities are a shared ownership. In condominium law it's called undivided interest—which is the joint ownership of common areas in which the individual percentages are known but are not applied to separate the areas physically.

You have a lot at stake, so you must find out what your rights are and how much your monthly association dues will cost. You'll also need to know whether or not there is a master hazard insurance policy insuring you against loss by fire and other perils. Are there any restrictions on your right to re-sell? Some condos require that the association be given the right of first refusal. Ask questions and read all the above-named official documents.

What type of condominium should you buy? This form of ownership is still new; and although it is rapidly gaining in popularity, impartial surveys continue to show that the most preferred style of living is that afforded by the single-family home. Buyers and renters alike, however, are flocking to condominiums. The two biggest reasons for this are that they often have no choice when the single-unit home is priced out of their reach; and secondly, some of the newer and more deluxe condo developments are extremely attractive to the younger—and older—families without children and pets.

When searching for a condo, keep in mind some of the reasons why many people still prefer the single-family home. They want the *privacy* and the *garage* or *storage space* a home provides. Many condos provide this also. So give top preference to the units that have enclosed double-car garages and some type of private courtyard. This doesn't mean you should reject all other units—each one should be judged on its own merits. I am just saying that the privacy and garage considerations are important and should be weighed heavily.

The type of condo you should avoid or take an extra hard look at is the one converted from a large apartment complex. Many of these will soon wear through their resurfacing job and become slums.

As surprising as it may seem, in almost every part of the United States condominiums are now appreciating in value as fast as single-family homes. Perhaps their time has come.

Many first time investors read a few books on the subject and then after getting emotionally worked up their "bubble is burst" in just one day after driving around town with an inept agent, looking at overpriced dogs and the absolutely wrong kind of property. This does not have to happen. —Dave Glubetich

8

THE SECRETS OF FINDING PROPERTY

Contrary to what some people may think—making money in real estate isn't really complicated or particularly hard to do. You can learn the ropes in a relatively short period of time. Still, some fear management responsibilities and the prospect of dealing with tenants, knowing that one serious blunder can put a destructive tenant into one of your rentals. And that bad tenant can cost you plenty in both money and temperament.

Once you get into investing, however, you'll find that management is one of the easiest things you'll have to do. The hardest thing today, believe it or not, is to find suitable property. It hasn't always been this way, and in some states or communities where assumable FHA and GI loans are still plentiful, it's still easy to buy property. But in other areas the realities of the eighties have set in. Few assumptions are available . . . interest rates are too high and significantly add to negative cash flows . . . and the really good buys are gobbled up (often by agents) before you even have a chance to see them. It doesn't have to be that way. In this chapter I'll show you how to find just the right property. But you'll have to work at it, because times have changed.

Following will be two basic techniques. The first will show you how to work with a real estate agent when looking for property. The second will give you a complete look at the "do-it-yourself" approach to house hunting. I am not going to endorse either method to the exclusion of the other. After reading this chapter you'll be able to easily see which method will work for you. You may even decide that a combination of both is best.

A Good Ally . . .
A COMPETENT AND LOYAL REAL ESTATE AGENT

In 1965 I was weighing the pros and cons of leaving my post as manager of a small chamber of commerce and going into real estate sales. At the same time my wife and I were looking at homes in the $15,000 to $17,000 price range. There were still some good pickings at those prices.

I clearly remember looking at one particular three-bedroom, one-bath home. The neighborhood was okay but this particular home backed right up to a busy freeway. I remember standing ankle-deep in weeds and trying to tell our agent, between the roars of passing diesel trucks, that I would not buy this property because it was obviously too close to the freeway. There couldn't have been more than 35 feet separating the rear door and the highway.

Our agent kept telling us that the noise did not matter . . . that we would soon get used to the sound. I thought it was ridiculous that we were even having this argument. Wasn't my agent supposed to find the kind of home my wife and I wanted instead of trying to jam down our throats what he thought was a good buy?

Needless to say, I didn't buy a home from that agent or any other. Instead I made a decision to go into real estate. I remember thinking that if he were typical of the agents I'd find in the business, then maybe I would do all right in that profession even though I did not have any sales experience.

My instinct proved correct. In the ensuing years I did enjoy a successful career. And to this day I still don't really consider myself a "salesman." In fact, the make-up of a successful agent includes many more important elements than salesmanship.

After more than 12 years in active real estate sales — eight of which were as the owner of a firm employing an average of 10 agents — I developed many conclusions about real estate agents. To wit:

The majority of real estate sales people are either too lazy, stupid or dishonest to ever be of any real help to their clients. I realize that is a strong statement but I am going to top it with an even stronger one:

An intelligent, professional and hardworking agent can guide you to more investment profit than you ever dreamed was possible.

I am completely convinced that if you can hook up with one of the super agents in this business, you will make a lot more money than you could by doing everything yourself or by using a mediocre agent.

In the next few pages I'll tell you how to find that terrific agent, how to work with him or her, what to expect in your relationship, and how to dump the agent who is not doing the job you require. For the sake of clarification, I'll refer to the super agent as *The Good Guy*.

HOW THE LAZY AGENT PERFORMS

Most of the poor agents are plagued by many of the traits I am about to list. The following items do not cover all of the possible problems, but just enough so you will know what to look out for when selecting an agent:

LAZY:
> Prefers the six-hour work day and spends half of that time socializing with the rest of the staff. Only tours new listings when he is forced to.

UNINFORMED:
> Always the last to know when interest rates or loan discount points change.

MOTIVATION:
> Has about as much get up and go as a turtle. Won't admit it but secretly desires to make only $10,000 yearly rather than the $30,000 he told his sales manager he wants to earn.

BAD HABITS:
> Likes the way he does things and has no real intention of changing. Would rather take short-cuts instead of doing things right.

FOLLOW UP:
> Returning telephone calls, checking on sales details, etc. takes too much time. Footwork won't be his strongest trait.

INVESTMENTS:
> Doesn't really understand investment properties or investors. When you tell him you want a single-family home as an investment unit, he'll show you the opposite of what you originally had in mind. Again it's too much trouble to keep informed.

CLOSING TECHNIQUES:
> He either does not use recommended sales techniques for closing a sale or he overdoes it in the hope he can make a quick sale and then "head back to the barn."

DISHONEST:
> You will find many more "bad" salespeople who are dishonest than "good" ones for two reasons: 1) It's easier than taking the time to be a good agent and, 2) The bad salesman does not have enough respect for the future *referral* business which a satisfied customer would send his way.

If you are currently working with an agent who fits into any of the categories just described, you had better ditch him unless he is your brother-in-law. Even then you would probably be better off with an agent who is not related to you or involved socially with you.

HERE IS HOW THE GOOD GUYS WORK

On the flip side of the coin are the men and women who are truly dedicated to their profession. As you will soon see, the difference between the two groups is like night and day. Unfortunately, though, there are more bad guys than good guys available.

MOTIVATION:

> The good salesperson is motivated by two things: Money and the satisfaction one gets from a job well done. Don't think that all good salesmen are making or want to make $100,000. Motivation includes the inner satisfaction one can get from helping people.

COMMISSIONS:

> He learns not to mentally spend the commission until the escrow is closed. A professional attitude is maintained this way. By prematurely counting commission income before the sale is completed, a salesman can get into trouble by overlooking problems instead of handling them.

FOLLOW-UP:

> This is of the utmost importance to the good guys because proper follow-up on all details of a real estate transaction will lead to a satisfied customer and then to future referral business. *Future referrals are "bread and butter" to the successful agent.*

KNOWLEDGE:

> He will be as up-to-date as possible on all aspects of real estate as well as on market prices and conditions.

INVESTMENTS:

> Many agents qualify as good guys even though they do not really understand investment principles. As an investor you will want an agent who not only understands how to make money with rental property but also has a feel for it.

PROVIDE EXTRAS:

> Many good agents go one step beyond what is expected of them. They will provide tenants, management service, etc.

It's hard to believe the difference between successful and unsuccessful real estate agents until you have a chance to see both types in operation. Until recently when I sold my realty office, a salesman worked for me who consistently earned over $60,000 each year and had more referral business than he could handle. On the other hand, I had three agents who between them could not produce more than $12,000 in income.

How can one salesman produce $60,000 worth of income while three others, supposedly working full time, could not do better than one-fifth of the production of one person? There are many reasons . . . but the list starts off with MOTIVATION.

The standout agents are certainly motivated by big commission checks. But it goes a lot further than that. They are motivated by an inner pride in the job that they do for their customers. They know, as professionals, that the name of the game is referrals. If they can efficiently sell a property, expertly handle all details, then their happy customer is bound to send his friends to that agent. One transaction well done can help bring five . . . ten . . . or even 20 more customers. Referrals are the name of the game . . . but sadly, many agents do not understand this.

I personally know one salesman who has done such a superb job for so many people that his biggest problem is turning away the business he doesn't have time for. His income in 1977 . . . $150,000. And all that was earned through residential sales, both to investors and owner occupants.

What sets apart these good guys from the run-of-the-mill agents? Here is a clue.

Visit a real estate office—any office. You will be approached by the agent who has what is called *floor time* in the trade. This means it is his turn to have the customer who walks into the office or calls on the telephone. From the real estate broker's standpoint, it is a fair way to let all his agents have an equal crack at new customers.

However, from the customer's standpoint it is almost like Russian roulette. You get what you get. You are not given the choice or even told about any choices. The particular office may have a couple agents who have worked successfully with a lot of investors in the past. They may really know their stuff. But they will quietly sit back and watch while their co-worker, Mr. I. M. Bored, greets you at the front door.

Mr. Bored has only been in real estate sales for four months, but you'd never know that from hearing him talk. After telling him you are looking for a rental unit which is to be priced less than $60,000 and is to have available financing (like an assumption or owner help), Mr. Bored starts into a long discussion of how he knows all about these things and what you really should have is a run-down fourplex which you can fix up yourself. "You'll make a lot more money doing it this way," he says.

The real tip-off, though, comes after you convince him you only want a simple single-family home, and he drags out his multiple listing book and starts thumbing through it. You don't have to be a genius to quickly find out whether an agent is a *good* guy or a *bad* guy. A good agent will inspect enough property daily so that he can tell you about several without needing to bury his head in a multiple listing. A bad agent doesn't inspect much property and will almost exclusively rely upon his listing book.

This is a bad sign and it indicates you'll be wasting your time by going out with him. Be courageous . . . tell any fumbling agents that you don't have time now. But you *may* get back with him when he has a chance to research your needs.

A SPECIAL WARNING IS IN ORDER: So that you can effectively

search for property, I must warn you about one of the biggest "traps" that has recently entered the real estate brokerage scene. And I say trap because it is a "tool" that many new and lazy agents rely too heavily upon. It is the computerized multiple listing book.

This method of sorting and keeping track of available properties became very popular in the seventies. It is a bound book which often is the size of a telephone directory. It is usually issued weekly and more often than not photographs of each listing are published alongside the data on the property. In my admittedly prejudiced opinion the efficiency of the average real estate salesperson dropped several notches when he started using the book.

The reason I am telling you this is that I sincerely believe that if you get hooked up with an agent who selects all the properties he or she is showing from this listing book, you are wasting your time and may easily get discouraged—thinking there are no good buys out there. "That Glubetich guy must not know what he is talking about!" you'll think to yourself.

Here are my reasons for this opinion: First of all, rarely do agents place their best listings on the multiple. They keep them exclusive for a period of time; and then if one proves not to be such a good listing, the agent may submit it to the multiple listing. (The only exception to this is when a Board requires that all listings be placed on the multiple listing.) A good agent knows this and will constantly seek out exclusive listings by calling other offices to ask for cooperative rights. More likely than not he may work on another company's exclusive. It takes time to find out about these properties, and remember that the bad guy is always looking for shortcuts—like his handy and impressive multiple listing book with all the fine photographs.

A second reason for disliking multiple listing books is that it is a slow method—unless daily updates are fed to each office. It usually takes 10 days to two weeks to get a new listing into the book. And, as many agents will admit, more than half of the better listings will be sold before their pictures are in the book.

The multiple listing book is best used to merely familiarize a customer with what type of home is on the market and what to expect in prices. And while occasionally a good property can be found through the book, a better use of it is to find properties that have been available for long periods of time (3 to 6 months). Often these properties will be vacant and the owner will be *very* anxious to deal—thus the multiple listing book can lead you to the type of situation where shrewd negotiations can get you a really good buy.

HOW TO FIND THE GOOD GUYS

Before you start your search, keep in mind that despite the masculine ring to the word "guy," these super agents can come in both sexes. You will also find that most of them have been in the business for over two years. They work out of both large and small, one-person brokerage firms. However, you won't find too many good guys working in so-called "body shop" offices which are largely manned by trainees.

Because detailed surveys have never been made (to the best of my knowledge) that classify agents by ability, income and knowledge, I am relying upon my experiences in dealing with hundreds of agents over the past several years. My educated guess is that only about 20 to 25 per cent of the active full-time agents in any given area will qualify as good guys. And in most communities only about one-half of the Board members are full-time. I have never known a part-time agent, regardless of his or her ability, to qualify as a good guy. That is because it's necessary to be in the market every day—full time—to be able to do the job correctly.

There are three basic ways to find these good guys:

1. ASK FRIENDS AND OTHER INVESTORS: If friends have a real estate agent they are happy with, you can bet they'll want to recommend him to you. Don't stop with just one friend—ask several. And if you still don't feel satisfied, locate every investor you can find (call on their "for rent" ads in the newspaper if necessary) and ask them if they would or even could recommend their agent to you.

Beware of superficial recommendations. Find out why a person was recommended. You're not looking for an agent just because he or she plays bridge with your next-door neighbor. Watch out especially for a recommendation for an agent who was successful in selling a friend's home by holding it open every Sunday until it finally sold. The use of the technique of holding homes open does not necessarily indicate a good agent. In fact, I doubt if you will find many good guys wasting a lot of time with open houses. Sure, sometimes it's necessary, but for the most part an agent's time can be better spent doing other things.

2. ASK A MORTGAGE BANKER OR LENDER: This may be your best source of finding good guys, but it is also the trickiest. Lenders and mortgage bankers (not mortgage brokers, who deal in secondary financing) are in contact with all active real estate agents in their territory. More than anyone else, a good lender knows who the best agents are. The problem is that they also have favorite friends in the industry who they might want to pawn off on you—good or bad.

To prevent a poor recommendation, ask three separate lenders in the vicinity where you intend to invest for the names of three qualified investment agents. Whatever name appears on your list two or three times is the one you want to call. I'll soon give you a list of questions to ask your prospective agents so that you can secretly determine if this is the person whom you should put your trust and time into.

The above criteria also applies to escrow officers. They too know who the best agents are and thus can be a good source for this information.

3. TRIAL AND ERROR: The third method is to place several telephone calls to the owners or sales managers of medium- to large-sized firms. Tell them what kind of agent you are looking for and what you expect of that

agent. Ask for a recommendation, but point out that you will not accept a salesperson just because he or she is currently on floor duty and is entitled to the call. Remember, each office you call will probably have an assortment of agents, ranging from very bad to very good. And don't fall for the line that "all of my agents are good because I personally trained each one." It just doesn't work that way!

If you don't get a satisfactory answer—then call another company. As a precaution you may also want to eliminate the person (broker or sales manager) with whom you are talking. They might be eager for a client and give you a song and dance on how good they are.

INTERVIEW YOUR PROSPECTIVE AGENT

One of the hardest things for most people, including myself, to do is to get really tough and put your foot down and say no. But sometimes it is necessary. For instance, I have known many clients who wanted to invest in property but became so discouraged after running around town for days with an inept agent that they simply gave up the idea.

I salvaged one such investor a few years ago. He came to see me after a Realtor discouraged him by saying that his $5,000 couldn't buy anything in today's market. Now this investor was somewhat short on cash but he did have a strong income and a real desire to buy property. I turned him over to one of my *good guys* and later that day the investor bought a nice 3-bedroom home with a huge backyard that in the near future might have commercial value. The property cost $50,000 but my agent got the investor into it for only $5,000 including closing costs. It was easy to do when the investor found an agent with enough intelligence to work out the financing.

The moral of that story is simple! Don't waste your time, money or positive outlook on a bad agent. If an agent doesn't meet your expectations tell him that he is not the person you are looking for. To help make that job easier, here are some suggestions.

Begin your interview by telling the agent that you are an investor and that you are looking for an investment-wise agent to help you locate property. Play it a little coy initially. Don't admit you have $100,000 to spend because he will do and say everything possible to keep you as a client. Nor should you tell him that you have only $3000 because he may then do everything in his power to get rid of you. Obviously, agents like big spenders. Until you make the decision to work with a particular agent, just let him guess how much money you have.

Before the agent gets too far into his interview of you (ex: How much money do you have? What type of investment property do you want to buy? etc.) create some ground rules. Tell him that you don't want to waste his time or yours and that you would like to ask him a few questions. Be polite; you don't want to antagonize a good agent. Tell him that you are very busy and this line of questioning is truly necessary.

Begin by asking basic questions like: How long have you been selling real estate? Do you work full time or part time? Are you working with many investor clients? Do you own any investment properties yourself?

One thing you want to determine, without being too obvious, is how much money the agent is making. Don't ask outright because he will probably resent it. All you need to find out is if he is earning at the minimum, an average middle-class income for your area. Anything over that amount is immaterial but less than that tells you one thing—he cannot be a full-fledged *good guy*. And you don't want to take any chances on getting hooked up with a lazy salesman.

After a round of preliminary questions, ask at least three loaded ones. Make them up if you want to, or use these three.

Question #1. Mr. Agent, as my Realtor, what will you do if you find the perfect investment property—one that you and I would both obviously want because it is in near-perfect condition and it is priced several thousand dollars under market value?

You will be able to tell a lot about the agent from his answer to this question. There is no absolutely correct answer . . . but his response should indicate that he would immediately contact you as well as any other investors that he is working with BEFORE HE WOULD MAKE ANY PERSONAL MOVE TO BUY THE PROPERTY.

If this agent is currently working with other investors (and he should be to qualify as a *good guy*), but he tells you that he will call you (a stranger) to give you and you alone the first crack at the property, then I would assume that he is lying or at least not really giving you a straight story.

If he answers the question by saying that he would buy the property himself and cut you out, then at least he is being honest. But I would look around for another agent.

Question #2. Mr. Agent, I would like to buy my first rental on minimum down FHA terms. Is this a good idea? (This is another loaded question that is designed to tell you a lot about your prospective agent.)

Immediately dump this person if he agrees with you! If you already own a residence and have no intention of living in the FHA-purchased property you cannot (under the law) purchase this home on government guaranteed terms. If the agent fails to warn you of this or is willing to let you go ahead and buy and thus risk the penalties, you want nothing to do with him. Thus this question will help eliminate the totally dumb or dishonest agent.

On the other hand, the more completely and honestly this question is answered, the better qualified this agent may be. For instance, he may point out that although what you have in mind cannot be done, FHA has a special program for investors. However, because of the high down payment and the loan discount points that the seller will have to pay, it's not always practical. He may then suggest assumption terms, contract of sale or new conventional financing with the seller carrying back a purchase money mortgage. It won't

88

take more than a few minutes of explanation for you to discover how good this agent is.

Question #3. Why should I use you as my agent? What can you do for me that others can't? This question is not a trick question, but one designed to start your relationship off on the right foot. Find out what the agent will or will not do from the beginning. Will he just "keep you in mind" and not call until he sees something that "he thinks" you might want (the kiss of death)? Or will he spend several hours a week in your behalf snooping around for the property you want? And will he report back to you at reasonable intervals, whether or not he found something?

Also from this question you may get an offer for low-cost management services or perhaps his help in finding your first tenant. Make notes on all these promises so you can remind him of them later, if necessary.

HOW TO WORK EFFECTIVELY WITH YOUR AGENT

So far I have given you a lot of pointers on how to find a good agent—a *good guy* who is capable of aiding you in your quest for bigger investment profits. Finding your agent is only the first step. You must next strive to establish a smooth working relationship with him or her.

Honesty is the best policy: There is a saying among real estate agents that: "Buyers are liars." The reason for this is that almost all agents are stung from time to time by clients who emphatically say, for example, that they will pay only $60,000 for nothing less than a four-bedroom home. The agent then spends a lot of time looking for such a property, only to find later that his client bought a three-bedroom home for $75,000 from another salesperson.

The moral of the story is this: Your agent will enter into his relationship with you with as much *suspicion* of you as you have of him. Break the ice by telling him exactly what you want and what you will do to help find the property. Find out what he plans to do for you and then step aside and let him do his job. Once you find your super agent—be honest with him.

Don't bug him to death: Keep in mind that a good agent will have many more clients than just yourself. He may not be able to call you every day or even every other day. So don't waste his time by constantly calling to ask what's happening.

Most agents will take only *one* day off each week. Be considerate! Find out what day your agent is off and then *leave him alone* on that day.

(I am sure that many of my readers have wondered why I am now writing instead of *practicing what I preach.* The answer is quite simple. After 12 years of working six days a week, most evenings and almost every weekend, I got tired, or as they say in the industry . . . burned out. I now enjoy weekend activities with family and friends and watching my children participate in their sports programs.)

Jump when he says to jump: If you have a good agent who is doing a more than adequate job in your behalf, then be prepared "to jump" when he says he has found that special property you have been looking for. Consider that your agent may have spent several hours finding it . . . and when he asks you to inspect it imagine how he will feel when you say you're too tired to see it until next week. If you put him off for lame reasons he'll dump you. On the other hand, if you feel that you are not getting the service you want, you are also free to fire him and find a new agent. Your relationship is a two-way street. Treat it that way.

Put it in writing: Many agents are what you could politely call *sloppy.* They will promise you the world. (Actually, wild promises can be interpreted to mean that the agent is not too successful and is thus resorting to bribery to make a commission from you.)

After working with any agent on one or two transactions, you'll get to know how much of what he says can be counted on. But until you find out, ask him to put all of his promises in writing. These would include offers to obtain tenants as well as estimated closing costs.

Helping your agent: If you want to take on some of the responsibilities for property hunting, then tell your agent exactly what you have in mind so that you will not duplicate his efforts.

I was always annoyed when clients called to have me check out ads in the newspaper. After many years of ad reading and writing, you get to know which are the exaggerated ones designed merely to bring in large numbers of new clients.

On the other hand I was always pleased to have a customer volunteer to drive through neighborhoods (ones that were mutually determined to be desirable) looking for new listings. When a new sign was discovered my client would call me and I would take over from there. This helped to relieve my crushing work load.

For sale by owners: In every community, at any given time, there are many for-sale-by-owner properties on the market. In the trade they are called FISBO's.

Your agent cannot realistically expect you to ignore these hot FISBO properties, but he hopes that you do. In fact, when there is a FISBO property near one he is showing you he will probably plan a driving route so that you won't even have to pass it. Out of sight, out of mind!

A good relationship with your agent should include a clear understanding of what he . . . and you . . . will be doing about FISBO properties. When you begin working with your agent you should let him know that you will be calling on FISBO's but other than that one exception you will remain loyal to him. You might even find it advisable to tell him when you find a FISBO you will then hire his services to negotiate the contract, find a lender and handle all details.

AN ALTERNATIVE—
THE SHOTGUN APPROACH

There is another way to work with real estate agents . . . and that's a shotgun approach where the client works with any number of salespeople who are willing. It's not my favorite way of doing business, but I know of several investors who successfully use this method. Thus it deserves mention.

The shotgun approach is best used when the client either telephones or personally visits as many agents as is physically possible over a two- or three-day period. For the sake of example let's say that an investor was able to talk with 50 salespeople. The conversation would go something like this:

"My name is Joe Investor. I've got $10,000 to spend on a single-family home which I intend to rent out. I don't want just any property but one which I can buy for at least $3,000 beneath its true market value; one which I can rent out for no less than $30 below my total debt service; one on which I will not have to spend more than $500 for painting, yard refurbishing, etc.; and, most importantly, one in which the seller will participate in some or all of the financing so I will not have to take out a new conventional loan."

Mr. Joe Investor would end the conversation like this: "I am asking several agents to help me find this home. I'll buy from the first one who delivers, but I don't expect to waste my time or yours looking for anything less than I just described. During the next week I can be reached at 666-1223."

It's like hunting for a needle in a haystack. But when you're looking for a hard-to-find property, your best approach may be to get as many agents as possible to help you. Even though most of the salespeople Mr. Investor talks with will not lift a finger to help him find a property, some will. Thus one important thing may be accomplished this way—the uncovering of a hidden exclusive listing; perhaps a "cherry" that was being purposely kept away from other real estate companies.

Keep in mind that real estate salespeople would rather get a full commission than just half of one. So if they can sell one of their own listings, they'll make more money than if a cooperating agent sells it. For that reason the best listings are not usually submitted to the multiple listing service. (An exception to this is in those Boards where *all* listings must be submitted immediately.) It is hoped that the listing salesman or his own office will sell the property. Some office commission divisions give the listing salesman more money when a cooperating salesperson in the same office sells a listing, as opposed to a salesperson from another office.

This commission division is only natural—I have no quarrel with it. But it does encourage many of the best listings to be kept under wraps. Depending upon office policy, when a salesperson from another office calls requesting cooperation rights, it may or may not be granted. The "how's" of getting this cooperation is a skill that is developed only after many months of trial and error. You've got to know who to talk with and what to say.

Do you now see the advantages of this shotgun approach? It gives you a way of getting to listings that you may not otherwise find out about. And this can happen in what may seem like record-breaking speed. But while this method may help you occasionally root out a good buy, its use will deny you the many benefits that can be had in a working relationship with *one* loyal agent.

THE DO-IT-YOURSELF APPROACH

I don't know how many times I have heard the buying public complain about real estate agents having all the advantages when it comes to investing because they can buy the good properties as soon as they hit the market. This logic has even been used as an excuse for not investing in real estate. Let's cast this wrong assumption aside for good.

True, the real estate agent has the advantage in having quicker access to new listings than does the non-licensee investor. They also have an advantage in that they can take a commission. Many times I have agreed on a net sales price with a For Sale by Owner and then added my commission on top. In that way I was able to get back part of my costs when applying for a new conventional loan. For example, I would agree to a $60,000 sales price and then tack on a six percent commission which would bring the price to $63,600. It is this higher figure which the sales contract reflects and upon which the savings and loan hopefully will appraise the property. Thus when the sale closes I get $3,600 to help reduce my actual out-of-pocket buying costs. And as a Broker with my own company I didn't have to share any of this. That helped too.

Needless to say these two advantages are big ones for the agent. But despite them I firmly believe that the non-licensee actually has as many advantages as does the agent. The best of these are: 1) Almost every property owner will talk with and negotiate with a principal but will not necessarily do these things with an agent; 2) When a commission is not involved more doors will be opened than if there were a commission at stake.

Let's take a closer look at these two non-licensee advantages, because a better understanding of them will aid in your search for property.

As to the first advantage, you must realize that every For Sale by Owner (FISBO) will greet a principal with open arms. But these same people are liable to shut the door in the face of any salesperson who dares to knock on it. As a principal, you can talk with anyone about buying their property. But as a licensee you are often dealt with at arm's length because it is believed that all you want is a listing. It is hard to shake this. Sure, an agent can deny he is one, but this deceit can only last a short while, and besides, the risks of this approach aren't worth it.

Also keep in mind that "ethics" normally prevent a licensee from talking offer, terms, etc. with the clients of another agent. Any questions or concerns one has must be channeled through the listing agent or the listing company. Believe me, this can be a severe handicap when you are up against an agent who is out of town or "out to lunch." Many a time I have spotted a listing that could make a great package with just a little imagination and help from the listing agent and his seller. But the agent makes decisions for his seller and responds with such comments as: "I won't ask my people to carry a second mortgage or even reduce their price. I personally checked other listings in the neighborhood and I'll have to recommend that they stay firm." Thus many times an agent can stifle your creative ideas without even giving them a full hearing.

Sure, the agent could bring in an offer to force the sellers to make a decision. But when dealing with a lot of customers, the *good guy* agent doesn't have much time to bark up wrong trees. This is the type of thing a principal does not usually have to go through. He is normally free to discuss offers with other principals—that is, unless the home is listed with a real estate broker. Even then he is more free than is an agent. For instance, as a principal you are free to go up to the owner of a home for sale and ask about price, terms, etc. If the home is listed for sale with a broker, you won't be able to buy it without having a commission go to the listing agent, but at least you can talk.

What you shouldn't do, however, is go back to a home you have seen with an agent and discuss terms or other details with the seller. That kind of action would not be well received by anyone. Your rights to access are restricted by common sense.

It should be obvious to you why a principal will have more open doors than a real estate agent. The answer lies in the fact that the majority of times an agent discusses real estate with a potential seller, he is looking for a commission. So most people view real estate agents as potential threats because rightly or wrongly they see them after only one thing—a commission. While an owner may want desperately to sell his property, he may avoid real estate people but negotiate with a principal whom he views as "safe."

It's strange sometimes how the mind works—but in this one instance it adds up to a big plus for the investor who is looking for a good property to buy. Doors for him will be opened and not closed!

The do-it-yourself approach to buying property does have a few advantages. But those choosing this path will wear out a lot of shoe leather. If you've got the time, the patience and the determination, then go ahead—I guarantee that you'll come up with some super buys. Here are some of the best ways to find them.

1. **THE "FOR SALE BY OWNER"**: This is everyone's favorite source. The agent looks here for a steady supply of new listings and the investor searches these properties for good buys. The competiton can be stiff. Yet

only between 5 and 15 percent of the properties for sale in your community will be of this type.

Most of the FISBO properties will be over-priced. Too many of the sellers will have relied upon hearsay and faulty information to set their prices by. All owners, it seems, think their home is better than Joe Neighbor's down the street. And when they find out Joe Neighbor got $75,000 for his they automatically think theirs is worth $5,000 more. Sure, Joe Neighbor's home may have been filthy dirty, but they forget about the big swimming pool he had in the back yard.

On the other hand there are always a few FISBO's that will offer their property at a bargain-basement price or will offer very favorable terms — such as carrying the entire loan balance at a low interest rate. These will get snapped up fast. So the only realistic chance you'll have to get one is to be the first (or at the very least one of the first) to see the property and negotiate with the seller. To do this you must read the first-edition newspapers before other people do. I know that's a tall order — but speed is important. Does your Sunday newspaper come out with a Saturday edition? If it does you'll find the very same classified ad section in the Saturday afternoon "Sunday paper" that's in the regular Sunday edition. But I'll tell you one thing — very, very few people will be reading those ads on Saturday.

One thing that most FISBO's seem to have in common is an inclination for being cheap. Even though they are trying to save thousands of dollars, they don't want to spend more than a few hundred to market their property. That's one reason they usually fail and abdicate the job of selling to a real estate company. Because of this trait you will usually find their ads in throwaway shoppers, posted on company bulletin boards and in the least expensive newspapers (if they have the choice). So don't let any source go unchecked. To save money most FISBO's will only run their ad one or two days each week. The only way you are going to catch these ads is to read these publications every day. And so you don't get confused, I recommend that you keep a record of each person you talk to. Do it by phone number rather than alphabetically. Start with the low numbers under the same prefix. Following the phone number you can jot down notes about the property and your conversation with the owner. Your records would look something like this:

> 357-2275   Mr. & Mrs. Sunshine. A two-story colonial style home. Asking $90,000 — too much home and too big a price for my purposes
> 357-3910   Mrs. Smith. Divorcee. Wants to leave area. Asking $50,000 for her two-bedroom home. In Pinewood area which is so-so. I think she may carry paper so it may be worth talking to her.

You'll be surprised at how easy your job can be with a system like this. Each time you spot what you think is a new ad you simply refer to your phone number file. If you don't find it you can presume it's a new ad. Be sure and leave plenty of space between numbers so you can add new ones. Or you may want to get a little fancier and use 3x5 cards which you can shuffle around as new names are added.

Also watch for the FISBO who will not use newspaper advertising but instead will pound a For Sale sign into his front lawn. These kinds of people were always my favorites when I was seeking listings because they usually didn't have the staying power to be a FISBO. So be alert for small, often hand-lettered signs. Don't assume you've already talked with them just because you have been calling on newspaper ads.

FISBO's are a challenge—and one that can bring you darn good results. But you'll also have to learn how to successfully negotiate with them—and that advice I will impart shortly in Chapter 11 which goes into negotiation strategies.

2. BIRDDOGS: I am not speaking here of the four-legged species which is the hunter's best friend. I am instead referring to the two-legged species who is often regarded as the investor's (or listing real estate salesman's) best friend.

A birddog, if you haven't already guessed it, is the name given to those who are on the lookout for property which may be coming up for sale. Usually these people are encouraged by payment of a small sum (anywhere from $100 to $1,000 for homes) when their tip leads to a sale or listing.

When looking for a good buy, this birddog system can be invaluable. Without much effort you can put dozens of people to work for you. Your friends and relatives (they may do it just because they want to help rather than for a fee), co-workers, neighbors, grocery store clerks, barbers, hairdressers, etc., can all be easily encouraged to "keep their ears open" for news of anyone who is talking about selling. When you get the tip you merely place a phone call to find out whether or not you can see the property and talk further. Don't be discouraged if most of your tips turn out to be bad ones. A few will lead you to the investor's pot of gold—a property in perfect condition, with desirable terms and an attractive price.

3. READING NEWSPAPER CLASSIFIED ADS: I've already told you about the importance of looking for FISBO ads in your local newspaper—but don't wrap fish in the paper after reading these ads, because you're not done with it yet.

Two excellent sources for leads which have provided me with good results in the past are *HOMES FOR RENT ADS* and *GARAGE SALE ADS.* The garage sale ads often (but not always) indicate that a family is clearing out their junk belongings in preparation for a move. The problem, though, is that most people have this sale after their house is sold. But if you are lucky enough to find someone who is selling his excess junk to make room so he can show his house for sale, you may have a live prospect.

The better of the two named sources is the "homes for rent" ads. Many of these are people like you—investors advertising for tenants. But in this group of landlords are two types that are very vulnerable to an offer to buy. They are the ones you are looking for. The first is the family which is moving across town or even out of town and never really did decide whether to sell or lease. The second is the tired landlord who isn't excited any more about owning rental property and will be happy to be tempted by a good offer. This is the person, incidentally, who will be most receptive to creative financing offers.

I know that some of my readers are probably wondering why, if property investing is such a good thing, would anyone ever get tired of it? The answer is simple—several million people own just rental homes, not even considering apartments. Yet few of these people ever read a book on the subject or attended a seminar. Their lack of professional skills often gets them in trouble. And for others, after twenty years of owning property and working with tenants, they just plain get enough of it. It may happen to you some day, too; let's just hope you make a couple of million dollars first.

How do you handle these two types of prospects? Simple! Just ask them if they would be interested in selling rather than in renting. If they say maybe, find out more about their property. If what you hear sounds good, go after it. Don't give up when they say no because "I just rented it last night." Wouldn't you rather have a property that is already rented? That depends on the tenant, of course. But at least don't let this fact stop your possible negotiations.

Newspapers are also good sources for information on distressed property (see next chapter) and for real estate company ads. Don't pay much attention, however, to the agent ads. Most are come-ons and I should know because I wrote these for eight years. If you are working with an agent, let him sift through the ads because he will be much more adept than you at determining which ones are for real and which ones are just a lot of hype. If you are not working with an agent, then still be careful about calling on ads, because you'll be verbally fencing with an agent who'll most likely want to show you five other homes. It's a fact that fewer than one out of every twenty people ever buy the house whose ad they responded to.

4. **PLACE YOUR OWN CLASSIFIED AD:** Some Real Estate offices consistently advertise in telephone books and classified sections to seek out distress property owners who are practically willing to give away their property.

They hook these sellers with such phrases as "immediate cash for your equity" or "we will buy your home at the top market value price." When the potential seller calls, he is usually discouraged because the offer often boils down to a two-month listing before actual purchase—which of course is then less several thousand dollars for commission and other expenses.

While most callers reject the proposition, some do bite. And these desperate sellers often give away $5,000 to $10,000 in equity.

When you are in the market for rental property, why not consider the following method of obtaining property: Place a small ad in the newspaper and let it run from one to two months. On long runs the rates are a lot more reasonable.

Here is an example of an ad that just might work for you:

Cash for Your Property

Private investor is looking for immediate purchase. Cash within 24 hours.

Just like the Real Estate company ad, yours is also a come-on to some degree. What you are offering is to buy the property (if you like it and the terms) at the close of escrow. Your deposit would be placed in the hands of a neutral third party (a title company) until actual title is passed. If the seller is truly desperate, you might consider immediately releasing $1,000 (but no more, as there are some risks to this).

If your terms call for assuming a government loan, then the sale can be finalized in a short period of time. However, if you must arrange for a new conventional loan, this escrow period may be as long as two months.

5. CANVASSING: Canvassing is what real estate agents call their listing efforts when knocking on doors in a neighborhood or telephoning from a reverse directory telephone book. No—I don't propose that you go that far in looking for property. If you did you might as well get a real estate license and change jobs.

But I am going to propose two types of canvassing which can be beneficial and a lot more easily accomplished by the part-time investor.

My first recommendation is to narrow down your search for property to just three or four neighborhoods. I am not suggesting you buy only in those neighborhoods, but that you concentrate your efforts there. You may pick a neighborhood because it's well kept and centrally located; the prices are right; and the demand for property there is reasonably strong. And by getting to know a few areas both inside and out you will be better prepared to make a sensible offer or buy decision when an opportunity presents itself.

A lot can be said about neighborhood specialization. But for now I'll just say that you should drive through these selected areas at least once a week when you're in the market for a property. This is a type of canvassing. When you see something that makes you think a family may be moving, stop your car and ask them. Look for homes which are being run-down by tenants; look for garage sale or FISBO signs.

My second recommendation is to visit new subdivision offices where moderately priced homes were sold with FHA or VA terms. America is mobile—people are always on the move. In California, for instance, it is said that home owners move every five years. This would mean that in a new subdivision every fifth house would come up for sale within the first year. Most likely one of every twenty homes would be for sale after four months. Good assumptions will be available . . . so will some real bargains where the new buyer put in $5,000 worth of extras but will be lucky to get more than $1,000 of them back.

You have two opportunities within these new subdivisions. First of all attempt to make birddogs out of the tract sales staff. You'll probably discover they are already giving listing leads to local real estate companies. These will be leads of people needing to sell both new tract homes and "older" residences. You can be successful—but you'll have to offer to pay some bucks to be so. It can be worth it, so negotiate.

Your second opportunity comes only with a little footwork. It will be worth your time to personally canvass these new neighborhoods door-to-door. Why? Because many will have realized they have made a mistake and will be happy to taken an offer for "their money back." Others will have the usual reasons for moving. The important thing is that many of these sellers are new to your community and they don't know any real estate people other than the tract sales staff. You'll have little competition for good buys which may pop up. If you don't feel up to walking door-to-door, hire a son or daughter. Give them a couple of hundred dollars if you end up buying a property. You can be successful—you'll just have to work at it.

*"When the recession everybody has been wait-
ing for finally hits in a big way, people will lose
faith in real estate . . . and there will be a lot of
distress situations. That's the best time to buy
real estate . . . when everybody else is disgusted
with it."*

*Bill "Tycoon" Greene in the
Impact Report HOW TO BUY
DISTRESS PROPERTY*

9

BUYING DISTRESS
PROPERTY

In 1975 B. J. Snapperhorne bought a big house that sat proudly on a
knoll which was right in the middle of one of the prettiest small suburban
towns you could imagine. But the story of Mr. Snapperhorne doesn't have a
happy ending.

A lot of unpleasant things can strike during the course of one's life. And
Mr. Snapperhorne was struck with his share. Three years after moving into
the knoll house, he lost his job. Mr. Snapperhorne then began to drink, just a
little too much at first, and then by the case. Next he lost his wife . . . she
moved out and filed for divorce.

Mr. Snapperhorne's troubles grew deeper—and soon he couldn't even
hold down part-time work. His beautiful knoll house went into foreclosure.
He had borrowed twice against the home, but now he couldn't get a loan or a
job. His estranged wife's attorney was making a last-ditch effort to get the
house for his client . . . and the bank was just days away from foreclosing.
Little equity was left—perhaps no more than $15,000. It didn't leave enough
to borrow against as Mr. Snapperhorne's home (now worth $90,000) was

encumbered with combined loans totaling $75,000. His story is one that happens altogether too often in America today.

Mr. Snapperhorne's house has become what is called a distress property situation. A trick on words, perhaps, because it's not the house which is in distress, but Mr. and Mrs. Snapperhorne's situation.

This story is fiction. But thousands of situations like this are happening all the time . . . in every community and in every state. And as a story like this unfolds, you can be sure that many individuals are swarming over the property like buzzards, eagerly awaiting their chance to profit. . . . Okay, okay. Let me back up just a little.

As an investor and citizen of perhaps the same town where Mr. Snapperhorne lived, did you have anything to do with his downfall? Could you have saved him from himself? Then why shouldn't you have an equal chance to benefit from this situation that you had nothing to do with in the first place? To hell with the bank or other lenders, they'll get their money back, so why shouldn't you have an equal chance to buy this property and make a few dollars?

A lot of well meaning investors will back away from distress property situations as though they were taking blood money. That's not the case. If you want to make money in real estate . . . and if you want to help provide decent housing for others . . . then take part in one or more types of distress property situations. When you can buy a property for $5,000 to $25,000 beneath market value, you can either turn around and sell it for a quick profit, or possibly rent it out with a positive cash flow (because you paid a lot less for the house, your loan amount and payment is apt to be smaller and can thus be covered by the rent payment).

For the purposes of this chapter I'll refer to distress property as that which is either discoverable through public records (such as probates, tax liens, foreclosures, bankruptcy sales, probates, etc.) or those type of sales which are often out of the hands of the seller (such as some divorces). In this chapter I won't go into those situations in which the seller could be described as highly motivated (the transferred owner who is now making two house payments).

While there are many different types of distress property opportunities, I have chosen to write about the four in which I have experience. I'll be writing about V.A. Repossessions, Divorces, Probates, and Foreclosure and Trustee sales. And I'll pass along some of the shortcuts and tricks that I have learned in my career.

The best advice I can give my readers who may want to get into distress property opportunities is to specialize. It's too difficult to try everything at once. Learn just one way (perhaps probates) and then after you get the techniques down learn about another type—maybe sheriff lien sales.

The details I relate in this chapter are admittedly light—and the reason is that all states have their own sets of laws, policies and methods for handling distress properties. While there are many similarities there are also many differences. Learn the laws and procedures in your state. Either "live at" a good library for a few days, or pay an attorney for a couple hours of consultation.

V.A. REPOSSESSIONS

There is no question about it . . . in most areas of the United States as of this writing it is difficult, if not impossible, to finance a sale with conventional loans.

Loan assumptions have also become more difficult to find, so many investors are seeking new ways of buying and financing real estate. And with these tough times and sluggish economic conditions have come some new opportunities for investors.

It is a known fact that when unemployment rates rise, more properties will go into foreclosure. A lot of good buys are then available at foreclosure and trustee sales. But competition sometimes gets plain nasty at these, almost impossible for the part-time investor to cope with.

Well, here is an alternate way to buy distress property. How would you, as an investor, like to buy a home which might be really worth $52,000 for just $50,000? And how would you like to pay just $5,000 down (that's just 10 percent) plus closing costs of less than $1,000? And for good measure how would you like the interest rate to be between 1 and 2 percent *less* than current rates charged by conventional lenders?

Does the above description sound like a dream? Well, it isn't. It's a V.A. Repossession property. When I had my real estate company my staff put together eight or nine of these a year. And many were sold to investors.

A repossessed property, incidentally, is a home or small rental unit that has gone through the entire foreclosure process and has been returned to the Veterans Administration. They got the property back because they were the guarantors of the loan. If a third party bid had been made at the foreclosure sale, then the property would never have gone back to the V.A. A major reason that some homes are not bid on is that there was not enough equity.

When you are fortunate enough to buy a V.A. Repossession you'll probably have a very good deal for yourself. Here's why:

1. You can sometimes buy these homes with less than $2,000 or $3,000 total cash investment . . . and you will probably never have to pay more than 20 percent total.
2. The Veteran's Administration carries back the first mortgage at an interest rate that is sometimes substantially lower than the current FHA-VA or conventional rates. But since the interest rate is independent of the regular VA interest rate it can sometimes end up higher than the regular rate, too.

3. Sometimes the properties are sold "as is" and are possibly priced a little beneath market value. Other times the properties are "fixed up" and priced at, or even a little higher than, market value. Through an *approved* real estate agent you can have access to inspect these properties. That beats most foreclosure homes in which the owner will not let you through the door.
4. Investors can often buy these properties with the same favorable terms that are available to owner-occupants. There is only one rub— in head-to-head bidding competition with a non-investor, the investor will lose unless he pays more money.

Buying a V.A. Repossession is not always easy. In urban areas there are usually a high number available, but in more affluent suburban communities there may be few available. From past experience I have found that in cities with a lot of repo's there are usually fewer people bidding on them. And on occasion a final sale date will pass without any bids received on a particular home. But the story is usually the opposite in affluent areas. There it is common for as many as 15 to 20 parties to bid on a property.

Following is a V.A. checklist which determines the priority in which offers are accepted.

PRIORITY OF OFFERS

"When more than one offer is received on a property, selection will be determined by the following priorities in the order listed," according to documents issued by the Veterans Administration Regional Office in San Francisco.

A. All cash offers.
B. Amount of purchase price (when 3 percent or more in excess of the list price). *For example*: Listing shows purchase price of $40,000; down payment of $2,000; maximum loan of $38,000 (3% of purchase price would be $1,200). Offer would show $41,200; down payment of $3,200; and the balance payable $38,000.
C. If on terms, the amount of the cash down payment, when it exceeds the required down payment by 3 percent or more of the list price. *For example*: Using the same listing shown in item B, the *offer* would show $40,000; down payment $3,200; balance payable $36,800.
D. Degree of acceptability of credit risk.
E. Purchase for own occupancy and use.
F. Veteran over non-veteran.
G. Among offers otherwise equal, time of receipt by VA will determine acceptance.

In addition to the above requirements, the V.A. demands that each offer be submitted on its forms by an *approved* real estate brokerage firm. The approved firms have special lockbox keys for access to the properties. The participating broker receives a 5 percent commission from the V.A. but he is required to do all of the escrow and settlement work. The V.A. pays no title insurance fees (they say they have good title) and does not require the buyer to have one either. Keep in mind, too, that the V.A. may change these priorities from time to time.

It's not difficult for a broker to be placed on the approved list. He need merely write the V.A. for the proper form, which says, among other things, that the broker will not discriminate against any buyer because of color, creed or religion, etc. As an investor, if you want to buy these properties, you must either find an approved broker or have your own agent (through his broker) get on the V.A. approved list. Incidentally, your broker (and his close relatives) are prohibited from buying repo's.

The most important things to keep in mind when bidding on a property you really want: Make sure your agent strictly complies with all V.A. requirements (like quintuplicate [5] deposit receipts) and deadlines and that you pay more for the property than it's listed for. (See item B of Priority of Offers.)

You almost have to be a good gambler to be a good repo buyer. You might find a perfect property which you want to buy, and the V.A. listing specifies only a $1,000 down payment. Now if nobody else bid on the property you could get it for just the $1,000 down payment. But if another bidder comes along and offers the same terms, he, if a non-investor, will get the property. Thus, you can greatly increase your acceptance odds if you increase the amount of money you are willing to pay for the property.

The third selection priority is to increase the amount of the down payment. You might offer to pay an extra $5,000 down, but if someone else comes along and offers to pay $1,500 over listed price, then you lose out. So if you really want a property and the figures justify it, raise your offer by at least 3 percent. You can often cover yourself by paying 3 percent or more of the required down payment or sales price. The V.A. won't consider anything less than 3 percent.

The V.A. selection committee has the authority to consider each investor on a "case basis." And this means that the investor will usually be required to make a down payment of at least 10 percent of the purchase price. So if you want a property badly enough, beat them to the punch with an offer which not only raises the price but which meets the "sometimes" 10 percent down payment rule. Keep in mind that once the sales deadline passes and the bids are opened, the bidding parties are arranged in order. It's too late at that point to come back with a higher bid.

DIVORCES ... ONLY FOR
THE THICK-SKINNED

If you think that calling on FISBO's is a tough way to find and buy real property . . . then you haven't seen anything yet. Pursuing divorce leads is definitely big-league. It's not for everyone! But I do mention this source because it's definitely one of the best for bargain property. I don't recommend you work with divorces, though, until you feel very comfortable negotiating with FISBO's.

It's certainly no secret—over a million marriages are splitting up each year. And with many of the divorces the property must be split also, so that the couple's assets can be fairly divided. Obviously this means a sale. But this is only half the story. In a lot of divorces the anger and hate is so dominant that monetary concerns are secondary to just getting away and starting a new life. Property is offered at bargain prices just to get it off their backs. Many times I have seen the husband and wife both pack up and leave . . . neither really caring what happens to their house.

A lot of the real property involved in a divorce never hits the formal market (listed by a real estate company). It's too good a bargain, so an uncle, brother, neighbor or the real estate company picks it up and it never has a "For Sale" sign.

Many times the wife, especially when she has children, will do everything in her power to keep the property. The continuity is especially important for the children. The court may request, however, the assets be divided, and unless this couple has a lot of assets (say a rental home which the husband could take) it may be a real problem. One way they can do this without forcing a sale of the home is to give the husband a note and second mortgage or trust deed for his share of the equity.

So in this way one ex-spouse takes the home and the other gets a note. Both now have something less than perfect. The one with the house may be saddled with extra heavy payments with the burden of a $10,000 note with 10 percent interest. But the ex-partner with the note doesn't really have a good deal either because notes do not appreciate in value as do houses, nor do they provide any tax shelter benefits. Thus many of these notes are sold at substantial discounts. (Divorces, thus, are an excellent source also for those who invest in discounted second mortgages, as laid out in my book *How to Grow A Moneytree*.)

I don't think I need to spend any more time telling you about the opportunities that can exist with divorces or about the problems you might encounter—especially when the irate ex-husband finds you at the home and confuses you with the boyfriend who set the divorce in motion weeks earlier. Let's get into the facts on how you find these leads and what you say to whom.

When a couple files for a divorce this information is usually printed in a local newspaper. It may read as: J. Jones vs. M. Jones under a heading *Dissolution of Marriage*. I guarantee you, however, that if you try to find the phone number of J. Jones or an M. Jones who's getting a divorce, you'll drive yourself crazy before you ever get started on this program. It's just too difficult this way.

Even if you do get the Jones phone number, direct personal contact will bring either the most success or the most trouble. You will force action fast when you hit them with the question "Do you want to sell your home?" Most will say no—but that's okay because what you are doing is playing the percentages. A percentage will say yes and a percentage of those will offer you the property, price and terms you are looking for.

(Keep in mind that you don't have to work this hard to make money in real estate. You can skip this entire chapter and trust the well-being of your portfolio to your *good guy* agent.)

An easier method would be to just drop a note to Billy and Bobby Joe. This note could simply say that you are an investor who is looking for property in the area and that if they are interested in selling, please call. This type of note will not force action like the personal visit or call would, but at least a percentage will respond. And besides, you can pay your teenage son or daughter to do all this for you. Teach them the ropes of capitalism at an early age!

What you must do to be successful is to regularly visit your county clerk's office. For some I realize this may be a fatal problem if the county clerk's office is 200 miles away. But it is at the county clerk's office (at least in my county it is—the information could be kept differently in your county) that this information is stored. The data will include the full names of the litigants, the names and addresses of their respective attorneys, and most importantly whether or not this couple owns any real property.

I'll give you a clue, however. If they own more real estate than their residence, they will probably have ample means to divide their assets. In that case don't waste your time.

Many counties also have legal newspapers which print all legal happenings and those things that are required by law to be recorded. This may also be a good source for divorce leads if what they print contains more detail than your local newspaper.

The trickiest part is yet to come. You have now found out that Billy and Bobby Joe are getting a divorce and that their home is at 1000 Elm Street. What do you do next? You actually have three choices: You can write a letter to the couple; contact the attorneys; or make a personal contact with the occupant of the home. This latter choice can be either by telephone or by just showing up at the front door.

But before you set out to talk with Bobby Joe, the probable occupant, you had better think about what you are going to say. "I am real sorry to hear about your divorce," just may be the worst thing in the world to say to an elated Bobby Joe who is finally succeeding in getting rid of that bum Billy. The best advice I can give you is to say nothing of a personal nature. A simple "I understand that you and your husband are getting a divorce" will do. But get ready for a door to be slammed in your face as Bobby Joe tells you "It's none of your damn business." It happens some times!

Your third choice is the most businesslike. That is to write or call the attorneys who are representing the couple. Tell the counselor that you are an investor looking to buy property and that you may be interested in making an offer for Billy and Bobby Joe's home—that is, if they are interested in selling. Remind the attorney that a quick sale could be very beneficial and would eliminate many future problems for his client.

When working with divorces you'll find that many couples will want to make fast decisions. But you can get into a lot of problems—especially when they won't speak to each other or when the opposite happens. The opposite being a reconciliation. And when the now happy couple reunites I can tell you one thing—they're going to want to get their house back. You can prepare for this latter problem by inserting a clause in the contract that should the couple reunite either before escrow is closed or before the divorce is final, you will agree to tear up the purchase agreement but you will get back any deposit or other expenses paid.

Yes, there are a lot of problems with divorces, but you'll also be pursuing an opportunity for great profit with little competition.

PROBATE OPPORTUNITIES

Probate is the legal settlement of an estate upon an individual's death. Following are techniques for buying probate property as it takes place in California. Keep in mind that every state has a maze of laws which pertain to probates. While no two states have the exact same laws, many are fairly similar. Thus this California example can be used as a rough guide for those in other states. However, if you plan to pursue probate opportunities, become familiar with the laws and procedures in your state.

As with all distress property techniques, you've got to find the source for the information. You can't just read the newspaper and then call Mrs. Smith and make your double offer—condolences and price. Just like divorces, probates can be touchy when you go directly to the heirs. But with probates the personal contact can also be eliminated when you buy only at court confirmation hearings. More on this later.

When one dies, his estate, regardless of size, goes through a series of legal steps under the watchful eyes of the court. This court might be the Surrogate's Court in New York, the Superior Court in California or the Probate or County Court in many other states. The name doesn't matter much—it's what happens. And basically what happens in court is that the will (if there is one) is declared valid or invalid; an executor is confirmed, or if the will doesn't name one, an administrator is appointed; all debts owed by the deceased are paid, after allowing creditors a limited, set time to file claims against the estate; tax returns are filed and paid to both federal and state authorities; etc.

This probate time can last from six months (which would be super-fast) to over several years. Contrary to what many people believe, real property can be sold and the title transferred long before the probate period ends. But you will always need court approval to do this.

Before I get into the California procedure, let's take a look at three ways a decedent's real property can be transferred.

Mr. and Mrs. Baker hold title to their residence in joint tenancy. When Mr. Baker dies title passes by *right of survivorship* to Mrs. Baker. Thus any title delays in probate are avoided. Whether or not Mrs. Baker decides to sell the property depends more on influences outside probate than within it.

The second situation is when the last survivor or a sole owner dies. Whether or not the decedent had a will, the property can be sold by the executor. The executor, usually an heir, is most likely interested in getting money for the property rather than retaining it.

This makes a lot of sense, considering that the survivors might be a son in Hawaii and a daughter in New York. If the property is in Colorado, what will they do with it? Most likely sell it. This so-called *private sale* is governed by the rules of the court. It is within the framework of this second described method for selling that the investor can contact the executor or administrator and negotiate a sale. A real estate salesman may also contact these parties and solicit a listing, as the courts in California, for instance, allow a commission to be paid.

What I refer to as the third way of buying probate property is actually the point in time when the court is holding confirmation hearings on previous offers to buy the property. At these hearings usually several probate property sales are being confirmed. A person may *overbid* at the hearing and buy the property. But the amount offered must be significantly higher than the price being confirmed in court.

All contacts with the decedent's family can be eliminated by the investor or speculator who overbids in court. He usually won't find much competition, either. But when he does, an auction-style, oral bidding contest can ensue.

THE NUTS AND BOLTS OF A CALIFORNIA PROBATE

In a California probate the executor or administrator may initiate the sale of a property unless otherwise forbidden by the will. This is called a private sale and may be conducted in any manner. In other words, the executor can offer the home to his next-door neighbor or he can place an ad in the newspaper or list the property for sale.

However, the law says that the real property in question must be appraised and that any offer to buy the property must be within 10 percent of that value. A home, then, that appraised for $60,000 could not sell for less than $54,000. That may not sound like a very big bargain, but here's the kicker. The law also says that the appraisal must be no more than one year old. So if the appraisal is made in January and the sale takes place in October, you can be assured that the value will be a lot higher—possibly $65,000 now.

These appraisals also tend to be low. The situation is different from when a home-owner guides an appraiser through the house, pointing out every good point so that the highest valuation can be given. When the estate is appraised it's a cold, vacant property, with no one to point out its good features. So look for many appraisals to be quite a bit lower than what is really the true market value. The only exeption to this might be when the executor, eager to get the highest price possible for the estate, personally sees to it that the appraisal is as high as possible.

Any offers to buy property must be in writing and they must be confirmed by the court in what is called *Confirmation of Sales of Real Estate*. It is at this confirmation that *overbids* may be made.

PROBATE STRATEGY

Before you can have strategy, you must know how to find probate opportunities. Again you'll have to either read a legal newspaper or keep a close watch at the courthouse where the confirmation hearings are set. Notices will be posted there. If you plan to meet with or call the executor or administrator you'll want to get that information from the county clerk's office. In my county the lady who keeps the dog license info is also responsible for the probate microfilm files. (You can see how difficult it may be to find the right place to look when doing this for the first time—but after you get the hang of it, it is easy.)

Once you get the information, the rest is routine. If you are contacting the executor, you just want to find out if the property will be for sale, how it will be for sale and can you inspect it. If you check out the property and like what you see, you should make every effort to get the executor to enter into a binding contract (subject to court approval, of course). If you negotiate a real sweet deal for yourself you had then better plan to protect yourself in court.

If you would rather overbid in court, you must find out exactly where and at what time the proceedings will be held. Even with this method it would be very wise to inspect the property. *It would have to be an awfully good deal for me to forego an inspection!*

Don't count on getting the chance to inspect the property, either. It's possible the home is being sold to a business associate of the executor and that the price is very very low. This does happen. And you'll be told there is no way for you to get into the home. You'll also be discouraged from bidding in court, but that's one right they can't take away from you.

One favorable thing about working with probates is that the dead can't rise up from the grave and change their minds.

FORECLOSURE OPPORTUNITIES

Joe bought a new car, but lost his job six weeks later. After he missed three or four payments, someone just drove his car away one night while Joe was sleeping. It was an agent of the bank . . . and it was perfectly legal as they hold title (the pink slip) to the automobile.

If Joe had defaulted on a personal obligation—like a department store account—the creditors would get a judgment against him. If he owned real property this judgment could result in a lien (a legal claim) against his home.

If Joe, however, defaulted on his mortgage payments, he would lose his home in what is commonly described as the foreclosure process.

Foreclosures are common in the United States. However, you'll find many more of them in recessionary periods when the unemployment rates are high and business is generally bad. While there are still foreclosures in "good times" there won't be nearly the number that are available in "bad times." A factor which limited the number of foreclosures in the late Seventies was that homes and other properties were appreciating so rapidly (increasing the owner's equity) that the debt-ridden owner was able to borrow easily against his increased equity. Thus foreclosures have not been plentiful in the past years. But times could change.

Foreclosure opportunities are largely cyclical. You've heard the expression, "when it rains it pours." That is the best way to describe what can happen with foreclosures. When times are truly tough, and when homes aren't appreciating by 10 percent and more, then you'll see five or six times more foreclosures.

Before I tell you of the best ways to capitalize on foreclosures and buy property for thousands of dollars under true value, I must briefly go into the technical side of mortgages and foreclosures.

MORTGAGES AND TRUST DEEDS

I often talk as though a mortgage and trust deed were one and the same thing. But this is definitely not the case. While both are legal instruments which when signed, acknowledged and recorded make a parcel of real estate security for full payment of the accompanying loan, there are many important differences. Most of these differences have to do with standardization and foreclosure.

The trust deed or deed of trust is very standardized. You will find little difference in this document from state to state. It is clean and simple.

The mortgage, on the other hand, often varies greatly from state to state. And most of these differences are in the area of forclosure.

Let's take a closer look at key areas where these differences are most pronounced.

1. *Parties:*

In a mortgage there are two parties, a mortgagor (borrower) and a mortgagee (lender). The mortgagor gives the mortgagee a lien upon his property as security for the loan. A lien can be thought of as a legal hold or debt against a property.

In a deed of trust there are three parties: the trustor (borrower), the trustee and the beneficiary (lender). The borrower conveys the title to his property to the trustee as security for the obligation owed to the lender. The title is "reconveyed" to the borrower when he pays off the debt owed to the lender.

In the event the borrower fails to perform as per the agreement, the property is sold at public sale by the trustee for the satisfaction of the debt. It is often a title company that acts as trustee.

2. *Statute of Limitations:*

With a mortgage, an action to foreclose is barred when the statute of limitations runs out on the principal obligation (the note). In a deed of trust the rights of the lender against the property are not ended when the statute has run out on the note, because the trustee has title and can still sell to pay off the debt.

3. *Remedy:*

With a mortgage, the only remedy the lender has is foreclosure, unless the mortgage contains a power of sale, in which event such power may be exercised. In a deed of trust, alternate remedies of trustee's sale or foreclosure are permitted.

4. *Redemption:*

Under a mortgage that has been foreclosed by court action, the borrower has a right to redeem for anywhere from six to 18 months. But with a deed of trust (or mortgage with power of sale) the debtor has a limited right of reinstatement of the loan after default is filed, but no right of redemption. The sale is absolute.

When a mortgage is being foreclosed, the proceedings are referred to as a foreclosure sale and it usually takes place in a court of law.

When a trust deed is foreclosed, the proceedings are referred to as a trustee's sale. The trustee, of course, is the third party in the deed of trust that actually "holds" title to the property as security for the performance of the debt.

Money lenders and property speculators both generally prefer a deed of trust or a mortgage with *power of sale* to a mortgage without a power of sale. That is because it gives the trustee or the mortgagee with power of sale the right to sell the property without court proceedings. To be sure, there are still legal steps which must be followed; but at least lengthy court proceedings are eliminated.

Mortgages with the power of sale are largely treated like a trust deed, giving the debtor no right of redemption. But there are exceptions, so check out your state laws *and* the individual note. Why? In Rhode Island, for instance, a borrower has a three-year right of redemption unless the document has the power of sale. So you would certainly want to know what kind of a mortgage you were dealing with.

The legal steps in California and many other deed of trust states go like this:

The trustee notifies the borrower of his default and records a copy of the notice of default. After three months elapse the trustee must publish a notice of sale of the property in a newspaper of general circulation. At least 21 days must pass between the first notice of sale and the actual date of sale.

At any time during the three months elapsing between notice of default and the first advertisement of sale, the trustor or borrower may stop the procedure and reinstate the loan by paying delinquent payments accrued to date along with certain costs. However, after advertising starts, he must pay off the entire loan and accrued interest and costs to keep the property from being sold in default.

To keep it simple, I am going to continue to refer to foreclosure and trustee sales by the popular connotation of *foreclosures*. I'll also continue to refer to mortgages and deeds of trust by *mortgages*.

MAKING MONEY WITH FORECLOSURES

There are two basic ways of making money with foreclosures. The first is what I call the *short circuit* approach and the second comes by participating in actual sale. Your success with either method will depend, to a large degree, on how well versed you are in your state foreclosure laws, how stubborn your determination is and how large is your reservoir of experience.

It's not hard to find out what the laws are in your state. Consult with an attorney or visit the library for one day. As for determination . . . you'll have to answer that one. Just remember, you'll have competition from "pros" who do this thing all the time, so if you get easily discouraged, maybe foreclosures aren't for you. Experience speaks for itself. After attending a few sales or chasing down a few owners who are in default, you'll begin to learn a lot. The more you know the better are your chances for success.

THE SHORT CIRCUIT APPROACH

At the end of the "foreclosure trail" is *THE SALE*—the time when a property is "put on the block." It's all over then for the defaulting owner. Either the beneficiary (the foreclosing lender), or a buyer present at the sale, will be the new owner. But it might be over then, too, for Johnny Investor.

There are two major problems with waiting until the foreclosure sale to make a bid on a property. First of all, a lot of properties—often the best ones—are purchased before the sale. And secondly, if a good property with a sufficient equity lasts until the day of the sale, it will almost certainly be bought by one of the so-called professional dealers who haunt these proceedings.

I like to short-circuit these professional dealers by going directly to the owner of the property to negotiate a deal. More often than not the owner will tell you to "get lost," but occasionally you will score. And some of those buys will put thousands of dollars in your pocket. But don't think that you'll be alone when you try to short-circuit the foreclosure sale, because this method is known. You'll still have to beat out competition—especially for the better properties.

Here's how you can be successful with this approach: You've got to get the jump on anyone else who may be doing the same thing. So you must find out about new foreclosures as soon as possible. You can do that by either subscribing to a legal newspaper which gives foreclosure data or to one of the many publications in larger populated areas which provide subscribers with all pertinent data on foreclosures and probates. Another method, although very time-consuming, is to go to your county recorder's office and sift through the daily recordings. The major problem with that is that only one out of every thirty or so will be a default.

With a deed of trust, incidentally, this data becomes available when the trustee files what is called a *notice of default*. In essence this notice tells the owner that the 90-day foreclosure period is beginning.

The most important tip that I can pass along is for you to be the first one to approach the owner. Some will resent what they feel is an intrusion into their personal lives. Others will tell you it's all taken care of—which more often than not will be a lie. A few will be honest and tell you of their hopes to arrange secondary financing.

I constantly stress the importance of being the first person to approach the owner. This is because a certain small percentage (perhaps between 5 and 15 percent) are desperately in trouble and are willing to negotiate a quick settlement to their problem. If the first person who reaches them is a real estate agent looking for a listing, that agent will probably walk away with one. If the first person to make contact is a second mortgage lender, then he'll probably convince the owner to borrow as much money as possible—because if he loses the property, at least he has salvaged something.

Now if Johnny Investor is the first one, he may be successful in arranging to buy the property, and for a pretty good price. He has a lot to offer a desperate seller . . . like a quick sale and an opportunity to avoid a degrading experience (the foreclosure) and a chance to redeem his credit. Nobody should want to have a foreclosure in his credit file.

Your chances will be good, if you get to the owner as fast as possible. But if you delay or if you are the tenth person to talk with him, what do you realistically think your chances are? Most of the 5 to 15 percent I mentioned will already be taken and other potentially good situations will turn sour. Why? Because very few people are going to sit tight and listen to ten people "pitch" them. They will probably listen to the first one and maybe the second. But by the time they're approached by the third or fourth person they just turn off. The fifth person will be told to scat and the door may be slammed in the face of the sixth because by this time the poor beleaguered owner has had it with all these people who say "they want to help me" but all along he realizes they are really after his property for a profit.

WHEN GOVERNMENT INTERFERES!

Passed as an emergency measure in 1980 to protect home owners against "unscrupulous profiteers," the California legislature enacted a law which in effect *sometimes* makes the California deed of trust more like a mortgage with a right of redemption.

The law basically deals with the *short-circuit* method of dealing with foreclosure properties before the trustee's sale. It practically eliminates a sale during the first 45 days after the notice of default is recorded. During this period the title to the property is not insurable.

After the first 45 days and up until the trustee's sale, the property is marketable but the law provides the seller with the right to rescind for three years an *unconscionable contract* made while facing a foreclosure. In typical fashion—the law does not define unconscionable, but leaves that up to the courts.

The law also contains many *ands*, *ifs* and *buts*. For instance, it does not apply if the property in question was not owner-occupied, and the rescission period will not apply if the property was acquired by the buyer for his personal residence.

Is there a way around getting caught in an *unconscionable contract*? According to my friend Bill "Tycoon" Greene, a renowned expert in California foreclosure law, the buyer should have the property appraised (to set the price) and then get a letter recommending the sale from the seller's advisor (perhaps his attorney).

The intent of the law was to prevent a homeowner under duress from rushing into a deal that might give the buyer too much of a bargain. California investors are urged to tread lightly when dealing with property about to be foreclosed. What the new law does is effectively prevent much of the help a down-and-out seller could once expect and thus almost insures that California will soon lead the nation in foreclosures. This is one California lead that hopefully won't be copied by other states.

A point worth mentioning is that these defaulting owners will be contacted by mail—especially by second-mortgage lenders. And it's easy *not to respond* to mail. So in reality you will have very little competition for these properties. Now as economic times get worse in this country, more and more foreclosure opportunities will pop up. But you won't necessarily have more competition because few who pursue these opportunities have the financial means to buy more than two or three at a time. Many of the properties that are into foreclosure are what is known in the trade as *dirty dogs*. These run-down homes need to be fixed up before they can be either rented out or sold. And that takes time.

Occasionally time is a factor working against you when buying foreclosure property. One of my favorite ways of speeding up the proceedings is to have the owner transfer his interests with a *quitclaim deed*. This deed is used to remove any "cloud on title" or any interest the grantor (seller) may have. Check this method out with an attorney or title company in your state, but it is usually a good way of removing the defaulting owner from the picture. Once this is accomplished you would bring the loan(s) current and cure the default. You will probably also have to substitute your name for his as either mortgagor or trustor. There will be a fee for this. Also be sure to record your quitclaim.

A word of caution. When dealing with a trust deed you should not take a quitclaim unless you check with the beneficiary (lender) first. If the foreclosure has gone beyond the 90-day period into the 21-day advertising time it may be too late. During this advertising period it's the lender's option whether or not to accept a transfer of title.

This is basically how you can short-circuit a foreclosure. The secret is really nothing more than getting the jump on any possible competition and doing a good job of negotiating with the owner of the property. Sure it takes a lot of time and it can be a lot of trouble. You can make a lot of money in real estate without getting involved in these, too, but if you are after a lot of money *fast* then there is no better way to do it. It's not uncommon for someone doing this full time to buy 20 homes or so during the course of a year— and then sell maybe 18 and keep two for rentals. The profit made on the sale of the 18 can pay his taxes, his living expenses for the year and to boot provide the cash to buy the two which he keeps.

BIDDING AT THE FORECLOSURE SALE

While I prefer to go after foreclosure opportunities prior to the final sale, many good opportunities are available on sale day. It's not uncommon to pick up a single-family home for about $10,000 less than its true market value, or a two-acre parcel of land for a $15,000 profit.

Keep in mind, however, that we are talking primarily about the foreclosure of trust deeds and mortgages with a power of sale. Mortgages without a power of sale are usually foreclosed in a judicial process (in court before a judge) that takes a long time. And after the sale the buyer must wait out a long redemption period (sometimes a year) in which the former owner may buy back his property.

As each state law differs some on this process, be sure to thoroughly check yours. Following is what happens in California, a process which is similar to those in states which use the trust deed.

For those bidding at a trustee's sale, the three biggest problems are *finding the sale*; *inspecting the property*; and possibly *meeting the cash terms of the sale.*

Every trustee has his own location for sales. The law only requires that the sale be held in a place to which the public has access. Sometimes the sale will be at the county courthouse, but occasionally the sale will be held in the offices of an attorney. The public has access—but have fun finding it. Why make it so hard? There have been (and will continue to be) occasions when the trustee and beneficiary did not want bidders at the sale. Greed can tempt almost anyone, especially when facing a chance to walk away with a $100,000 piece of property for just the cost of a $50,000 mortgage plus maybe $3,000 in delinquent payments and foreclosure charges.

To find out about these sales what you really need to do is track down *notices of sale*. The notice of sale sets forth the date, time and place of sales and describes the property which will be sold. The law in California requires that these notices be published at least once a week for at least 20 days prior to the date of sale, in a newspaper of general circulation published in the city in which the property is located. The notice must also be posted 20 days prior to the sale in some conspicuous place on the property and at one public place in the city where the property is to be sold.

If you ever had a secret desire to be a detective, you ought to do well with foreclosure sales. When a large, reputable bank, savings & loan, or other lender or individual who truly desires to just get their due monies back is foreclosing, you'll probably find their notices of sale published in the largest daily newspapers in your area.

On the other hand is the beneficiary (maybe someone who buys existing notes on default property just so he can have this opportunity) who does everything possible to hide the sale—and the fact that there may be $25,000 equity in a property. He and the trustee whom he can control will do everything required by law. They'll advertise all right, but in a smaller newspaper where few people will be looking. And they'll hold the sale in a public place—in a small out-of-the-way town inhabited by only 3,000 people.

Yes, this type of thing happens. An acquaintance of mine, who describes himself as a professional dealer (the pros who follow the foreclosure sales) told me about a sale that was once held beneath a large bridge at 2 in the morning. It doesn't take much imagination to realize why the sale was taking place in such an unusual public place.

This problem of hiding good buys can sometimes be eliminated if you are fortunate enough to have a clipping or foreclosure service in your area. For a not-too-small fee you can subscribe and then not have to read all those newspapers.

The next problem a potential bidder has is to inspect the property and to assure himself that the title is in order. This can be a major obstacle because you just don't have the right to go over to Mr. Ted Debtor's home and go through it because it's in foreclosure and you want to make a bid. Granted—you should try to see it. But odds are that the occupant will not let you inside. You'll have a much better chance if it's vacant, then you might be able to pick up a key from the trustee.

So unless you are fortunate enough to get inside a property, you may have to take an educated guess as to its condition and value. For this reason alone I do not recommend that the amateur investor go after foreclosures. They are a good source, but I personally feel that it is too difficult for the beginner. Get some experience in real estate first.

The trustee will also not guarantee title nor express any opinions as to its condition. Thus you should always plan to get or buy at the very minimum a preliminary title insurance report. Do this also when you're buying directly from the owner. The prelim does not provide insurance but at least it will give you a fairly accurate look at the condition of the title. It will tell you whether Ted Debtor really owns the property or if it is owned by his estranged wife, Susie Debtor, who could drop in some day and take her property back. Unlikely, I admit. But don't take the chance. This prelim will also reveal any other concerns, such as existing rights of way, easements, etc.

The sale itself will be held by the trustee or one of his representatives. It will be held in an auction manner with the property going to the highest bidder. This amount is usually set at that figure which will pay off the entire indebtedness (all loans), delinquent payments and foreclosure costs.

Clarification should be made here. All beneficiaries are not automatically paid off from the sale proceeds. It is possible a third lender, for instance, will be wiped out if he is not doing the foreclosing. Foreclosure action is often initiated by the original lender, say ABC Savings & Loan. This will most likely be followed by any junior lenders filing their own action. They simply bring payments current on ABC's loan, pay delinquent loan payments and foreclosure costs and then initiate their own action. They were probably alerted to the foreclosure by a notice from the county. This happens when the junior lien holder files a request for notice of default and sale.

If, for example, a third mortgage holder failed to participate in foreclosure, he would be paid off only if the sale proceeds were high enough to cover his loan. For instance, consider a home encumbered by a $40,000 first; a $10,000 second; a $5,000 third; and charged with $3,000 in back payments and foreclosure charges. This amounts to $58,000. But if the third lienholder is not foreclosing, the bidding will start at $53,000. The property may sell for this minimum amount and the third lender gets wiped out. If it sells for $62,000, the third lien holder gets his $5,000 and the former owner will get the $4,000 balance.

The third problem a potential bidder has at the foreclosure sale is that he will usually have to pay for any purchase on the spot—with cash or a cashier's check. There are exceptions, of course. But they depend upon who the lender is and whether or not the loan has an alienation clause which will be enforced. In other words, do the terms of the note and trust deed allow a transfer of title with assumption of existing terms? If alienation cannot be enforced, then an assumption of a loan is possible and less ready cash will be needed. These are some of the many things you will need to find out in advance.

Your degree of success will also largley depend upon how much competition you have and occasionally who that competition is. The professional dealer that I mentioned before is very adept at getting the property he wants. If, for instance, a home comes up that has a $30,000 equity, the competition can become furious. The pros, who know each other, will undoubtedly get together and decide among themselves who will take the property. They may even draw straws for it! They're too smart to bid the price up. But you can be sure they'll dip into their bag of tricks and come up with one or more that will get them the property. These tricks have been known to include such things as bidding the price up to discourage the amateur, and then rescinding their bid and later taking the property at the minimum price. Other tricks can include such things as paying off potential buyers by giving them a few thousand dollars for not bidding.

Outside of the pros, who are usually around only for the best deals, you will not have much other serious competition. Whether you are competing with just one or ten others largely depends upon the population of your community.

Despite the competition, the pros and the technicalities, foreclosure properties do present fantastic opportunities. It's *just one method* that takes dogged determination and a degree of experience. But it is also a way of buying property dirt cheap.

*"The prize for investing in real estate goes
to the investor who KNOWS—not who
guesses—the current market price."*
                    —Robert G. Allen
                 in NOTHING DOWN

10

DETERMINE THE VALUE

So you want to be an investor? Okay, then you'll have to become an amateur appraiser. Even if you work exclusively with a real estate agent, you are going to have to develop some skills at recognizing property values.

Can you visualize an investor buying fourplexes when he has no idea of their value? Can you imagine how successful he would be if he constantly paid $4,000 to $5,000 more than true value? Selling would be a chore, too, without knowing what the property was worth.

To develop this skill, you'll have to understand the ins and outs of *fair market value*. Fair market value is sometimes defined as the amount which a knowledgeable buyer would pay a knowledgeable seller for a property after the property has been on the market for a sufficient time. The key here is the phrase *sufficient time*. A property may appraise out at $60,000 but sell for $50,000 because it was sold under distress conditions. The value, however, remains $60,000.

The determination of real estate values is not an exact science. With single-family homes, particularly, the price someone is willing to pay depends upon many factors, such as the exterior and interior design, room layout, landscaping, view, physical condition, age, built-in features, location, neighborhood, school district, etc.

Despite the complexities, you'll have to become a near-expert. You'll be surprised, though; it's not that difficult. I am going to give you some shortcuts which will help you be reasonably sure of the value of most homes or small income properties you will be dealing with.

There are two basic ways to determine value; one way is market value through property comparisons and the second way is a more complicated process known as *replacement value*. A strict replacement cost estimate of value will tell you what it would cost to reconstruct your present building and improvements. It will not tell you the probable sales price of the house and lot together. Thus this method is usually not helpful to the typical investor and we will dispense with any further discussion of it in this chapter.

WAYS OF DETERMINING VALUE

Here are five basic and simple ways that most small investors can determine market value.

1. TRUST YOUR REALTOR: Many investors place their full trust and confidence in their real estate agent. What he says goes. The hours spent in an investment program will be minimal when you rely upon someone else. How easy it can be! But is it wise?

A competent *good guy* agent can do many things for his client—and one of those things should be a recommendation on the value of a property. But we are all human, and thus we can make mistakes—even the highly touted M.A.I. appraisers. Two heads are certainly better than one. My advice is, don't box yourself in. What if you lose your agent? At least gain some knowledge of ways to determine value.

2. TRUST YOUR OWN INTUITION: Again, this is not the best way to determine value. But it is a start.

By intuition I mean the informal collection of data which is stored in that grandest of all computers—the human brain. If, for instance, you tour thirty or so properties in a given time in a specific community, you can soon develop a fairly accurate opinion of their value.

It certainly isn't scientific and you'll have to allow a percentage for error, but surprisingly that percentage can often be less than two percent. That's $1,000 or less with a $50,000 property.

This intuition doesn't just happen. You will have to make a conscious effort to develop this skill. Here's how to do it. Whenever you inspect a home or income property, make a mental note of the asking price in relation to key features such as *location*, approximate *square footage*, and general *condition*. Try to lock this information into your subconscious memory. If your memory needs help, jot down some notes.

You won't get enough data until you inspect about thirty different properties (or maybe as few as eight if you are only dealing with one moderate-sized subdivision of about 400 homes). For maximum accuracy this whole process should take place in a two- to three-week period. If you looked at just one house a week I don't think you could take in enough concentrated data to make effective price judgments.

This knowledge will also be helpful a year later. Sure, your memory will be rusty and prices will have changed. But you will find it is relatively easy to recall facts and start the intuition process over again. It will be easier the second time. You may need to see only a dozen or so properties to jog your memory and give you enough new data so you can mentally update prices.

As you might have guessed, there is one thing wrong with this method so far. That is because the discussion to now has been about *asking prices* and not *sales prices*. It is comparable sales prices that are used to determine market value. So to take this intuition process out of the backwoods and make it a fairly reliable method, you are going to have to make some adjustments. You'll have to discover the eventual sale prices of the homes which sold after you inspected them. (If you are working with a sales agent ask him to supply these figures to you as they come in to him.) The second thing you should do is learn the sales price of each "sold" home you drive by. Just go up to the door and ask.

Does this sound complicated or impossible? It really isn't. With a little experience you'll be doing it like it was second nature. In fact you've probably done this before when looking at property. The only difference is, I am recommending that you now make a conscious effort, dig a little deeper for selling prices, and realize that you are not an expert in judging values until you see enough properties. After following these simple procedures you'll soon realize that you possess a previously hidden, uncanny ability to determine property values.

3. **COMBINATION OF THE ABOVE TWO METHODS:** While still not a very scientific method for determining value, a combination of the two previously described ways is probably more than sufficient to meet most of your real estate requirements. (Since this is a how-to book rather than a text book, I can get away with such unprofessional statements. But being very practical, there are few times when you will need more scientific data.)

Two heads are certainly better than one. The biggest drawback to two heads, though, is when you or your agent go into a purchase (or listing) without enough "property experience" and neither of you wants to admit it. If you don't have enough mental data, don't try to bluff each other because you're afraid to be embarrassed. Ask: "Have we seen enough property and have we reviewed enough sale prices to make a conclusion about this property?" If the answer is no, or if you are dealing with a unique situation or property, either hire an appraiser or do a market comparison study.

4. **FEE APPRAISAL:** An appraisal is an opinion of value from someone competent to make that opinion. A fee appraisal is not—I repeat—is *not* an opinion of market value that can be obtained free of charge from most real estate agents. It can be obtained from either an M.A.I. (a member of the American Institute of Real Estate Appraisers) or a S.R.E.A. (a member of

the Society of Real Estate Appraisers). For a simple appraisal of a single-family home your cost should run between $75 and $250.

Keep in mind that an appraisal is an estimate. It is an opinion. It may or may not be accurate. The appraisal's accuracy depends upon the basic competence and integrity of the appraiser, and by the soundness and skill with which he processes the data. Its worth also is influenced by the availability of pertinent data. And, I can add, the willingness of the appraiser to make data available. Some won't spend much time digging. So if you want a high appraisal and if you know of any recent sales which would support a high valuation, give this information to the appraiser *before* he gets under way.

5. **THE MARKET COMPARISON APPROACH**: Most of the time you are buying or selling property, any one, or a combination, of the above methods will be sufficient. When you need an accurate valuation on a large or difficult property, don't hesitate to bring in a qualified fee appraiser. Many of your situations, though, are an obvious cinch—like a distress property which can be purchased way under its true market value. Use the intuition approach on this kind. Why waste time or money otherwise?

There is another method which fits in between those described. It is the market comparison approach. This method is scientific—unlike the intuition method. It is also one of the basic ways a fee appraiser uses to determine fair market value. But it is also a relatively simple method which you can learn to apply and get almost the same results as the professional would. It takes a fair amount of time and effort, but the cost savings and accurate results may well be worth the trouble.

Without going into 40 to 50 pages of explanation and diagrams and charts, there is no easy way I can teach you this system. So instead I am just going to outline this method here. For those of you who are serious about doing your own market comparison appraisals, I will recommend a very good book on the subject. It's called *How to Appraise Your Own House* by an M.A.I. friend of mine, Richard Maxwell Rhodes. It's published by Delphi and is available at many bookstores, but for $9.95 (includes postage and handling) you may buy it from Impact Publishing Company.

The market comparison method basically means that you are comparing similar properties to a subject property which you are evaluating. The theory is that if properties B and C are very similar to your subject property (A), then the value of A should be the same as B & C. One thing you can be sure of is that it usually gets more complicated than that. For instance, if home B has a swimming pool but home A doesn't, you have to adjust for that difference.

This method requires a lot of foot work, as you cannot properly use it unless you have fairly similar homes for comparison. And these properties should be homes (or like properties) that have sold within a six-month period. Thus to get these comparables you may find yourself poring over sales data in real estate offices, knocking on doors, or visiting the county recorder's office. And to be accurate, you'll have to get out a tape measure and find out the square footage of the properties. It's a lot of work—but it can be fun. And it might save you a few hundred dollars . . . or even more if it prevents you from buying an over-priced property.

Another method for determining value—which I won't be going into—is the INCOME or CAPITALIZATION approach. They are formulas which are basically used for larger rental units which are valued by the income they produce rather than by the market value approach.

AN APPRAISAL USED AS PROTECTION AGAINST A POTENTIALLY BAD SALE

The reason for an appraisal is to let you know the accurate value of a piece of property. Thus if the value is not up to your expectations, it should provide you with the reason to back out of a sale. This is your right; however, most buyers get foxed out of this opportunity to rescind. Here's how to get back that right.

It all has to do with the words *subject to.* When you buy a property subject to obtaining a new conventional loan in the amount of $60,000, that home must be appraised for $75,000 if you are paying twenty percent down. If, for instance, your purchase agreement says that *you and the property are to qualify for a new conventional loan in the amount of $75,000*, and if the appraisal is short (say a $69,000 valuation) you'll have to keep trying other lenders until you get the $75,000 appraisal. The only other two alternatives are losing the sale (the home didn't appraise) or negotiating a new contract. A new contract could end up mostly in your favor—like buying the property for just $69,000—or perhaps in the seller's favor with you paying additional down payment to buy the property at an amount over the appraised value.

(Keep in mind one important thing—it appears that banks and savings and loans appraise tighter when they are short on funds and are more generous in their figures when they have a lot of money to put out. I can't prove it . . . but I have definitely come to that opinion over the years.)

Technically you can shop different lenders until time runs out on your contract. You are locked into this contract because the wording said buyers and property to qualify for a new conventional loan. The key here is *a new*. If the phrase were more specific and called for a new loan from ABC Savings and Loan, you would be released from your contract if ABC came up with the short evaluation.

What about those many times that you are not applying for a new conventional loan? It's even simpler! In chapter 12 I'll be writing about "escape clauses." But there is probably none more basic and above board than an appraisal. When buying a property, unless you are absolutely sure of the value, it is always wise to make the sale subject to a formal appraisal. If the property doesn't measure up—you are not obligated to buy. As the sellers may not trust a market comparison prepared by the buyer, they can hardly argue with an appraisal submitted by a professional.

You could word your sales agreement something like this to avoid a lot of potential hassle: *This sale is subject to the buyers paying for and receiving an appraisal within 10 working days. If the appraised value is not $75,000 or higher, this contract is null and void.* Check local customs or consult with an attorney before doing this. The wording may vary, but the concept is universal. You don't need to buy anything unless you have a fairly clear-cut idea of its value. While there will be many times that this precaution would be a waste of time, there will come a time when the "escape clause" may be most welcome.

"When negotiating many strange and weird things will happen to you that are not supposed to happen and are not written up in the textbooks. Be prepared and don't get rattled. Maintain your adult personality."

A. M. Barr
from his real estate course

11

HOW TO BE A WINNER WHEN NEGOTIATING

Do you want to be a winner . . . do you want to double your money in real estate every two years? I presume you do, or you probably wouldn't be reading this book. Then pay attention, because in these next few pages I'm going to show you how to successfully negotiate for those things *you* want. You'll be getting *your* way for a change!

"Is this important?" you may ask. "I can use an agent," you may say, "Someone who is already adept in negotiating who can do all this for me." But in return, I ask . . . Who motivates the motivator?

You'll be a winner when *you* understand all the *gives and takes* of negotiations. Whether you use this knowledge yourself, or you set this knowledge in motion through your agent (like charging him up and pointing him in the right direction), having it is important.

It's important, that is, if you would like to save an extra thousand dollars or two the next time you buy a property.

Before I get into specific strategies, like ploys to use with *sellers, buyers, tenants,* etc., I am going to make a few general comments. We'll find out whether you have the "raw material" to be a good negotiator. To be honest with you, not everyone has the basic stuff. It can be developed, though. But it will take a little longer while that person without the raw material fights his inner self to change some attitudes.

Remember the self-defeating negative attitude I talked about in Chapter 1? . . . Well, you can be dominated by negativism. If you are the type of person who constantly reaches for an excuse, you're not on the right track.

You can be shy, introverted, outgoing, slightly pessimistic; you can even stutter 'n' stammer a little—but you can't be afraid of people. A negotiator must be able to firmly say, yes, no, or perhaps, and not be too timid to speak his mind.

A negotiator should be an honest person—because many can see through deceit, lies and half-truths. But at the same time it doesn't hurt if the negotiator is a good poker player.

A good negotiator can be stubborn, conceited, casual or formal, but he must know how to gracefully "bend" and compromise, because that is what negotiations are all about—getting people to do what you want them to do while sometimes *appearing* to be compromising your original goals.

How do you stack up? If you've got what it takes, then let's get deeper into the subject. I'm going to start with a discussion of *motivation* and what motivates sellers. After all, how can you expect to win if you don't understand your opponent?

FIND OUT WHAT MOTIVATES THE SELLER

You will never be a top-notch negotiator until you learn what motivates the seller to sell. As a rookie salesman, this was driven into my head. It seemed as though every day I heard, "You can't squeeze blood from a turnip so find out what you are dealing with. Don't bother with the turnips."

I became a believer . . . and to this day I can't walk through a home for sale without asking the preliminary question my sales manager taught me to ask: "Where are you folks moving to?"

The ethics of my profession did not allow me to come right out and ask questions that were too direct, such as: When do you have to be out of the house? Will you carry paper? For a quick sale would you take $3,000 less than your asking price?

But this simple inquiry was my first step in finding out about what is called *seller's motivation.* I needed to find out whether the sellers might be candidates to carry back paper, or I wanted to find out whether they were firm on their price. Their answer could be a clue as to what to expect if I brought an offer in on their home.

If I was told they were transferred to Little Rock and the husband was already there looking for a new home, I could surmise that they were highly motivated and might accept a lower offer—that is, if the transferring company wasn't buying the home after a month or two on the market.

Another answer might indicate an early retirement and a move to a country home under construction. This answer indicates both a plus and a minus. The minus was that the sellers may not be in a hurry to sell and might stay fairly firm on their price. But on the other hand they were good candidates for carrying a second mortgage.

This line of questioning could also uncover divorces, remarriages, foreclosures, health problems, etc. Once upon a time my Board of Realtors published this motivation information on the listing under *reason for selling*. Believe me, it was a big help in deciding what kind of an offer to bring in and how to structure negotiations. It was dropped, though, because many sales people didn't think it was pertinent. They just filled in the blank with the word *moving*. Incidentally, over seventy percent of new salespeople in most Boards fail or quit during their first year. I rest my case.

Following are seller motivation factors plus my interpretation of what they mean:

When a seller is motivated by the following factors he is not a good candidate for an investor buyer. This seller won't swing on financing, although he may drop down some in price.

- Moving to a bigger or more expensive home
- Job transfer to another city or state

If the seller's motivation is as follows, he may be a candidate for creative financing, but not a very strong one. You can offer less price on the last two.

- Moving to smaller home/apartment/condo
- Divorce, probate sale or pending foreclosure
- Selling because of financial difficulties

Here is the cream of the crop for investors—at least as far as terms go. This group will be the most likely to carry back paper or the entire loan, give you an option, take a wrap-around loan or otherwise participate in the financing. They may be a little tighter on their price, though, than the second group.

- Tired landlord—wants out of management problems
- Absentee owners—especially after they realize they won't be moving back to city where property is
- Investor selling off part of portfolio
- Seller with tax problems—can't take any capital gains

Please don't treat these criteria as firm. I don't like any method, system or what have you that is not flexible. There are always exceptions; it's just that from my experiences I find that those in the last group are more inclined to "play ball." The sellers in the first group will rarely carry back a second mortgage, for instance, because they usually need every penny they can get for their next purchase.

Once you find out why a person is selling, you can plan your negotiating strategy. It helps to know this before your offer to purchase is written. Sometimes, though, you won't know until your offer is being presented. But it's not too late—you can always regroup.

NEGOTIATION STRATEGIES

In the next few pages I'll be passing on to you some of the negotiating tips and ploys I have learned over the years. I am sure there are many other techniques which I don't know about . . . but by mastering (and using) these few concepts you will be able to out-fox and out-maneuver almost anyone you ever negotiate with.

I'll start with some general tips, ones you can use in almost any situation. Then I'll go into specific ideas which you can use in particular situations— like when you are negotiating with a FISBO. There is no significance to the numerical order.

IN GENERAL:

1. *Find out the needs of the other party.* This is important. Determining needs can be described as delving into what motivates someone. For instance, if a seller is selling only to raise $10,000 cash for a business venture, you can assume he might "carry back" the rest of his equity . . . with a little persuasion. You can't buck basic needs, but you can cater to them, especially when they are parallel to your needs.

2. *Always start out negotiations slowly.* Be relaxed. Get the other party involved before you get tougher with your demands.

3. *Learn the art of compromise.* Don't associate compromising with being weak. Instead it should be part of your strategy. For instance, when selling, set a false goal, but don't reveal that it's false. This might be a $75,000 asking price on a property—where your real goal is to get $72,500. Thus after a round or two of negotiations you can magnanimously offer to reduce your price to $73,500, still leaving room for further compromise. "And now that I have broken the ice with a $1,500 reduction," you can say to your opponent, "perhaps you can meet me half way." It can be an effective strategy—what you are really doing is giving up something you never intended to keep in the first place. But your opponent doesn't really know this and may respond to your kindness with a concession on his part.

4. *Use trade-offs.* Trade-offs are what I describe as mini-compromises, or a series of little concessions you can make which will hopefully be matched by similar concessions from your opponent. For instance, "If I let you keep the draperies and kitchen curtains, then I would like you to leave the refrigerator with the property."

5. *Learn the art of patience.* My biggest fault as a negotiator was that I wasn't patient enough. I knew several real estate salesmen who had reputations as great listers. What they did that I didn't was to stay in negotiations for five, six, seven hours, or however long it took until they either got the

listing or were kicked out of the house. Now I'm not recommending such stubborn staying power, but I think the example makes its point. You will not always come to an agreement in a half-hour. Be patient, and be mentally prepared to stay with it for three or four hours. There may even be times when all parties sit in silence for several minutes—even though it may seem like an eternity. That's part of the negotiations—make a point or an offer and then keep quiet until you get a reply, even if it takes ten minutes.

6. *Don't negotiate when you are emotionally upset or sick.* Sure, there may be a time when you have no choice, but if at all possible stay away from the proverbial negotiating table when you are unable physically or emotionally to handle it.

7. *A little intimidation doesn't hurt your cause.* If you are like me when it comes to seasoning, you like a little salt on much of your food. Without salt, baked potatoes taste bland. Too much salt and they're ruined, but with just the right amount they taste great. The same principle applies to intimidation. It's a good thing if your opponent is slightly in awe of your investment knowledge or if he respects your ability to handle negotiations and business affairs.

Your opponent should be properly intimidated so he will think twice before trying to fool you. He won't try to bluff you if he knows that your knowledge of real estate values and/or financing is solid. How do you become the intimidator? Not by being too outspoken, a braggart, conceited or domineering, but by casually giving a little background on yourself before you get into more serious discussions. Take advantage of those first few minutes where there is a lull before the first serious round of discussions. During the "small talk" drop a few comments about how you are buying property, how you have checked on neighborhood sale prices or tell a little story about some of the financing problems you've had on another property.

8. *Set the tone by letting your opponent go first.* Let your opponent begin the serious negotiations and let him make the first concession. He might get into the habit of conceding, and it's better he do it than you. Another important reason for doing this is that often you don't know the price or terms a seller will accept until he states this. For instance, you know that the particular seller you are negotiating with is soft on his $75,000 asking price—only you don't know how soft. So if you speak first and offer $74,000 you could be a big loser if he were mentally prepared to accept $72,000. Sometimes you'll be surprised at what price or terms are offered you. So be patient and let your opponent make that first offer.

9. *Listen more—talk less.* This rule is closely associated with the previous one. It's a time-honored rule of salesmanship—but one many people have a hard time obeying. To put it simply . . . keep your mouth shut and let the other person do the talking. Your opponent will appreciate the chance to talk and might just talk himself into a corner. You'll learn a lot which will help form your later actions if you'll just be quiet and *listen.*

10. *Keep personalities and personal attacks out of your strategy.* It should go without saying—but often in the heat of negotiation one party resorts to personal references. For instance: "Mrs. Smith, the reason I will not pay more than $73,000 for your home is that it's in worse condition than a pigpen. I'll have to spend days and hundreds of dollars getting this place cleaned up."

Mr. and Mrs. Smith stop negotiating in good faith (or even at all) after that statement. Avoid personal references unless you can be very adept at skirting the edges. The following statement would have done that: "Mrs. Smith, I can only afford to go $73,000 because I am setting aside quite a bit of money to renew the landscaping, repaint the interior and fix those broken doors and windows. I want to have this home in tip-top condition for my first tenant."

11. *The flip-flop approach to negotiations.* As I said before, be patient in your negotiations and let the other party lead the way. But you should strive to control the basic direction you're going. For instance, when buyer and seller get together the one biggest question in the negotiation is price. It's to settle that question of price that you are negotiating—it is the pinnacle you are reaching for. But if you can't get your opponent to accept the price you want him to, lead the negotiations away from that question. Tell him, "Let's forget the price for a moment and take a look at the occupancy date."

Get away from whatever point you're deadlocked on and go to a more minor point and try to settle it. When this is accomplished on one or two points, *then* go back to the question of price. Everyone's mind has been off that question and you can start over again from a fresh direction. If you deadlock again, flip-flop back to more minor issues. Keep doing this until you run out of minor points.

12. *Put it in writing and then move on.* Don't make any real estate agreement that is not in writing. It doesn't matter that you don't have the proper forms—put it in writing even if it's on a paper napkin, and then have all parties to the agreement sign it. This is usually done at the conclusion of the negotiations when everyone is exhausted. So after everyone has a copy of what was agreed to, say goodbye and leave. Don't rehash what has already been done or your opponent may be reminded of something he wanted to add to the agreement and you could destroy what you've already accomplished.

NEGOTIATING TIPS FOR DEALING WITH SELLERS

13. *An agreement can't be signed over the phone—so don't sell over the phone.* The biggest mistake novice salesmen and investors make is revealing their price and terms over the telephone. They'll say something like: "Mr. Morris, I want to offer you $73,000 for your home and if it's okay, I would like to talk to you about it."

Mr. Morris will almost certainly answer with something such as: "Let's not waste our time, I want $75,000. If you are willing to pay that, then we can talk." The end results of the short phone conversation is *failure*.

That's not negotiating . . . that's being stupid. You might be surprised at how many people (and even real estate agents) present their offers on the telephone. They rarely succeed.Both parties need to negotiate in person, at a place and time when an agreement can be signed. It's to everyone's advantage. In the above example the buyer needed a personal confrontation to have any chance of getting his price. And the seller needed a face-to-face meeting so he could make his higher price bid.

14. *Meet with all owners.* More often than not, you will be dealing with a married couple who own the property jointly. Then why negotiate with just one? Don't meet and discuss any terms until both husband and wife or all available owners can be present. Also, when inspecting the property prior to submitting your offer, don't make any remarks or give any hints as to what your terms may be. If you tell the wife, for instance, that you may be interested in buying the home if they carry some paper, you are giving them a lot of time to create reasons why they shouldn't do it.

15. *Bring a written offer to the negotiating table.* Don't make verbal offers . . . you'll probably get nothing but a verbal response—and you can take that and a quarter and buy a cup of coffee (maybe).

Put your offer in written form and present this to the seller at the beginning of the negotiations. If you are not a real estate salesman or if you aren't chummy with one who can give you some kind of a purchase agreement, buy a supply. Some business supply stores carry them, or write Professional Publishing Corporation, 122 Paul Drive, San Rafael, Calif. 94903. For just $2.65 plus $1 postage and handling (plus sales tax for California residents), you can buy a pad of their form 101 called Residential Purchase Agreement and Deposit Receipt. It's easy to use and should be legal in every state.

16. *Don't let them sleep on it.* In real estate, the kiss of death comes after three hours of emotion-draining negotiations when one of the sellers abruptly stands up and announces: "Let us sleep on it."

Don't let them do it. Both buyer and seller deserve more than that. After several hours of difficult negotiations both parties should be able to come to some understanding, even if it's an agreement to have no agreement. It's not like the sellers were taken by surprise. If the home has been on the market for any time at all then they have had plenty of time to realize exactly what terms and price they want. So get an answer, because if they go to bed to think about it odds are that they'll be more negative the next day and you'll lose a deal. Following item 17 will give you a workable tip on how to get quick action.

17. *The two-offer strategy.* You're not going to come out ahead in too many negotiation encounters if your opponent knows that he has you in a

corner. If he feels that you want his property badly enough, he will undoubtedly remain firm in his demands.

Thus you must adopt an attitude of *I don't care too much because I have another property which I will place an offer on if I don't get yours.* I am not saying this has to be true and I'm not saying you should lie. Be a good poker player—let your opponent know that you saw other properties you liked and that you may put an offer in on one of them. You must *infer* that your opponent's property isn't the only game in town or he'll probably get a lot tougher in his demands.

18. *When to put "give-ups" in your contract.* It can often—but not always—be beneficial to present the owner with an offer which contains several "give-up" points which you can graciously shed at critical points in the negotiations. For instance, you may not give a darn about keeping his ten-year-old refrigerator, but it looks good when you can say, "Okay, you can keep the refrigerator if you'll let me have occupancy by the 25th of June rather than July 10." People will often respond with a kind gesture on their part.

But let me warn you of one time when you should not fool around putting "give-ups" in your offer. That is when you are in a seller's market and you have just found the ideal property. The problem is, you have competition. If you want it, you had better not fool around with negotiations and low offers. *That's the time to come in with your best offer—one designed for the seller to accept without counteroffers and a lot of hassle.*

19. *How to knock "ever so gently" your opponent's property.* Most sellers strive to get top dollar for their property unless they are in some sort of distress situation. From my experience I have found that most FISBOs used very faulty methods to set their asking price. They may choose a $79,000 asking price because a neighbor on the next street got $79,000 and that home wasn't half as nice as theirs. But if you look into the situation, the truth is that the neighbors started out asking $79,000 but finally sold for $74,000. When other neighbors asked what they sold their home for, they said, "We got what we were after." Thus the rumor started that they got $79,000. A second faulty method for setting an asking price is to rely on what real estate people say the property is worth. Agents seeking listings will always give a high price so as not to insult the owner and maybe lose the listing.

Most sellers aren't trying to get more than their property is worth—they are just trying to get what they think is a fair price. Thus the best ammunition you can bring to the negotiation table is a detailed list of what similar properties sold for, preferably homes in the same neighborhood. This list can be powerful and will help to get a big reduction in price where nothing else you could say or do would. And it's a way of knocking the house without insulting the owners.

It's not always easy to compile this list, but the place to start is a real estate office which will be kind enough to give you this information from their files or multiple listing sources. Your second method is to drive around and look for *sold* signs. If you can't find any or enough (you should have three comparable sales on your list) ask a man cutting his lawn whether he remembers any homes selling in the past few months. Ask around, but only go after sales which took place in the past six months.

20. *The dramatic close.* For a moment, let's suppose that you have been in negotiations for over two hours with a seller who you think may just be more stubborn than a mule. He is asking $80,000 and you brought in an offer for $72,000 but expected to pay around $75,000, which you feel is the correct value of the property. Except for minor concessions on personal property, you succeeded only in lowering the price to $79,500. You're finished! Almost everything you can think of saying or offering has been done.

It's time to go, because you have wisely decided not to pay more than $75,500 for his property. Secretly, you want to call the "stubborn mule" a few choice names, but you don't. Instead, you muster up all your emotional strength, stand up, and put on your coat without saying a word. You take your pen and scribble your final offer (which you have saved for this moment) of $75,000 on the purchase agreement and then gently toss it on the table. Then you announce: "I am leaving now, and I am also leaving with you this agreement with my best price. It's a fair price and it's as high as I am going to go. I'm going to give you the rest of this evening to accept or reject it. You can call me at this number tonight." After that, you head towards the door. You have broken off negotiations and will probably not get together on the price. But you still have a chance, as a lot of things happen in the last few minutes of negotiations. So make those last few minutes your strongest.

HOW TO INSPIRE YOUR AGENT

The preceding information will be extremely helpful when you personally tackle a FISBO. But how about those times when you are working with an agent? Well here are two ways to look at it.

First of all, if you are working with a *good guy* agent, he or she will probably know a lot more about negotiations than you do. So much the better, then. You can ask him to review any strategy he plans to use to get your offer accepted. You might even suggest a new wrinkle that will help.

On the other hand, you might be using a green agent or one who doesn't inspire much confidence. You would feel better presenting the offer yourself, except that you can't. Most new agents hate to admit they haven't sold a home before—they're afraid the client will dump them. So you will probably do him (and yourself) a favor if you can detect and confront this inexperience. Once the embarrassment of discovery is over with, a plan of attack can be developed. What you don't want is for that green agent to walk into a room with the seller and his agent, hand over the contract and ask: "What do you think?" And believe it or not, I have seen that happen many a time.

Unless you want to place your financial future in the hands of lady luck, you had better make sure that you—or your agent—enters each negotiating session armed with reliable facts and a workable strategy.

*"Real estate cannot be lost or stolen, nor can it
be carried away. Managed with reasonable care,
it is about the safest investment in the world."*
                                 —Franklin D. Roosevelt

12

CLAUSES, CONTRACTS & WARRANTIES

At the heart of every real estate transaction is an agreement which defines the rights and responsibilities of all parties concerned.

Once signed, this agreement, or contract, becomes binding and locks into place all prices, terms and conditions. Whether it be a good or bad contract, all parties will have to live with it. Any changes will be difficult or impossible.

The problem most investors have when buying property is that they spend a lot of time with details such as price, condition of the property, occupancy dates, and a multitude of emotional considerations. But usually no thought is given to the legal agreement. It is assumed that "everything will work out okay."

But once a contract is signed—beware to the person who breaks any part of it. It takes its place next to God's own laws. Break the covenant and go to court.

I am not saying this is wrong. What I *am* saying is that more attention should be paid to the many details making up a contract than is usually done. I could cite numerous examples, but the first story that comes to mind happened to a salesman who worked for me in the mid-seventies.

Sam listed a home and convinced the owner to sell with FHA-VA terms. This meant the seller had to pay what is known as loan discount points. At that time this amounted to four (each point represents 1 percent of the buyer's loan amount). The seller signed a listing agreement (a legal contract) in which he agreed to pay four points if the home were sold via FHA or VA financing.

Several weeks later Sam found a buyer for the home. He submitted an FHA offer which was a few thousand dollars beneath listed price. The seller accepted the price offer and signed the purchase agreement.

Just before the transaction was to "close," someone noticed that the purchase agreement made no mention of the seller paying loan discount points. Even though this was spelled out in the listing, it also had to be written in the contract because points can fluctuate almost daily. The seller may agree to pay a set amount, like a maximum of 5 points, or even to pay *necessary points*, but this must be spelled out in the contract. Without mention of points there was no agreement because current FHA and VA requirements say the buyer cannot pay these. So either the seller—or the agent— had to pay the points.

I suppose you can guess who paid most of the points. Sam took it on the chin! The seller did agree, after a lot of debate, to pay some of the cost. But it was Sam who paid most; thus he ended up selling a house for no commission.

Contracts are important. But this book is not a textbook. It is a how-to book, one that allows the author to express a certain amount of opinion. So here is how I am going to give it to you.

Learning what you should know about contracts is a tedious thing. They are even more dull to write about. So I recommend that you find a book on real estate law and contracts that spells out how these things are done in your state.

I also recommend that you put contracts in their proper perspective. You don't need to know a lot about them—you merely need to respect them. For instance, virtually all contract forms are developed by competent attorneys. They are then made available in easy to use form so that basically inexperienced people can learn to fill in the blanks. Thus, you don't need to have knowledge of contract law to be a real estate investor. But you do need to have respect for the agreement. And you need to be aware of some of the pitfalls that you may run into. So in this chapter I am not going to give you a lot of legal jargon which I'm not qualified to discuss in the first place, but I'll just point out areas where you had better pay attention when buying or selling.

Whether you use an agent or not, this information will be valuable. While your agent (and settlement attorney in those states that use this system) will probably be competent at filling in the blanks in a contract form, it doesn't hurt to know the danger signs, because they are easy to overlook or forget when everyone is excited about important things like MONEY.

The printed portions of most contracts you will be using in real estate are important, but they are not as critical as what is later written or typed in the blank space provided. It is in those blanks that your artistry is displayed.

That is where your creative terms are spelled out, where various clauses are inserted and where your price is stated. Thus, it is with these blank areas you'll be filling in that we should concentrate our efforts. The thrust of this chapter, therefore, is to alert you to some of the many clauses which you may or may not want in your agreement.

THE ESCAPE CLAUSE

I'll soon discuss a number of clauses which you may or may not want to use. Most of them will qualify as *escape clauses*. An escape clause or weasel clause as it is sometimes known is the part of your agreement which lets you back out of a sale if you should so desire. A proper escape clause will let you back out without recourse, without being penalized or losing your considera-tion deposit. Sometimes this type of clause is obvious—like when you ask for an inspection and the results turn out to be of a negative nature, you may declare the contract null and void.

Sometimes the escape clause is not so obvious—like when a purchase agreement says that buyer and property are to qualify for a new conventional loan in the amount of $65,000 at an interest rate not to exceed 12.5 percent. Now if all available interest rates in your area are 13 percent and higher, this contract is really no good from the beginning unless the buyer wants it to be—as at any time he can agree to pay the higher interest rate. It's a one-way street. An alert listing agent (when an agent is involved) would spot this and have his sellers insist the buyer either increase the rate or simply state *pre-vailing rate*. Without an agent, there is a good chance that this sort of ploy can pass by undetected.

There is nothing wrong with a fairly conceived escape clause that is used to give the seller a few days' extra time to check out questionable details about a property. Escape clauses are most necessary when buying run-down property—what are called "dirty dogs" in the trade. For instance, you may have found a broken-down older home in a very expensive neighborhood. At first glance it appears there is too much work to be done, but you are impressed with the surrounding homes which are valued between $125,000 and $175,000. The dirty dog you are inspecting has just been put on the market at $89,000. Too much money to keep it as a rental, but by fixing it up and putting it back on the market you should be able to get over $130,000.

The question now comes down to money. What will it cost to properly restore this once magnificent old home? You sense that time is running out because in the hour you were looking at the property, there were also two other agents with clients. And since they were walking around with mile-wide smiles on their faces, you assume they too are interested in the house.

The house is already priced low because of the condition, so your agent recommends that you come in at full price and you agree, but only if . . . if you had some idea how much the repairs would cost. Knowing that much more than surface repairs are needed, you realize you'll have to run a virtual army of experts through the home before you can get even a half-way accurate idea of the extent of repair costs. With your agent's guidance, you realize that to sell the home for a minimum of $130,000 and turn a decent profit, you should not spend more than $14,000 on repairs. This way you could make a maximum profit of $17,000 after paying the real estate commission and allowing another $2,500 to cover the mortgage payments while the home is vacant.

Note that this profit figure of $17,000 is 100 percent more than the $14,000 *rough* estimate for repairs. A lot of things can—and usually do—go wrong when rehabilitating a dirty dog. If you cannot foresee making at least 100 percent more than you know you'll be spending—you shouldn't even consider the task. And don't forget to add a dollar value for the *time* you will be spending on the project.

Would you personally buy a property to rehabilitate for which you would make a 20 percent down payment, spend another $5,000 on materials, and devote 200 hours of your time . . . just to make a $3,000 profit? I hope you wouldn't!

When rehabilitating property you have to estimate the *end results* before you get there. If potential costs add up until it looks grim, you'll want to have one or more escape clauses which can get you out of what might be a bad deal.

Here is a simple way to estimate your end results. Basically what you want to do is decide what kind of profit you must have to make the entire project worthwhile. But before you can do this you have to make a detailed list of what you'll be doing and what it will cost. The more carefully you compile the costs, the more accurate will be your estimate of end results. But other factors come into the picture.

If you found a good, but run-down, home which you want to fix up and keep in your portfolio, for instance, you can obviously work on a slimmer profit margin—especially if you got unusually good financing. But when you are fixing up a property for resale, you had better make sure you can get enough money out of a sale to cover your expenses and time.

Basically, I don't believe in formulas. Take a commonsense approach instead. For instance, allocate a dollar amount to your time. Is your time worth $10 an hour, or perhaps $25. I am not crazy about doing this type of "handiwork," so I estimate my time at $50 an hour. So if I were spending $5,000 on materials, plus $10,000 for the property, plus $10,000 for my labor (200 hours × $50), I would want to cover my time ($10,000) plus make enough to justify the use of the other monies involved. The money could have been invested in seconds or T-Bills, so I would personally want at least 20 percent on the $15,000, which would be $3,000. It doesn't matter that this whole process might take less than a year—base your figures on one year.

So there it is—not a strict formula but a commonsense approach to a short-term investment. If I don't have a chance of turning a $13,000 profit (profit on money and reimbursement for my time) then I wouldn't go into the particular property. I would instead use one of several escape clauses to get out of the contract. Following are several important clauses you should be familiar with, most of which can be used to escape from a deal.

REAL ESTATE CLAUSES

FINANCING: The question of how you will *finance* a purchase is the starting point of any real estate contract. While some may not think of financing as a clause (because there is no correct and neat package of words to describe it), it is certainly your most important one. You might consider it a free form clause, because you can cover the subject in a multitude of *ways* and with any verbiage you want. Just make sure the language is clear and covers all important points. For instance, just don't say *the sale is conditional upon purchaser obtaining a new conventional loan in the amount of $62,000.* Instead spell out the complete terms such as: . . . *a new conventional loan in the amount of $62,000 at an interest rate not to exceed 12.5 percent and for a term of 30 years, with loan origination fees not to exceed 1½ points.*

If you know which lender you will be seeking a loan from, put in the name. Describe the method you will be using to buy the property. For instance, will it be an assumption, a contract for deed or whatever. While it may appear that a tight contract may favor the seller, you certainly wouldn't want to buy a home and have the seller agree to carry back the loan but through an error fail to say when the loan would be due and payable. An error like this often leads to either a court battle or the sale falling apart.

So start out on the right foot and completely describe the financing terms and method of buying the property. Take time to think about what you are saying or not saying in the contract.

PEST CONTROL INSPECTION: Here is an important clause. Sometimes this verbiage will already be in your sales agreement, but if not, follow the custom in your state. The important things are to not overlook the inspection, who will pay for the inspection, and who will pay for any corrective work. (Incidentally, pest control inspections go beyond looking for bugs, the inspectors are also after a more serious problem—dry rot. So don't skip this if the seller says "I don't have any termites.")

Occasionally it will be necessary to limit the amount of money that will be paid to correct termite problems. A seller may agree to your low price but balk at the idea of possibly paying more than $3,000 to $4,000 in "termite costs." If that is the case, limit the amount he will have to spend. If the bill exceeds $2,000, for instance, you will have the option of picking up the balance. Be creative, don't lose a deal over a termite clause or repair costs.

Incidentally, the company who does the inspection doesn't have to complete the work. I find that most termite repair estimates run very high. But you can get around these excessive fees. What I normally do is get a bid from an appropriate small contractor. With a problem like a rotted bathroom floor, it is possible you'll need to get three separate bids: one each from a carpenter, a linoleum company and possibly a tile installer if the shower has tiles. It's probably not worth doing this when the total repair estimate is less than $250. But when facing one of those really big estimates (like over $2,000) you will usually be able to save quite a bit of money by getting competitive bids. I've known sellers who have saved over 50 percent on the termite company's cost estimate.

Here is another way to make money when a big repair bill is at stake. Ask the seller to set aside an amount of money equal to the termite expenses. Then you assume liability for the work and any money saved is yours to pocket. The repairs are not begun until after the sale is closed and you have the deed. Get competitive bids. This idea is only worth pursuing when a large enough sum of money is at stake or when the lender will let you close before the termite work is done. Some lenders will go along with this as long as the funds are held by a neutral party (like a title company). The seller is apt to go along with this if he can be convinced that it's a lot nicer packing and moving when there are no workmen running around the house. It's worth a try when facing big (like $2,500 plus) repair bills. And with a little effort you might be able to make $700 or so.

CONTINGENCY-RELEASE CLAUSE: This clause is used when an offer to buy is contingent upon the sale of the purchaser's property. For instance, you decide to sell one of your rental homes and buy three more. But instead of waiting, you start looking for the best available property. When suitable property is found, you make your offer contingent upon the sale and closing of your rental home. If another offer comes along (and it often does) you will be given notice (as required in the release clause) to either go ahead with the sale or void your contract. The buyer is usually given from 3 to 5 days to make his decision. Although the option belongs to the buyer, few will be able to come up with the necessary money to complete the purchase if their home isn't sold yet.

Properties with a contingent sale remain on the market even though the owner has accepted a contract. But from my experience, many salesmen won't show property with a contingency-release clause. Therefore some listing agents strongly recommend that their clients reject contingent sales. So when you want to buy property this way, prepare for the negotiation table with strong arguments why your contingent sale should be accepted. The strongest argument you can present is that your "for sale property" is priced right and is being marketed correctly and should sell any day. If you can prove that—then you can probably get your contingent offer accepted.

INSPECTION REPORTS: Not only are inspection reports your typical *escape clause*, but they are important to protect you against any known or unknown problem which could lead to your spending a lot of money. It doesn't really matter who pays for the inspection or who pays for the repairs. What is important is that an inspection takes place and the results either give you peace of mind, or alert you to a problem. If the problem is big enough to warrant it, you may choose to back out of the sale. But only if you worded your inspection request as an escape clause—with wording like the following: *Seller agrees to release buyer from this contract if electrical and heating inspections reveal any recommended repairs in excess of $500.* You don't even need a dollar limit—just the fact that work is necessary can be enough.

Typical inspection reports would include, but not be limited to, the following: air conditioning system; built-in appliances; electrical system; heating system; roof; plumbing; structural and foundation; and soil. Occasionally you can find qualified people who will make multi-inspections, thus saving you the time and money you would otherwise have to spend on separate ones. Many structural engineers, for instance, will make detailed inspections of all parts of a home. Here's a clue to finding one. Don't call a large firm, but look for a small independent operator. He is your best bet. Also ask your real estate agent—he should know qualified inspectors.

When are inspections necessary? I don't believe in wasting the time or money or even jeopardizing my negotiations by asking for unnecessary inspections. I only ask for one when I need an escape clause or when I suspect a problem. And my suspicions increase with the age of the home or when an owner himself has added on to or remodeled his home.

INTERIM-OCCUPANCY CLAUSE: One of the trickiest obstacles a real estate agent sometimes has to deal with are consecutive strings of dates on which buyers, sellers and tenants will be moving. Sometimes five families must all coordinate their moving date, and like a string of dominoes, if the first falters then they are all in trouble. And hell has no fury like a family who just put their total belongings in a moving van and then found out that they can't move into their new home today but must wait three more days.

Often your biggest headache when buying rental property, especially single-family homes, will be coordinating moving dates. For legitimate reasons, it may well be possible your seller cannot move out of the house when you close escrow. Thus the interim-occupancy clause comes into play. This important clause is often printed as a separate addendum to the purchase agreement. In that case the complete rights and obligations of all parties are spelled out. Sometimes this clause is printed in the sales agreement, as with many Agreement of Sale forms. When this clause is available in the sales agreement or by separate addendum, your problem is more than half solved. Just coordinate the moving date with the seller.

If he stays on he should pay you rent. This, however, is a matter to be negotiated. Perhaps he will stay rent-free for a month, as a trade-off for the low price you paid for his home. Maybe he will give you the same amount he has been paying on his old mortgage or perhaps this interim rent will be increased to equal what the new payment is. These are negotiated items.

When you develop the clause from scratch, consider the following wording: *The seller shall remain in possession for _____ days after the recordation of the deed. The seller agrees to pay purchaser $ _____ per day from recordation to the date possession is delivered. Seller also agrees to leave this sum in escrow, to be disbursed either monthly or on the date possession is delivered to the buyer.*

Interim-occupancies can be done in reverse, too. You might want to take occupancy a few days or even a few weeks before the sale is final. This early occupancy can be especially helpful when you need time to fix up a property or for getting a tenant so you can avoid a lengthy vacancy after closing the sale. But be extremely careful when doing this.

Some agents will, as I did, do everything in their power to discourage early buyer occupancy. And this is because the buyer often uncovers "problems" he didn't recognize when he first inspected the home. Some will then say: "Hold it, I am not going to go through with this sale unless the seller fixes or replaces the water heater, the broken garbage disposal, the . . ." Thus with early buyer occupancy, the seller risks all kinds of potential headaches.

But because the advantages of early occupancy are many, and this book is written for the buyer more than the seller, I am going to recommend that you seek early occupancy when it is in your favor to do so. To pull this off, you must be prepared to offer something of value to the seller. You must also be willing to insure his "peace of mind."

The best ways of accomplishing this are to pay XX amount of dollars for the privilege and place the entire amount of money you'll need to buy the property in escrow or with your settlement attorney. You might also agree to sign a statement which would read something like this: *In return for early occupancy, I hereby agree to accept the property in "as-is" condition, except for items previously listed in the purchase agreement dated _____.* You have to give a little to get a little, so if you want early occupancy to fix up or rent a property, plan to offer something of value to the seller.

(For a good book which will help you *write* these clauses, terms, etc., get a copy of the *Realty Bluebook*. This is the "Bible" for many real estate agents. It contains over 350 pages of charts, amortization tables, proration tables, checklists, tax effects and the exact wording of the many clauses or statements you may want in your purchase agreement. See the back of this book for information on how you can order the *Realty Bluebook*.)

WHERE THE PROBLEMS ARE . . .
AND HOW TO SOLVE THEM

Following is a brief rundown of some of the many problems you might encounter when buying property. In almost every real estate transaction I was involved with, there was something new to learn. I don't care how much you read, you'll never be prepared for *everything* that could happen. But at least you can be trained to look out for the most common problems. Here they are:

ACCEPTANCE: It is in your best interests to convince a seller to make a *yes* or *no* decision on your offer at the time it is presented. Sleeping on it won't do anyone any good. The important facts and figures the seller must mentally sort out will be cold after *sleeping on them.* So if the seller can't say *yes* then ask him for a counteroffer.

Have all parties to a contract sign the agreement or the counteroffer. Without signatures you have no agreement. An exception, at least in California, is a telegram which can convey acceptance when negotiating by telephone. The out-of-town seller (perhaps the husband) may in effect give his signature on the telegram. This is because the signatures on a purchase agreement do not need to be notarized as they do on a grant or warranty deed.

COPIES OF AGREEMENT: It is a good practice (and usually required by law) that all parties to an agreement receive a signed and dated copy. Don't forget. California real estate salespeople can have their licenses revoked for forgetting this.

CONSIDERATION: You cannot have a valid contract without exchanging something of value—like money. While $1 may satisfy legal requirements, most sellers will throw you out on your ear if you bring in an offer with a consideration deposit of just $1. A $1,000 check is better . . . but $1,000 in cash is even better. I know an investor who doesn't use a typical deposit but instead brings the entire sales price in cash. Can you imagine how impressed you would be if someone came to your house and emptied a sack of $20, $100 and $500 bills on your coffee table and said: "This is yours if you accept my offer."

The catch, of course, is that this shrewd buyer uses this gimmick to discount prices—by several thousand dollars. But what better way is there to "convince" a seller to accept a lower offer?

WHO GETS THE CONSIDERATION DEPOSIT: I don't care how careful you are when negotiating a deal and drawing up the purchase agreement . . . during the month or two that follow you are apt to have a lot of problems—some of which can threaten the sale. Sometimes the problem is nothing more than *remorse*—that feeling one of the parties gets when he thinks he has made a mistake. So play it safe and never allow the seller to hold the deposit. See that it goes to a neutral third party. That can be a title company, escrow company, attorney, real estate office or whatever, but not the seller unless you have agreed to give him a non-refundable deposit. But those cases should be rare.

ESCROW AND TITLE INSURANCE: Escrow is where a neutral third party acts as a *stake holder* for a buyer and seller and processes all papers and monies to complete the sale. Many states exclusively use this system. And most escrows are handled by highly trained title company employees.

The costs are typically about $440 on a $60,000 sales price, almost $300 of which is for a title insurance policy and $140 for the escrow services. These fees are inseparable when a title company handles an escrow.

While you can buy property directly from an owner and avoid escrow by doing all the paperwork yourself, it would be foolish to do so. The knowledge and expertise you get from a good escrow officer may be the best bargain you'll get from anyone in a real estate transaction. And that's not a putdown of others, just a pat on the back to those people who spend hours behind the scenes making sure your papers and escrow instructions are correct. The title insurance? I think it is over-priced. I cannot remember any of my clients ever benefiting from it. Yet it is important and I certainly recommend buying a policy. Your lender will insist on it. Title insurance, incidentally, protects you from any errors in the public records plus many off-record hazards such as forgery; if an imposter sold you a home he didn't own, you would be protected.

In some states escrow is not used and closing is handled basically by a settlement attorney. Just as with an escrow officer, a good settlement attorney is well worth his fee. But as with any law firm, go to one who specializes in settlement and not one, for instance, who exclusively handles divorces except for your closing which he'll do as a favor.

HOLDING MONEY AFTER ESCROW CLOSES: One of the best safeguards you have to guarantee that all items in a contract are completed is the power to insist that the seller leave XX amount of dollars in escrow. The money remains there until specified contract provisions are satisfied. For instance, the seller agrees to replace two broken windows and to repair a damaged fence. How do you know he'll do it? In the purchase agreement you get the seller to agree to leave a sum of money in escrow as sort of an insurance policy. If the work is done by closing, then the seller gets his money back. If not, this money will remain in escrow until either the items are fixed or until after a specific number of days (perhaps 30) pass, then the money goes to the buyer. It's a good safeguard, but to use it effectively you should request this provision when the sale is consummated and not try to force the seller to do this the day before escrow is to close. It's too late unless the seller has enough guilt to voluntarily put the money in escrow.

WARRANTIES: There are basically two kinds of warranties which can protect the investor-buyer against unforeseen property problems. The first type is known as a *home warranty*. It is usually purchased by the seller for the buyer. It's a good gimmick for a real estate office to advertise that "this home comes with a full two-year warranty to protect you against unforeseen problems."

These warranties, however, are better tools to help agents sign up listings than they are protection devices for the buyer. That's because many warranties will not cover a home which is non-owner occupied, Some warranties have deductibles (even as high as $100) and others require owners to pay service call charges which are often $25 or higher.

Even if you did find a policy that covered tenant-occupied property, and did not have either a deductible or a service charge, the odds are that many specific break-downs would not be covered, because so many items, like air conditioning, are often exempt.

If the seller has already purchased a policy (the prices range from $150 to $250) don't look a gift horse in the mouth—take it. But don't expect much. As some are better than others, you might luck out and get a good company. If you think I am being harsh on warranties, consider this fact. A warranty is really nothing more than an insurance policy which states that if you pay $200 the company will take care of some equipment break-downs you have inside the home (not outside). These must happen within one year and you must pay a $50 deductible (thus the most common type of problems you'll face, like a drippy faucet which the plumber can repair for less than $40, will not be covered). The company is betting that their combined customers during the course of the year will have few problems (probably averaging $50 or less) and that the remaining $150 will cover their profit and over-head. Personally, I'd rather chance paying for problems out of pocket. In typical rental property you won't have a lot of expensive built-ins to break down. Your biggest problems will be the water heater and furnace. And these can be partially warranteed in this second manner.

Regardless of local customs, you can agree to just about anything you want to with the seller as long as what you agree to is lawful. In my area many Realtors put warranty agreement clauses in their purchase agreements which read as follows: *Seller warrants that grounds and improvements will be maintained, that the roof is watertight, and that all appliances and heating, plumbing, sewer, and electrical systems shall be in working order at close of escrow. Seller agrees to permit inspection thereof prior to close of escrow and to pay for any necessary repairs.* While this guarantee is important it still will not give you all the protection you'll need. It protects you from the time you sign a purchase agreement to the time escrow closes, although the agreement has no teeth unless you go one step further and require that a few hundred dollars be kept two weeks or so past the closing date.

So you *can* put teeth into the agreement, but in one respect it's still not as good as a home warranty because this one ends when the buyer takes title to the property. But as I said, you don't have to follow local custom. Why not create a warranty that will be in effect for one year? There is nothing stopping you from entering into an agreement with the seller which says he will warrant the water heater and furnace, for instance, for one year after close of escrow. This agreement, again, will lack teeth. If the seller moves out of state and does not honor the warranty, what do you do? You may decide the legal expenses are not worth a $300 water heater. As you can see, there is no per-fect way to protect yourself, but at least you can try. Most people are honorable and will meet their obligations. Probably nine out of ten will pay for a legitimate break-down that happens during the first year.

The above example was designed to show you how flexible your agreement can be. I personally would not have a seller warrant items after close of escrow. I feel that this kind of request puts too much burden on negotiations. You'll have a better chance at getting your price if you're not asking for too much. The way I would cover a potential water heater and furnace problem would be to have them inspected prior to close of escrow. If my contract called for the seller to pay for any repairs found necessary at close of escrow, then the matter would be settled very easily. If an Inspection Report (my escape clause) reveals that they are in working order but, as they are old, may not last more than a year, I would then have to decide whether or not I wanted to buy the home with these potential problems. A *yes* answer would indicate the risk was worth taking, considering the total package I was buying (price, property and financing). A *no* answer says I feel the price is not worth paying . . . and that the total deal is not good enough to risk even the possibility of replacing a water heater.

As you can see from the material in this chapter, an investor should take great care when negotiating and executing a legal agreement, because the ramifications can be many. Take your time, read over (in a private, quiet room) any agreement, including the small print, before you sign it. A little care here will help to insure your success, as you won't get bogged down with court battles, hassles and arguments.

PART III
Being Creative Pays Off

"There is little good news about working with the institutions. The interest rates are the highest, the closing costs most expensive and a lot of personal guarantees and mickey mouse paper work are required. When using them, you must be aggressive in seeking out the best available interest rates and lowest closing cost. Keep in mind that ¼ of one percent in interest on $60,000 is over $12 per month cash flow you give up for the life of the investment."
—John Schaub from Impact Report
"Investing in New Homes"

13

THE BASICS

If you follow football at either the college or professional level, you probably know that the best teams use powerful, yet basic, plays. Teams which consistently win don't use very many triple reverses, fake field goals and Statue of Liberty type plays. They just run or pass the ball right down the opposition's throat.

Real estate can be a lot like football. You might find 100 ways to buy one house . . . but why waste the time and effort when *you can just come straight in* and assume (take over) the first mortgage. A simple assumption may not always be possible; but when it is, it's your basic way of buying investment property. There are no better ways of buying . . . taking over a high balance but low interest FHA or VA loan rates a "10" any day.

True, this isn't always possible. Sometimes you have no choice but to buy with a wrap-around or multiple trust deed, especially in tight money markets. When seeking new rental property always think assumption. You may not find one, but you should never let the vision of a classical assumption escape your mind. By *thinking* assumption, you just might uncover one when you least expect to. I have, several times, but I don't think I would have succeeded if I hadn't kept thinking assumption with every home I looked at.

One day I found one—a $5,000 VA assumption, but the listing agent had disguised the fact because his sellers wanted to retain their full GI loan eligibility. I recognized the lender as a mortgage banker who dealt almost exclusively with new FHA-VA loans. I called the listing agent and pressed for an answer. He finally admitted that the loan was VA, but that the sellers did not want it assumed. The home, however, had been on the market for over two months and the agent said no offers had come in yet.

Why not, I thought to myself. And so I did—I presented a full-price offer on the home subject to my assuming the VA loan. The now-anxious sellers said okay.

In this chapter I'll discuss the basics. I'll start out with FHA and VA assumptions and then discuss ways of buying property with conventional financing. Once you understand the basics, you'll be ready for the following chapters which will show you how to blend your understanding of the basics with a touch of creativity.

FHA LOANS

The familiar FHA initials stand for Federal Housing Administration. In reality it doesn't exist anymore, as it has been absorbed by Housing and Urban Development (H.U.D.). So much for semantics, though, because FHA programs and loans are still very much alive. And for the investor they are number "1." Here's why:

FHA loans are fully assumable. There can be no increase in the interest rate and the lender cannot turn down a buyer because he is *not qualified*. You can come straight off the unemployment lines and still assume one of these loans. It's possible a lender could try to bluff the buyer with a credit application and personal history form, but they cannot turn down a buyer.

Another attraction is the low cost involved when assuming a loan. At this writing you may be charged a $35 assumption fee and a $15 loan statement fee with a $60,000 home. A buyer can typically save more than $1,200 in closing costs when assuming a loan rather than buying with a new conventional loan.

Although the interest rates for both VA and FHA loans are usually the same, the FHA borrower must pay a ½ percent monthly insurance rate. Therefore FHA loan payments are a little higher than a VA loan payment at the same rate.

For investors the big question about these loans is their availability. Millions of loans are made each year—but investors must catch them on the rebound. In 1979, for instance, 446,000 homes were financed with FHA loans. (This money, incidentally, comes from private sources. The loans are merely *guaranteed* by the government.)

Out of those 446,000 loans probably close to 75,000 will be resold during the year. Because the owner-seller didn't live in the property long enough to pay in a great deal of equity, most of these 75,000 homes will be sold with assumption terms. How much money the assumption will take depends upon many factors. One of the most important is the fact that with high appreciation rates, many houses will have gained so much in value that the asking price will be substantially higher than the existing loan balance. Thus when homes appreciate rapidly, in one year it can easily take more than $10,000 to assume a $60,000 loan. On the other hand, in a slow market, or in an area which has slower appreciation rates, it might only take $3,000 or $4,000.

Presently the maximum FHA loan is $67,500. A home priced at $67,500, for instance, can be purchased with only a $2,875 down payment plus closing costs (which are sometimes paid for by the seller). Because of this relatively low maximum loan, you won't find too many homes being purchased with FHA financing in high priced areas. Another limiting factor is loan discount points, which I'll be explaining shortly.

If you live in or near communities where a lot of FHA-VA transactions take place, you are fortunate. Always look for these assumptions when buying property. For you others—keep reading!

VA LOANS

VA loans can also be assumed without the interest rate being raised. These loans differ from FHA loans in that the borrower is not paying for an insurance premium. Instead, the government is guaranteeing the loan in case of default.

Another difference is that the veteran buyer does not have to make a down payment. The VA does not have any loan limits, only limits on the amount of guaranty. At this writing the guaranty limits are four times the maximum of $25,000 . . . which means that a vet can buy a home for $100,000 without a down payment.

As with FHA loans, the vet buyer must sign a statement that says he is purchasing the home for use as his principal residence. Thus investors are prohibited from directly using this minimum down payment, government-insured financing. However, should the veteran later move to another residence, he may rent out his old home which was financed by the VA loan.

While a person may have an unlimited number of new FHA loans during his lifetime, the VA puts limits on how a vet can buy additional property with a VA loan. This is done through a somewhat complicated *entitlement* program. The VA may permit restoration of a veteran's full entitlement if the property has been sold and the previous loan has been paid in full. However, if a non-vet assumes the loan, the vet will not get his full entitlement back and if he buys GI a second time he will at best get what is known as partial entitlement. But even a partial entitlement can be a good deal as the vet will get the relatively low interest rate provided for GI loans, plus his down payment will still be relatively small when compared to a conventional loan. I won't be going into this partial entitlement formula because it's rare that an investor would be buying property with a new VA loan. If one does, and does not occupy the property, he can expect a visit from the F.B.I.

Don't assume that a seller with a VA loan will always insist on getting back his entitlement. Many don't . . . and that's because a successful vet moving up the corporate ladder isn't thinking about entitlements when shopping for $150,000 homes. Nor is a financially troubled seller—all he wants is a fair price for his home.

WHAT YOU SHOULD KNOW ABOUT ASSUMPTIONS

Taking over or assuming a loan should be one of the smoothest of all real estate transactions. This is especially true with an FHA loan. But you begin to run into trouble with conventional loan assumptions, especially those with enforceable due-on-sale clauses. Here's a look at different aspects of "assumptions" which you should be familiar with.

ASSUMING A MORTGAGE

While I speak throughout this book about assuming mortgage loans, I am not specifically (unless I so identify) referring to the formal method of *assuming a mortgage.* Assuming a mortgage (or trust deed) is when a formal agreement between the buyer and lender is executed. It takes the seller off the hook for any remaining liability! This formal assumption often takes place when a loan with a due-on-sale clause is being assumed, and the new buyer will be faced with an increase in interest rate, approval of credit, plus an assumption fee and a costly loan fee which usually amounts to 1 percent of the existing loan balance. (I've always thought it was very generous of the big lenders to raise their interest rate three or four percent and then top it off with a big assumption fee.)

So by *assuming a mortgage* the legal responsibility for making mortgage payments passes from the seller to the new owner. While this may be important when a property has a thin equity (less than 15 percent of value), it should not otherwise concern sellers. In the future, when I refer to assumptions I am not making a statement as to whether a loan was formally assumed, but just to the fact that a buyer is taking over an existing loan.

TAKING TITLE SUBJECT TO

This is the opposite of *assuming a mortgage.* It's when nothing is done except transference of a grant, warranty or quit claim deed. It's the method used most when one assumes an FHA or VA loan.

When Mr. Jones buys a property by taking title subject to (assuming without a formal agreement), the primary responsibility for the payments stay with the original maker of the loan. Technically this can only occur when the note does not contain a due-on-sale clause or when court decisions (as with Wellenkamp vs. Bank of America in California) allow conventional loans to be taken over *subject to*. In the event of a default, the lender would foreclose. If the property does not yield proceeds to cover the loan balance, the lender may get a deficiency judgment against the original borrower.

The odds of the above deficiency judgment happening are remote at best. The most probable way of its happening would be if Johnny Investor takes title *subject* to an existing FHA loan by paying just $3,000 cash to loan for the property. He rents it out to a gang of motorcyclists who practically destroy the home in three months and so Johnny (who didn't read *The Monopoly Game* and didn't have a good insurance policy which covered vandalism) lets the property go into default rather than dig into his pockets for $6,000 or so to fix it up. The result is a deficiency judgment against the surprised original borrower.

Occasionally you are going to come up against a seller who will insist you go to the trouble of taking title by formal assumption. If you are only paying a few thousand dollars for his equity, you might find it difficult to argue against this request. But if you are paying more than 20 percent down for the property, you can make an ample case against the formal assumption. You can tell the seller that with homes appreciating in value he should never have to worry about a deficiency judgment, because the equity (his ultimate security) will grow each succeeding month. If your arguments fail to move the seller, however, go along with his request. It won't be much of a bother. And FHA and VA interest rates will not be changed, regardless of how you take title.

DUE-ON-SALE CLAUSES

California's famous Wellenkamp decision struck down that state's due-on-sale clauses because they were "unreasonable restraints upon property title transfers unless the lender proved security impairment." The decision emphasized that due-on-sale clauses discourage property transfers because (1) the lender can demand full payment, (2) they increase interest rates, and/or (3) assumption fees are charged if the property is sold. The significance of this decision was that state chartered banks, savings & loans, etc. were not allowed to enforce due-on-sale clauses, thus paving the way for buyers to take title subject to the original loan.

Prior to Wellenkamp, it was practically impossible to assume (by "subject to") a conventional loan in California. As almost every lender had a due-on-sale clause in the trust deed documents, there was hardly a way a loan could be taken over without a formal assumption. And why bother with a formal assumption when there were usually no benefits—it would usually cost the buyer as much to assume as it would to get a new loan. And you weren't cutting any red tape, either. For awhile many buyers were using a contract of sale (see chapter 16), which did not impair the lender's position, to get around the due-on-sale clause. Now these diversions are unnecessary when dealing with state chartered institutions—a buyer can assume (subject to) these loans today with hardly a whimper from the lender. And I am happy to say that the Wellenkamp decision is affecting due-on-sale clauses in many other states, with the courts in Florida, for instance, recently entering favorable decisions against restrictive due-on-sale clauses.

Check on the laws in your state. If due-on-sale clauses are still legal, find out whether there are ways of skirting the clause (as with a contract of sale in which the deed does not pass from the seller to the buyer) and if not, find out what kind of lender you are dealing with. Don't spin your wheels trying to assume a loan in which the lender will jump the interest rates to 14 percent *and* charge a two-point loan fee. A two-point loan fee (they may even call it an assumption fee) would amount to $1,500 on a $75,000 loan. If the lender has an enforceable due-on-sale clause, back off unless you decide the property is well worth the added costs. Instead, concentrate your efforts on FHA and VA loans.

NEW TYPE OF LOANS

The world doesn't stand still! New types of loans are being tested and introduced at a fairly fast clip these days. Two significant, and often assumable, types that you should know about are: the *Graduated Payment Loan* and the *Variable Rate Loan*.

Let's talk about the *Graduated Payment Loan* first. It is an FHA creation that is designed for the young family which expects a rising income in the future; a family supported by a college graduate, for instance, who is just starting up the corporate ladder and can, in all probability, expect their income to almost double in five or six years. The Graduated Payment Loan lets these buyers pay less in the early years (less than the actual amount of interest needed to cover the loan) and more in the later years.

There are five plans from which the buyer can choose. They are:

Plan 1 — Monthly payments increase at a rate of 2.5 percent per year for five years.

Plan 2 — Monthly payments increase at a rate of 5 percent per year for five years

Plan 3 — Monthly payments increase at a rate of 7.5 percent per year for five years

Plan 4 — Monthly payments increase at a rate of 2 percent per year for 10 years.

Plan 5 — Monthly payments increase at a rate of 3 percent per year for 10 years

Graduated Payment Loans are popular now and you will be seeing a lot of them. They are just as assumable as a regular FHA loan. They are good for the investor, too, because he will have less negative cash flow in the early years of the loan. As the payments increase, the rent can be raised.

The worst thing about a Graduated Payment Loan is that if the investor believed he had assumed a regular FHA, he might be fairly shocked when his payments jumped 5 percent. But when you know what you are getting into, you can plan accordingly. So always find out what type of FHA loan is on a property.

Variable Rate Loans are also growing in popularity. Basically these are loans in which the interest rate over the term of the loan may vary depending on conditions in financial markets. Currently these are conventional loans (not those which are government insured like FHA). When the loan's interest rate moves up or down, the monthly payment either moves up or down accordingly, or the borrower is allowed to extend the term of the loan instead.

There are three basic types of Variable Rate Loans with which you may come in contact. They are:

Straight Variable Rate Loan: This is one in which the interest rate changes periodically, with the moves based upon some change in a basic reference index, such as the rates on savings certificates.

Escalator Loan: This one allows lenders to change the rate when they can justify that economic conditions warrant such a change.

Rollover Loan: This one may become the lender's favorite! It is renegotiated after the end of a specific period of time (usually three to seven years). The new rate may be tied to change in a basic reference index or it may be the current mortgage rate.

These Variable Rate Loans are both bad news and good news for investors. The bad is easily understood—you won't be able to lock in a low interest rate that a fixed rate mortgage provides but will be at the mercy of an economy which seems to always bring higher costs and interest rates. But many of these loans have a limit. I have several straight variable rate loans and in each case the lender is limited to a maximum interest raise of 2.5 percent over the life of the loan. And these changes can be made only in small increments (¼ percent) in any six months.

Here's the good news. When the interest rates increase, the buyer is given up to six months to sell without a prepayment penalty. In California now, if the lender is chartered in that state, these loans, of course, are fully assumable at any time.

Incidentally, as more and more states outlaw due-on-sale clauses, more and more lenders will be going to variable loans. This way they will still have a way of eventually getting their higher interest rates. Another long-term advantage of variables is that more mortgage money will become available, because lenders won't be fearful of having money tied up at a low interest rate for long periods of time.

THE BASICS

LOAN DISCOUNT POINTS

You can't have a discussion of FHA and VA loans without getting around to the subject of loan discount points.

Points are an adjustment paid to the lender to increase the yield of a loan. Each point is one percent of the loan amount. By charging *points* the lender is able to increase his yield on FHA-VA loans so that they are as attractive as conventional loan yields. This is necessary because Congress keeps FHA and VA interest rates artificially low—usually one full percentage point below standard conventional rates.

Now one thing Congress can't do is put a gun to a lender's head and tell him he must put money into the government insured-type loans. But Congress can pass laws which say that buyers cannot pay these points, and that they must instead be paid for by the seller. But because sellers don't like to pay five to seven points in a strong *seller's market*, many simply do not offer their homes for sale with FHA or VA terms. Each two points, incidentally, normally represent ¼ percent of interest. So when FHA rates are at 11 percent and conventional rates at 12 percent, you will probably find that lenders are charging 8 points. With a $60,000 loan that will come to $4,800. RIDICULOUS!

This has been the system for years. It's sheer hypocrisy that on one hand the government appears to be so concerned that young and low-income people are having a hard time finding and affording homes, but on the other hand they hold up the one reform which could help millions of home buyers over the next few years. (And I am not even talking about the many investors who would later benefit by buying the resales.)

The reform I speak of is allowing FHA and VA interest rates to freely float with conventional rates. Then there would be no need for sellers to pay points and many thousands more homes could be offered for sale with this type of financing. The best reason I have heard that Congress does not do this is that they don't want to release their control. They like to tell their constituents that they voted to decrease the interest rate. Of course when the rates are increased, they won't say much.

Why doesn't this system change? Probably because nobody complains. I have the feeling that the real estate industry has accepted the facts of *points* and is concentrating their efforts on other areas. If you wake up to a rainy Saturday morning sometime with nothing in particular to do, why not write your federal representatives and ask them to change this archaic system?

DISCOUNTING HOMES WITH POINTS

There is one other important aspect about loan discount points which the alert investor should be aware of . . . and that is the opportunities to "discount" these points and thus buy property $3,000 to $4,000 beneath its true market value.

The government will not allow a seller to increase his price beyond market value to make up for the points he must pay. If the market value for a particular home is approximately $58,000, there is no way that the seller is going to get an appraisal for much more. Anything higher would be a pure and simple mistake! Thus if current points were eight, in reality this seller is offering to sell his home for $58,000 (the listed price) less $4,640, the amount he would pay for a no-down-payment GI buyer.

What may not appear to be an assumption—a property with a $40,000 loan balance offerd with FHA-VA terms (points) at a price of $58,000—may very well turn out to be an ideal assumption. I find that almost all sellers will discount the price of their home by at least the amount of current points at the time they are considering your offer. The two problems you will face are when the seller's company is paying the points (then there is no chance of getting a discount), and when the seller cannot visualize the math involved.

The math is really simple, but you would be surprised to find how many people cannot understand. They seem to realize that when the home is sold for $58,000 they will have to pay points representing XX amount of dollars. But they find it hard to realize they will be netting the same amount of money (actually more if a commission is involved, because it will be smaller) when they accept an offer to sell for the price of $53,360. You can succeed, however, if you or your agent takes enough time to simply explain the math involved.

If you are dealing with a "heads-up" seller, you should be able to get the price discounted more than just the amount of points. And that's because of the uncertainty that exists with FHA and VA appraisals. Following the "a bird in the hand is worth two in the bush" principle, a seller can be convinced the odds are great that his home will not appraise for $58,000, but perhaps $56,000 or $57,500 instead. This is not uncommon. And it usually takes three to five weeks to get back the results of this appraisal—an appraisal which may be low. Selling FHA-VA is definitely a gamble. The buyer may not qualify after "tying" the seller's home up for two months. And with an FHA appraisal it is very likely that corrective conditions will be called for—like requiring the seller to replace cracked windows. Complying with these conditions takes time and money. If the repairs are not made, the buyer doesn't get his loan and the seller doesn't sell his home.

A seller who does not want to gamble can easily be persuaded to take what at first glance looks like a low offer—because that bird in the hand *is* worth more than the two in the bush. When the seller's loan is assumed and the seller does not have to sell via FHA and VA, he relieves himself of the following problems:

- Costs—no loan discount points to pay
- Hidden costs—no surprises or unreasonable conditions
- Uncertainties—the sale would not be subject to an appraisal which could very well be lower than anticipated

- Time—no waiting for Uncle Sam's bureaucrats to process (and sometimes re-process) paperwork
- Changes—no potential market changes to cause problems—like renegotiating a sales contract because interest rates dropped so the seller's loan discount points jumped from three to nine.
- Disappointments—eliminates disappointments when buyer is rejected after waiting two months for his application to be processed.

The above arguments can help you trim a lot of fat off a sales price. Whether you are buying via a new conventional loan or are assuming a loan, you stand an excellent chance of discounting the price of a home when you go after sellers who are offering their property with FHA or VA terms. How do you know? Usually the ad or the listing agreement will invite FHA or VA buyers or will say that seller will pay necessary (or perhaps a fixed number of) loan discount points. Find those properties and take a close look at them. Most likely the home being sold on FHA terms has an existing FHA or VA loan. When loan discount points are at their highest, you can have a field day buying property 5-6-7 percent under market value, and probably getting an assumable loan too.

In the example of the $58,000 home on which the owner agrees to pay eight points or $4,640, it is conceivable that an investor could reduce the total price further to just $52,000 by using the above arguments. When a seller is anxious to close escrow and get out of town, a sure thing like an assumption and a two-week close is very appealing. Giving up an additional $1,300 or so for a "sure thing" is often well worth the price.

FANNIE MAE LOANS

The Federal National Mortgage Association (FNMA), which is commonly known by the nickname "Fannie Mae" is another entity which the investor will most likely run into.

While Fannie Mae actually is an agency that purchases FHA, VA and conventional loans in the secondary market (so that the investor-lender can go back into the market and make additional new loans), I'll be writing here of the conventional loan which has been prearranged to meet FNMA specifications. This so-called Fannie Mae loan will be made by a private lender (often a mortgage banker rather than a typical savings bank) and then sold to FNMA.

These loans are sometimes important to investors because they can be assumed, although technically the buyer is supposed to occupy the property. Regardless of what conditions may be in the original note, FNMA will not enforce prepayment or due-on-sale clauses. All the investor must do is convince the lender that he will be living in the property. Sometimes that's not hard to do!

I mention these loans here because they are fairly numerous today. That's because the original borrower can borrow up to 95 percent of the purchase price up to a maximum loan of $75,000. And at this writing a qualified buyer may borrow up to 90 percent of the purchase price up to a maximum loan of $93,750. This program more or less is the government's answer to what happens after FHA loans leave off. Remember, at this writing the maximum FHA loan for a single-family home is $67,500. This figure will be raised, however.

CONVENTIONAL LOANS

Conventional loans are those made with private investment funds which are not insured by the government as FHA and VA loans are. These loans are usually made by banks, savings and loans, and mortgage bankers. I like to think of this source as the second basic method for buying property—the first being FHA-VA assumptions.

In the late seventies, many investors could not find lucrative assumptions so they began to look for alternative ways of buying. For a while the favored method was new conventional loans. This method had many advantages at the time, because the buyer could shop the entire market and not have to limit his search to assumable FHA and GI loans. While the buyer was saddled with higher closing costs, the interest rates were nominal (8 to 11 percent), the qualification standards were lenient, and the investor could get decent leverage, as most lenders allowed up to 10 percent of the purchase price to be carried back in a second mortgage.

For awhile the advantages of conventional loans actually outweighed the disadvantages (higher costs), but then the inevitable happened. Prices were soaring and money was being used up—often by investors or short-term speculators. So, one by one the conventional loan industry put up "Investors Not Welcome" signs. If a buyer was not going to personally occupy the property, he had to pay a premium for his loan, which usually included a higher down payment and a higher interest rate (sometimes a full 1 percent more).

This tight conventional money for investors carried over into the new decade. But one additional problem popped up then—with a national inflation rate (as measured by the cost of living index) at over 13 percent in 1979 and at this writing heading for a possible 18 percent in 1980, Uncle Sam stepped in and tightened the screws on consumer spending. Better a recession, the thinking went, than out-of-control inflation. The results were that buying income property (let alone a residence) was out of the question with interest rates as high as 13 and in some cases even 18 percent. With interest rates that high it's necessary for the investor to seek out FHA-GI assumptions or use creative financing methods which are explained in forthcoming chapters.

The following table will give you an idea of how crippling high interest rates can be, especially when one is trying to hold down negative cash flows.

Monthly Payments for a $70,000 loan, amortized 30 years

At 8% interest $513.64
At 10% interest $614.31
At 12% interest $720.03
At 14% interest $829.42

Note that the difference between 8 and 14 percent is $315.78. That's enough money spent on additional interest to discourage any investor—that is unless he has a chance to buy a $100,000 property for $75,000. So there are exceptions, but the investor should generally concentrate his efforts on getting lower payments that won't kill his program over the long haul.

Speaking of interest rates, here is a prediction. While we will never see rates as low as eight percent again, I don't believe that over the next five years (until about 1986) we'll have to worry much about 15 percent rates. Everyday rates will be relatively high, I would suspect about 11 to 13 percent, but not much over 13. Also expect cycles; when the economy is sluggish and inflation is not a problem, you will probably find that buying via new conventional loans will again be the way to go, and investors will probably be able to get these loans without penalties, just as they did in the mid-seventies. However, when other outside occurrences happen, like oil embargoes, runaway inflation, tight money, etc., watch for investors to be kicked out of the market again, and for interest rates to go to higher levels.

THINGS YOU SHOULD KNOW ABOUT APPLYING FOR A CONVENTIONAL LOAN

A while ago I interviewed a loan agent who had worked for a large California Savings & Loan. Following are some of the highlights that appeared in the Update, the eight-page newsletter that accompanies IMPACT REPORTS (for more details see back of this book). You'll find the tips passed on by this anonymous lender quite helpful when you are applying for a new loan.

Question: Is there any inside information or tips available that if properly utilized by an investor would enable him to get more desirable treatment in times of tight money . . . such as being able to get loans with better terms than another investor might get who was not privy to this inside information?

The preceding question was the central theme of my article. To get "the inside information" I interviewed an experienced loan agent who until recently was employed by one of California's largest savings and loans. For reasons which will become obvious as you read on, our subject has asked to remain anonymous. I'll refer to him as Bob.

Bob has been employed as a loan agent for the past eleven years. During this time he was on commission rather than salary. The meaning of this should be obvious—Bob only gets paid when a real estate transaction is completed (recorded).

I began the interview by asking Bob to explain what is going on with the "thinking process" of the lending institutions and what an investor might do to better his chances of buying property with conventional loans.

"The current outlook is not good for investors," according to Bob. "The main reason is that the primary function of savings and loans is to provide funds to borrowers who are going to be occupants. Therefore non-occupant loans and refinances normally play a secondary roll.

"Investors cannot really expect very much good news from the savings and loans — at least while there is a heavy demand for mortgage money. But there are exceptions," Bob pointed out. "One month my firm allowed investors to borrow at the same terms and conditions as owner-occupants — loans to 80 percent of appraised value with secondary financing for an additional 10 percent of the property value. Our office was swamped with investors that month, with them making up about three quarters of our volume.

"It was like a giant spring clearance sale — when the merchandise (in this case, money) was gone, the sale was over. This will happen from time to time. Except unlike a store sale, this one was not advertised. The word was spread by our loan agents as they made their routine contacts of real estate offices in their territories."

During the interview, Bob stressed over and over again that each loan association is governed by different policies. "Because of these important differences," he said, "an investor must learn to shop around. That is very important! You'll rarely find two associations with exactly the same interest rates, loan fees, qualification requirements or investor loan policies. By having your agent shop around . . . or even by doing most of it himself . . . an investor will usually come out many dollars ahead.

"It is also very important," Bob pointed out, *"For an investor to keep in close contact with his real estate agent, because in the example I just gave, the agent could have told the investor about the loan 'sale.' "*

With many associations today imposing such tough requirements for investor loans, there are always rumors about people buying homes as owner-occupants but then not moving into the property. "Most lenders," Bob said, "require that borrowers sign a statement which says that you are going to live in the property. The lender can deny your loan if you refuse to sign the statement. And if you sign the statement and they later find out that you are not occupying the home, they have the right to call that loan due and payable — usually within 30 days after discovery or from the time you are notified that they are exercising this right."

"However, from my experience," Bob pointed out, "I have never seen a lender recall a loan. They may give you a bad time — they may never make another loan to you, but they probably won't recall the loan.

"Periodically the lenders do check to see that the borrowers who are supposed to are actually living in the property. But even when they find someone not living in a house who should be — what does it prove. Perhaps their move was delayed or maybe they changed their mind after they moved into the home—and moved out right away. There are many legitimate reasons why a person may decide not to move into a home he just bought. Of course, this person could be an investor who is just making excuses. But I think you can see how difficult it can be for the lender to police this provision," Bob said.

"The lender has a better chance," Bob pointed out, "of stopping an investor at the very beginning—when the application is submitted. It's almost impossible, for instance, for a wealthy investor to hide the fact that he is not going to live in a home. You just can't make a lender believe that you are going to sell a $150,000 home to live in a $60,000 one. These facts are like waving a red flag in front of the loan commitee . . . and a lot more questions will be asked.

"*Another investor might get away with it,*" he said. "*Take an investor, for example, who lives in an apartment. This person could probably get a lot of loans without arousing much suspicion, as long as he didn't keep going back to the same association.*

"If an investor wants to take a chance and lie, that's up to him and his conscience," Bob said. "The fine print in the loan application states that everything submitted is 'true to the best of my knowledge.' There are times, however, when even people who would not lie about occupancy to get a loan might consider telling a little white lie—or at least not supplying certain information.

"A case in point," Bob said, "is the investor with a sizable portfolio who does not want to list all of his properties on the loan application. I have been guilty of this myself. Here's why: Suppose a person owns real property with outstanding loans totaling $500,000. The properties might even provide a positive cash flow—but that might not matter to some conservative-thinking lenders. To these lenders all that matters is that this investor with a large portfolio might get caught with several properties vacant during hard times. And even a $40,000 salary, they reason, would not be able to take care of several vacancies over a period of time. So sometimes a big portfolio can work against, and not for, the investor-borrower.

"Another reason for not listing some of your properties is to hide the fact that your credit rating may be slow. By not submitting this information on the application it will probably not show up on the credit report.

"You have to be careful with credit reports," Bob reasoned, "because excluded items can come back to haunt you. You might choose to omit a department store charge account because you know your credit rating there is slow. But just because this information was not submitted does not guarantee that it won't be picked up and appear on your credit report. And if it does show up there is a good chance the lender will reject your loan application because you did not include this information.

"A lot of these credit report problems," he explained, "can be eliminated by working with a loan agent who is paid by commission rather than straight salary. A commissioned agent has something at stake—like money—so if the customer does not get the loan he does not get paid.

"Experience is important too," Bob said, "because the agent's skills can make the difference between the borrower getting or not getting his loan.

"This commissioned agent," Bob pointed out, "could get his hands on the credit report before it went to the committee to make sure that items left out of the loan application (but that appeared on the credit report) were added to the application so that the borrower would not risk rejection for non-disclosure.

"A good agent—especially one who is working on commisssion—is usually on the borrower's side. When filling out a loan application, the investor should verbally discuss his entire financial situation with the agent—and then he'll probably help fill it out. There are a lot of tricky questions," Bob said. "For example, consider a divorced person who has not remarried and is paying $300 monthly child support. If this information goes on the application, it will then most likely also appear on the credit report and thus become a liability to the borrower and maybe even tip the scales against his getting the loan. So sometimes it is best not to put this information on the application. A cooperative loan agent will tell you when those times are.

"Finding a commissioned agent is usually not too difficult," Bob pointed out. "Usually your real estate agent knows who they are. More likely than not these people will be working for savings and loans and not banks."

According to Bob, every loan agent has a superior who is an underwriter (he has the power to say *yes* or *no* on a loan application). At most savings and loans this "loan committee" is a person who works in the same building—even in the same room—as the loan agent. For instance, Bob had a boss and the boss had an assistant. Both of these men were the loan committee, according to Bob, and either could approve or disapprove a loan.

"Sometimes a loan agent can influence the committee's decision," Bob said, "but not nearly as much as the selling real estate agent thinks. The committee may go along with my special request for an approval if *he* is in a good mood that day. But if he has had a fight with his wife, it could be a different story."

Although a loan agent might sometimes influence the loan committee, Bob said that is not the same case when it comes to the appraiser. "The loan agent has virtually no influence over the appraisal department," Bob said. "For one thing it is a separate department and usually has separate offices. On rare occasions, I have been able to get a friend to bump a valuation a little. But I feel that those guys seldom under-value a home anyway, so a low appraisal is usually not a problem.

"If an investor buys a rental home by declaring that he is going to live in it . . . and then he doesn't . . . and he gets caught . . . he will probably just get his wrists slapped," said Bob. "I am not condoning this method, I am just telling it like I have observed it for eleven years.

"On the other hand, an investor should not submit false sales prices. I know this is done but the results are not worth the risks. What happens is that some investors, in an attempt to get maximum leverage, talk the seller into writing a second contract— which shows a higher sales price than the real one—and then submit this higher contract to escrow. If they get away with it, the buyer gets a higher loan amount and the seller kicks back the extra money (under the table) to the purchaser.

"This is called defrauding the lender," Bob emphatically stated. "If a person gets caught, the penalty can be severe . . . he can be prosecuted for fraud by the district attorney. I strongly recommend that this is one technique which investors should avoid.

"If an investor wants to get better leverage, he should consider placing a second mortgage or trust deed on the property shortly after the sale is recorded," Bob said. "Even though the lender may not have allowed a second as part of the original loan and sales package, once the transaction is closed the first mortgage holder no longer has anything whatsoever to say about other loans recorded in a secondary position. So a smart investor may have his leverage (second money) all lined up just waiting to be recorded the day after the first loan records."

*"With Secondary Financing, the buyer and
seller can come to terms which will benefit
BOTH of them without mandatory regulation
imposed on them by conventional lenders."*
— *Al Brown*
Creative finance educator

14

SECOND MORTGAGES

What can give your real estate portfolio *liquidity* . . . often solve your negative cash flow problems . . . and at the same time help you buy . . . and buy . . . more and more property?

The answer is second mortgages and trust deeds. They are the "magical tool" you can use to accomplish almost anything you want to with your investment properties.

Virtually all successful real estate investors that I have ever met use second mortgages (or deeds of trust) to advance their investment goals. While some use second loans just occasionally, others use them so extensively that every property they own is encumbered with one or more of these secondary loans.

In real estate slang, second mortgages and trust deeds are often referred to as "paper"; paper which has legitimate value for the holder because it is secured by real property and because this paper has value it can be used as the down payment on other properties.

Second mortgages can also be structured to reduce your negative cash flows, thereby helping the investor on a tight income-and-expense budget buy more property. I'll show you how to do that a little later.

In *The Monopoly Game* I told the reader how important second mortgages were to the investor who sets his sights on creating a small fortune. In my second book, *How To Grow A Moneytree*, I told the reader how lucrative second mortgages can be as an investment. In *Moneytree* the complete workings of the mortgage and trust deed were explained . . . certainly a help to the property investor. But an important gap still remained!

This chapter will fill that gap, plug the missing holes! I'll show you *why* you should use secondary financing in your investment portfolio . . . and *how* to use it . . . and *where* to get the money.

Seconds, or junior liens as they are also called, can be utilized by property owners at almost any time, for any reason, with almost any property in nearly all markets. They give property owners an important degree of versatility. For example, following are eight accomplishments they can help you realize:

1. *Peace of mind:* Your property is always a source of cash via secondary money. Because the investor knows that he *can* get a loan against his property at any time, he receives a valuable sense of security and peace of mind. It makes your investments "liquid."

2. *A way to raise cash—for any purpose:* Want to go on a costly vacation? Or perhaps you want to buy more property? Your rental property (and often your own residence) is a constant source for this cash. You might have to use a costly licensed mortgage broker—but if you have a reasonable amount of equity in your property, he has the cash.

3. *Seconds can help you sell property:* As a seller you can participate in the sale by carrying back what is called a purchase money note and second mortgage. It's called purchase money because the terms of the note were arranged as part and parcel of the sales agreement to buy your property. In many states (such as California) any interest rate goes with purchase money loans because the terms of the note are considered to be part of the sales agreement rather than just a loan which may or may not come under the scrutiny of the usury law. Usually, though, the seller carries this note at a reasonable interest rate because the purpose of the secondary loan in the first place was to facilitate the sale.

4. *You can use your paper to buy other property:* You will often be able to use paper you own as the down payment on property you are buying. But be prepared to discount it! I'll tell you more about this later in the chapter.

5. *Seconds are excellent investment vehicles in their own right:* As all types of interest rates crept to record-breaking levels in the early eighties, many states either threw out or revised their archaic usury laws. Where it was only possible to get 10 percent before in many states, it is now possible for a second money investor to get 15 percent interest and more. And by intelligently buying "discounted notes" many investors are able to get annual returns of over 25 percent. Investing in seconds does not give one a tax shelter, but neither does it require as much personal attention as some properties (and tenants). For more information, I heartily recommend my book *How To Grow A Moneytree.* You'll find a handy order coupon in the back of this book.

6. *Seconds can greatly aid one in accelerating purchase time tables:* I won't go into a lot of detail here, but keep in mind that the investor who goes out and borrows money via creative second mortgages will be able to buy

many more properties than the investor who sits idly by waiting for his properties *to mature* to the point where he can either sell or refinance to raise cash for additional buys.

7. *Junior liens can help you reduce and even eliminate negative cash flow:* While borrowing money to reduce expenses may sound counterproductive right now, I'll soon demonstrate practical methods which can enable you to do just that—borrow money to reduce nagging negative cash flows.

8. *Seconds can help you put together a purchase that couldn't be done any other way:* Actually there is quite a list of *things* that you can do with second mortgages to help "glue a deal together." I'll be going into several of these at the end of this chapter.

SOME THINGS YOU SHOULD KNOW ABOUT SECONDS

Before I get into the many creative usages of junior liens, the following information should be kept in mind. As the old saying goes, "An ounce of prevention is worth a pound of cure."

FINANCING IS GOVERNED BY STATE LAWS

The only type of real estate financing that is the same nationwide is the Federally insured loan programs such as FHA and VA. Most regulations and laws dealing with conventional loans and *ALL* laws regulating secondary financing are administered by the state in which the property exists. Thus the owner of an Illinois property who lives in Missouri, but borrows money from a Kentucky man, would be required to abide by the laws of Illinois.

Laws, practices, maximum interest rates, security devices (mortgage or trust deeds), mortgage redemption periods, etc. vary quite a bit from state to state. You must take time to learn the basic laws in your state.

In Texas, for instance, there is a Homestead Law which makes it impractical to borrow money which is secured against one's personal residence—but the law offers no barriers to making the loan on a rental property. In California, under most circumstances a hard money mortgage loan broker cannot make a loan to an owner-occupant that is not equally amortized over the term of the loan. But that same borrower could secure the loan against a rental property and receive an interest-only loan (considered a balloon payment loan) from the same mortgage broker. In Nevada, the owner-occupant can obtain a secondary loan with interest-only terms from a mortgage broker.

These examples could go on endlessly. Take my word for it, I will give you ways to creatively use junior liens, but you will have to research your own state laws. And it's not that hard to do—simply pick up your telephone and call a mortgage broker (not a mortgage banker who deals primarily with first loans) and ask him what the basic laws are in your state.

POSITION OF LOANS

A second mortgage is only a *second* mortgage because another loan has already been recorded against a property. Traditionally first loans are for larger amounts, lower interest rates, longer terms and are usually originated by a standard lending institution. However, a secondary loan can fall into first place in the unusual event that the original loan is paid off.

A third mortgage is the same thing as a second mortgage, except for one small detail: it was recorded at a later date than the second loan. Priority in default goes to the loans in relationship to the order in which they are stacked against a property. Thus the first loan gives a lender more security than the second loan, which in turn affords more security than does a third or fourth loan.

But the problems of security can become academic if, for instance, a property has a value of $100,000 and the first loan is for $25,000; the second loan for $10,000; the third loan for $10,000 and a fourth loan for $10,000. The total of all four loans equal only $55,000 thus leaving $45,000 in equity.

ASSIGNMENT OF LOAN

Since a mortgage is considered to be an asset owned by its holder, he may dispose of it in any way he sees fit. This is known as an assignment when ownership of the note and security device is transferred to a second party. One important detail that must be followed through when transferring a junior lien is that the assignee record his assignment at the earliest possible moment with his county recorder's office.

This right of assignment is important to the investor because it gives him a great deal of flexibility. And because junior liens can easily be assigned (and discounted to increase the face value yield) these instruments can be treated almost like money, which is why the phrase "buying property with paper" is used. I'll soon show you how to use second mortgages to buy property and how to avoid "cash in escrow" problems created by outdated policies of some banks and savings and loans.

HOW TO FIND SECOND MONEY

You can make a fortune with borrowed money! But first you must know where to find it and then you must act upon a plan which properly utilizes this borrowed money.

Shortly after I began my real estate career (in 1965) I began to realize that a lot of money could be made by owning rental properties. Properties were only appreciating then at about 4 percent annually in my area, but the handwriting was on the wall. Rentals were so scarce then that tenants would fight over them. FHA-VA assumptions were readily available for as little as $1,000 to $1,500. Negative cash flow was unheard of and the average home price in Pleasant Hill then was only $17,000. Today the average price is well over $90,000.

I had a dream back then, but unfortunately it was only a dream. I would imagine how much money I could make in 5 to 10 years if I could borrow one million dollars, and with that money buy as many single-family homes as I could . . . probably about 400. After a few years of appreciation I would sell some of the homes to pay back the loan plus interest.

If only I realized then what the future would hold. If only any of us did! If I had acted on my hunch . . . and borrowed a million dollars . . . and bought 400 homes as fast as possible . . . that investment today would be worth (without considering any refinancing or trading for more homes) more than 40 million dollars.

But *IFS* and *HINDSIGHT* cannot play any part in our thinking. It's a new day . . . and a new ballgame . . . and opportunities are good today, too. We must recognize this and take action.

If you want to make money . . . I mean really big money . . . you don't need to sit idly by waiting for your rental homes to mature to the point where you can sell or refinance to buy more. Go out and borrow what money you can today—and then buy today. Prices aren't coming down!

And keep in mind that when you borrow money via a second mortgage, there are no immediate tax consequences. You are getting tax-free money with which to expand your holdings. It's only when you sell a mortgaged property that you must bring the mortgage into the picture when reporting your capital gain or loss. And you can go Uncle Sam even one better by refinancing and thus put off the tax collector.

Here are some ideas on locating second money:

1. MORTGAGE BROKERS:

State licensed mortgage loan brokers are always available to give you the money, for a fee, if the equities in your properties are sufficient to meet the security standards that the broker sets to protect his investors. The mortgage broker often requires that you have a minimum of 20 percent equity in your property. Some will accept a minimum of only 15 percent equity. This means with a property valued at $75,000, the broker who requires 15 percent equity in the property will not make a loan for more than $63,750.

Always have an open mind when considering mortgage brokers as a source of borrowed money. Sure, the expenses can be high; perhaps as much as $1,800 on $10,000 borrowed. But there comes a time and place where this hard money source can be invaluable. For instance, you might stumble across a classic "steal" in which you can buy a property for $8,000 beneath market value, but only if you act today. And your private money sources may be "out of business" for a few months. So what really is $1,800 when compared to making a quick $8,000?

2. PURCHASE MONEY LOANS:

A purchase money loan is one that is carried back by the seller. It is a method in which the seller "carries some equity" to help the buyer and to put together a sale which might not have been made without this help. (Note: purchase money loans can also be *first* mortgages, as discussed in the next chapter.)

As purchase money loans are usually intended to put a sale together rather than be an investment vehicle for the seller, they are often poorly drawn. They might be for 8 percent interest in a state that allows 10 percent; they might lack a prepayment penalty or late charges. Just by the fact that a junior lien is a purchase money mortgage, it is a red flag to a note investor.

Carrying back a purchase money second:

A property investor who finds that he must take back a purchase money second to sell a home or apartment should be very certain that his note is properly drawn, carries the highest possible interest rate and contains both a prepayment penalty and late charge. There should also be sufficient equity in the property.

Why all these precautions? Simply because you'll want to use this paper later as either collateral on a loan or as a down payment on another property. A well-drawn second can be either used at full value or may need to be discounted slightly. But a poor one can cost you as much as a fifty percent discount.

Buying Purchase Money Seconds at Discount

I am always fascinated by "rags to riches" stories. I once met a man who claims to have made over a million dollars profit in fewer than five years by buying notes at big discounts. What he did was make a lot of offers to buy (at a discount, of course) purchase money loans. Often his offers would be accepted. Usually he got them for 30 percent discount, but some were picked up for as much as 50 percent. The reason he went after purchase money seconds was that the great majority of the holders of these notes were not investors but property sellers who were pressured into carrying back a second. Most were reluctant to keep these notes but very eager to accept a good cash offer for them. Thus when this alert note investor was able to discount a 10 percent second by even just 25 percent, he was able to get a real yield of 20 percent on his money. I don't want to sound like a broken record, but *How To Grow A Moneytree* goes into all these exciting "discount" details.

The reason I bring up this discount idea here is to demonstrate yet another way an eager investor might raise cash to buy property—and that is by taking a few thousand dollars and going out in the market and buying as many discounted notes as possible. With clever buying, selling and trading, it is possible for someone to quickly turn $5,000 into $25,000 in a relatively short period of time. To do this one will have to carefully read the classified section of every local newspaper, talk with real estate agents in his area and even go so far as checking with the county recorder's office. (As all loans are recorded this information becomes public, thus there is a way to trace those who have purchase money loans.)

3. PRIVATE MONEY SOURCES:

The name of the game is M O N E Y!! Some investors use as much borrowed money as they can get their hands on. It makes sense . . . if you can borrow money at a low cost and then turn that money into an even greater profit . . . wouldn't you be ahead of the game?

If you could borrow $10,000 at 10 percent interest for five years with interest-only payments, wouldn't you do it? At the end of five years you will have paid back $10,000 in principal (in one lump sum) plus you would have paid $5,000 in interest (at $83.33 per month) for a grand total of $15,000. But in that time span you could buy a property for $70,000 which will, with very conservative calculations, be worth $90,000 after five years. And that's with less than 6 percent appreciation per year.

Now in this example you paid $70,000 with the $10,000 used as a down payment, leaving you with a loan of $60,000 which will be paid down to less than $59,000 in five years. Subtracting the $59,000 loan from the $90,000 value leaves $31,000. Repaying the principal and interest on the second ($15,000) leaves a $16,000 profit—all realized without spending any out-of-pocket cash.

As you will see there are many, many creative ways of making a profit with borrowed money. But for now, I am going to concentrate on how you can find that money. To start with I am going to tell you about a secret weapon you can have at your disposal . . . and that's a copy of *How To Grow A Moneytree.*

I know that the preceding statement sounds like a clever way for me to boost book sales—but it is not intended to do that. The point is that to get money you'll need to cultivate private individuals who most likely are putting their money in bank or savings and loan accounts. They need an "education" or else you'll have little chance of getting them to lend you money.

And the best "door opener" that I know of is *Moneytree*. It may accomplish two things. First of all, it can open their eyes to better investment returns and secondly, it can assure them that it is a safe, sound and practical investment.So don't be shy about asking a friend to read the book. It just may be your first critical step in getting secondary financing. Here are some ideas on where to look for the people who might have the money you want to borrow.

1. *Relatives:* Always start here! You will have a good idea in advance which uncle, aunt, distant cousin or parent might have some extra cash. You will also have the best chance with relatives to borrow at an interest rate less than market in your state, which in some is now as high as 15 percent.

Keep your relationship, however, on a business level. Don't take advantage of a relative just because they may not like the idea of making a profit off you. Treat them fairly and be sure that the loan you set up is properly drawn and recorded. And don't you do it. Have it done by a title or escrow company or a real estate attorney.

2. *Friends:* Make a list of all your friends or get out your Christmas card list. Try to determine in advance which ones might not only be able to but would be possibly willing to lend you money.

3. *Neighbors:* Probably your third best source for private money, try to determine in advance which neighbors would be likely to lend you money. Then approach them the same way you would a friend. Tell them what you are trying to accomplish . . . tell them that you are looking for a source of money . . . and lend them your copy of *Moneytree*. Ask them to read it and tell them you will confer with them in a few days to see if they would be interested in your proposal.

4. *Co-workers:* Another good source. You probably spend more time talking with co-workers in a week's time than you do with friends or relatives in a month's time. Thus you should have a good idea in advance who can or possibly will lend you money.

5. *Advertising:* If all the above sources fail, consider placing a small advertisement in your local newspaper. Let it run for at least one week or longer. It could be worded in the following manner:

> Private party needs $10,000, secured by 2nd trust deed (or mortgage) on clean three-bedroom home in Pleasant Hill. Will pay 15% with interest-only payments for 5 years. Call Dave at 345-6789.

Advertising is unpredictable. You might get five or six calls or you might not get any. The above ad is designed to limit calls, however, as it spells out the terms you want—specifically limiting your requests for interest-only loans. You could broaden the ad by not setting forth the terms you want and thus get more calls. You could then try to convince the caller that it would be a good deal for them to lend you money on interest-only terms.

HOW TO SWEETEN THE POT SO YOU CAN GET THE MONEY YOU WANT

When dealing with friends, relatives, neighbors, etc. you will often run into stumbling blocks, like either an unrealistically low interest ceiling (such as 8 percent) or perhaps the exact opposite—too high a limit (as much as 18 percent).

With a low limit a "market wise" friend may point out that he could get a U.S. Treasury bill (currently one must put up $10,000 for a minimum of six months) or whatever other investment commodity is currently paying returns in excess of 10-12—or maybe 14 percent annually. So why, he may ask, should he lend you money at 8 or even 10 percent? If you get caught in this squeeze, you'll have to agree he has a good point. I'll give you the answer to this dilemma in a moment. First let's look at the high interest problem.

When the market interest rate is as high as at this writing in California, where for practical purposes there is no usury ceiling (a voters' initiative removed the old 10 percent limit), an investor could well get stuck with an 18 percent loan. With a $10,000 interest-only loan this would mean repaying $150 monthly. At the old rate (10 percent) this would be $83.33 monthly— a much easier figure to live with. If this $10,000 loan carrying 18 percent interest were fully amortized for five years, the monthly payment would be about $250.

To make a long story short—the figures just may not work out for you at the higher rates. And when your legal state rates are very low you just can't get anyone interested. But there may be a solution which will work for you. That is to offer your lender an extra incentive. Offer a small percentage of ownership in the property you will be buying in addition to the interest rate agreed upon in the note. For example, let's say that in your state you can pay up to 18 percent interest but you feel this amount will cause excessive negative cash flows. You want the money, but 12 percent is your limit. So you offer your friend a 12 percent note in addition to a small undivided interest in the property you are buying. He is protected because his name will be on the deed.

This can be done by taking ownership in the property by what is known as *tenancy in common*. With this method of ownership you can give your note investor a specified percentage of ownership in a particular property . . . for instance, a 1/20th interest. Thus if you buy a $70,000 property with a $10,000 down payment, you are in effect initially giving away 1/20th or $500. In time, as the property appreciates, that $500 or 1/20th interest will grow to perhaps $2,000 or $3,000.

As you can see, this method can often push a "fence straddler" over to your side. But let me caution you to check with legal or tax counsel, as property held in this manner is subject to probate and the inherent problems of probate in the event either party dies. In the long run you may feel it is not worth the risk.

An alternative to the tenancy in common method is a partnership or limited partnership agreement. Again you will need legal counsel. With a partnership agreement you are basically giving your note investor a bonus as in the tenancy in common example, but with this method you will be able to take title in any manner you wish. A separate partnership agreement will set forth terms in which you specify how much interest your note investor would have in a particular property. For example, you might agree to give him 1/25th of either the profit or total monies pulled out of a property when sold. Or if you refinance in five years rather than sell, you might offer a straight dollar amount like $500.

ACCELERATING PURCHASE TIME TABLE
AND LEVERAGING TO THE HILT

You've heard it said before: Money is made in real estate when you get as much leverage as possible. TRUE! Provided that negative cash flow does not eat you alive and that homes continue to appreciate at rates of 6 percent or more annually.

Please keep in mind that an investment plan which "digs out" all available equity for buying more property contains some risks. It is not for the conservative investor . . the empire could crumble in bad times. Serious recessions are not exactly unknown! So before I get into the hows of leveraging to the hilt, let me make one suggestion. Take a percentage of your investment cash . . . at least 10 percent or even as much as 15 percent . . . and keep it liquid. Keep it handy in case you need to bail out your investment portfolio if things go sour. I am not issuing this warning because I feel that real estate is a bad investment or that disaster is around the corner, but because most investors, when you analyze their portfolios, don't have enough cash to bail themselves out of trouble when they must evict a bad tenant, or need to put on a new roof, or when they have a two-month vacancy. So if you want to get rich fast, go ahead and play for high stakes, but cover yourself by leaving some money at home.

By constantly working at your portfolio, it is possible to leverage your properties up to 90 percent of their combined values. As previously stated, most professional money lenders (second mortgage brokers) will not advance any secondary money if the total amounts of the first and second loans exceed 80 percent of the value of the property. But many private sources (your friends, relatives, etc.) will not be so leery in these days of escalating home prices. You can convince most of your private sources, and with solid reasoning, to advance secondary money up to 90 percent of the value of a home or building.

So with plenty of private money sources at your beck and call, you can keep pouring your equities into more properties.

Following is an example where an investor with $14,000 cash buys his first rental property for $50,000 by paying 25 percent down to a 75 percent conventional loan. In this transaction $12,500 is down payment (now equity in the property) and $1,500 goes to closing costs.

Our leverage-minded investor has now bought his first home with terms that don't really add up to good use of leverage . . . *but* . . . *Mr. Investor has been quietly working in the background to develop private sources for secondary money.*

Within a few days after settlement (close of escrow), Mr. Investor carries back a second mortgage on the property for 15 percent of the sale price ($7,500). He arranges terms that allow him to make monthly interest-only payments ($62.50 based on a 10 percent interest rate) for a term of five years. So he now has $7,500 available for his next purchase, and his first property is encumbered by loans totaling 90 percent of value.

NOTE: While banks and savings and loans may limit or completely disallow secondary financing from the time they take a loan application through close of escrow and disbursement of funds, after the loan is recorded and the sale is final, they are virtually helpless in stopping the new owner from placing additional loans on the property.

Once the property is yours, there are no laws or provisions that I am aware of which would restrict, limit or prevent you from placing a new junior lien on the property. But don't act on just my word . . . make sure there is no law preventing a quick secondary loan in your state and also read carefully all the fine print in the note accompanying your mortgage or trust deed. If the language is unclear, consult an attorney or switch lenders.

Obviously this method of investing—loading your portfolio with balloon payment secondary loans—depends upon a reasonable amount of inflation so that the home values will appreciate to the extent that in five years the properties can either be sold or refinanced in order to pay off the junior liens as they become due.

Mr. Investor now has $7,500 to buy his second property. He could look for an FHA or VA assumption for that amount of cash, or even one where the seller would carry back a purchase money second for any additional monies needed. But so I don't spoil my hypothetical example, I am going to have our investor buy his second property also with conventional terms.

We will assume that Mr. Investor has shopped all the major banks and savings and loans in his community and that he has found that the best he can do is still with his original lender who requires the 25 percent down payment from non-occupant buyers. And because Mr. Investor has done a good job of lining up private money sources, he has another 15 percent (or $7,500 loan) ready to go when needed.

But this is where he gets into his first real problem. Mr. Investor has only $7,500 cash in his possession, since the money for the secondary loan will only be made available to him after close of escrow when he can deliver a signed note and mortgage to the lender to be recorded. But he will need to have $14,000 in his possession (assuming the second buy is also a $50,000 property which will take $14,000 cash including closing costs) at the time he fills out the lender's loan forms. There are many creative solutions to this problem. Here are two of them:

If Mr. Investor owns his own residence, he can temporarily borrow against his home with a properly drawn and executed secondary loan from his same source. After escrow closes on the rental home purchase, this second can be in effect transferred from the residence to the rental property. Although the practical effect would be a transfer of money, in practice the second loan on the residence would be released (with a reconveyance deed) and then a new note would be drawn for the rental property.

A second solution would be to pledge the first rental property as security for the $7,500 cash advanced to Mr. Investor a month or so prior to close of escrow on the second property. This security could be in the form of a personal note (not secured by any real property) or preferably a quit claim deed which in effect relinquishes any and all claim that Mr. Investor has in the rental property. The quit claim deed, of course, would be in favor of the lender who has advanced the $7,500. This deed should be completely filled out, signed and notarized *but not recorded.* It should then be placed in the hands of a neutral third party (an attorney, for instance) who would record the document only in the event that Mr. Investor defaults on his obligation. And his obligation in this case would be to take title to the second property for which the loan is intended to be used. A previously agreed upon set of instructions should be left with the neutral third party which would automatically set into operation either the release of the quit claim deed or its recordation. Of course, the quit claim deed would be destroyed (or returned) if the $7,500 is paid back immediately or if the second sale goes through as originally planned so the note can be recorded on the intended property.

Mr. Investor has now, within a relatively short period of time, bought two $50,000 properties with his original $14,000. Disregarding closing costs, he has approximately 10 percent equity in the combined homes. His next logical step would be to wait perhaps one year until the value of each of the homes increases to about $55,000. An additional $500 would be paid down on the principal of the first loans of the homes by that time.

Mr. Investor will then have:

First loan of	$37,250	
Second loan of	7,500	
Totals	$44,750	× 2 = $89,500

Value of both properties $110,000
Total encumbrances of both homes .... − 89,500
Equity now in both properties $ 20,500

As our hypothetical investor is pulling out all the stops to make as much money as he can in the shortest period of time, he is now ready to go on the move again. Even though his homes have appreciated well in one year (10 percent), he does not really have enough equity in any one property to borrow against it alone. So what he does is go back to his private sources and arrange a third junior lien which is recorded against the two original properties. This is often referred to as a *blanket mortgage* as it covers more than one property. In this example it would be a blanket mortgage in third position. In the event of default, the blanket mortgage is often arranged so that both properties would be equally subject to foreclosure.

Following the unwritten Glubetich rule that the investor maintain at least a minimum of 10 percent equity in his properties, all he would be able to borrow after one year is $9,500. See below:

Total values	$110,000
Less 10% equity	− 11,000
	$ 99,000
Less total of all loans	− 89,500
Amount borrowable	$ 9,500

With $9,500 Mr. Investor is off and running again. His best bet would be to look for an assumption. And if he came up a few thousand dollars short, he could buy a property where the seller would carry back a purchase money second.

Leveraging to the hilt is a good way of accumulating a great deal of property, but there are problems. One of the most common is excessive negative cash flows (the amount of money you would need to add to your portfolio each month to make up for the difference between your higher mortgage payments and lower rent receipts). Now if Mr. Investor had a high income (say $75,000) and very little tax shelter prior to buying his properties, his negative cash flow situation wouldn't be too bad. In fact, it would help to greatly increase his tax shelter.

Mr. Investor might also live in a community where all the properties he buys would return him a positive cash flow. Most likely his only negative flow would be from the interest-only payments he makes each month to his private money lenders.

On the other hand Mr. Investor might live in an area where each property would bring a $250 negative cash flow. Thus if he were not in a high income and tax bracket category it would appear there would be no way for him to pursue the above-described plan.

Following, however, is a way you can turn the tables on negative cash flow and still use junior liens to advance your real estate portfolio. It's like having your cake and eating it too!

REDUCING NEGATIVE CASH FLOWS

I talked earlier about cultivating private sources for secondary loans. Again we must go back to that source—but this time you will have to be much more selective.

You will need to locate a fairly well-to-do individual who is approaching retirement; someone with a good income who has four to six years left before he turns himself out to pasture. More likely than not, this person will soon be living on a lot less income than he presently earns. For instance, he could be earning $35,000 now but will only get $25,000 after he retires. *And don't forget inflation.* That $25,000 in five years may only buy 1/2 as much as his $35,000 buys now.

This person is a likely candidate to lend you money with a big balloon payment at the end of five or six years. In other words you will not make any payments—not even interest—for the term of the loan. And that's only logical! Why? Because if your prospect does not have a large tax shelter base now, he will be paying taxes on the interest he gets. And he's in a much higher tax bracket now than he will be in in five or six years. And secondly, he is going to need the money (and interest too) much more after retirement than before retirement.

What I am describing is a *straight note.* With this type of note the whole shooting match—interest and principal—is due in one lump sum *balloon* payment at the end of 3 . . . 5 . . . or however many years the note was negotiated for.

To reduce your negative cash flows, here is what you do after you find a lender who is willing to go along with a straight note. Let's assume that you have $10,000 to buy a home with. But the average home in your community sells for $70,000. And even if you buy a more modest $60,000 property, with $10,000 down, your negative cash flow will be about $150 per month—not a particularly small amount when you're living on a fixed budget.

What you do is borrow $10,000 with the above-described terms, and put $20,000 down instead of $10,000. With a mortgage rate of 10 percent, this additional down payment will cut your $150 negative flow by $87.76 to a more liveable $64. As with the investor who is leveraging to the hilt, you will need to sell or refinance the home in five years to pay off the note. But you will still be far ahead in the long run.

This concept is important because many investors are living on a fixed income or they live where there are excessive negative cash flows—mostly caused by the tremendous 25 percent-plus home appreciation rates recently experienced. These people want to invest, but when one spends all but $200 from a $1,800 income on basically just food and shelter, obviously little extra money can be set aside for negative cash flow. So, finding ways to reduce it is important, because it's always better to invest in some small way than to not invest at all. (See Chapter 16 for r ore ways of either eliminating or reducing negative cash flow.)

That's an important lesson—remember it! Don't fail to get into real estate investments because of a lack of time or money. *Do what you can—even if it's just buying one small property.* Someday you'll be glad you did.

SOME OF THE MANY WAYS SECONDS CAN HELP SAVE THE DAY

Through junior liens you can borrow money to buy property, pay off debts or visit Aunt Mary. You can buy property with them . . . or you can use them to sell property. They can give you greater leverage . . . they can help eliminate negative cash flows . . . and without a doubt, they can give you greater flexibility. Following are a few ways in which second mortgages can help you. Perhaps these methods will crank up your own imagination.

PAPER AS A DOWN PAYMENT

To set the background for this example, let's assume that you recently sold a rental property and carried back a purchase money second mortgage at 8 percent interest in the amount of $10,000. Since the property needed a lot of paint and repairs, you found that you had no choice but to participate in the financing if you wanted to sell at a figure close to your asking price. In addition you were out-negotiated and left with an 8 percent interest rate.

You want to buy another home with the $10,000 note or use it as part of your down payment. Your first logical step is to find a private party or mortgage broker who will buy the note at a reasonable discount. But after several discussions with investors and mortgage brokers, you find that because your note lacks a prepayment penalty and has a low interest rate, the best offer you get is for a 30 perent discount, thus leaving you with a net of only $7,000.

Rejecting the offer for a 30 percent discount, you begin looking for a suitable buy in which you can offer your $10,000 note as part of the down payment. The first problem you run into is that the sellers of all the nicer homes are not interested in your note. Why? Because most of them know that they will be able to sell without getting involved with your "white elephant." And some of the sellers need all of their cash out of the sale so they can buy another property. So obviously you are barking up the wrong tree again. Incidentally, you will have much better luck buying with "paper" when you're in a buyer's market. Sellers will not be able to be as choosy then.

Your next logical step is to examine properties which have been on the market for three months or more; or to look for properties in which the seller does not need all of his cash; or to locate property that is in the "dirty dog" classification.

After going through a dozen run-down properties you find one that can easily be fixed up by doing some yard work, replacing worn-out carpeting and painting the entire inside of the home. You learn that the home has been on the market for five months and the seller is discouraged. The seller is ripe for an offer. He's the perfect one to offer your second mortgage to as part of the down payment.

After carefully inspecting the property and neighborhood, you find that fixed up (it would take about $3,000 to do so) the home would be worth approximately $60,000. The asking price is $55,000 but obviously soft because of the time the property has been on the market. But you also have a weakness (a $10,000 note which is really worth only $7,000) so you decide to offer $55,000 for the property provided the seller takes your paper as part of the down payment. Your agent makes a good case for the logics of taking the note and so the seller accepts your terms. Up to this point all is well and good. But possible problems again loom ahead as you select a lender.

GETTING THE LENDER TO ACCEPT PAPER

There are as many different lending policies as there are lenders. And not only do policies greatly differ on the local level but they can be as different as night and day when comparing region to region.

While many lenders will accept your purchase money second (or any other paper that you may own) as part of your down payment, there are some who will not. Some lenders will allow the paper to be part of the transaction as long as the buyer shows at least 10 percent of the purchase price in cash. Others will allow any amount of paper as long as it is secured by another property other than the one being purchased. That's the key in this discussion—your note will usually be considered as good as cash *if it's secured by another property*. If it was secured by the property you were buying, the lender could rightfully say that you were not putting any of your own money into the sale and thus their policy (and eventually security) may be jeopardized.

How do you get around this problem? The first and obvious answer is to shop around for the best lender. When you get one who insists on all cash in escrow, rather than paper . . . drop that lender and find one who will allow the note. After all, the note represents a true asset and not borrowed money.

Your only other way around this possible dilemma is an illegal maneuver which depends upon the cooperation of all parties to the transaction (except the lender, of course). It starts with a good escrow officer who is willing to show the lender what he wants to see.

For instance, let's assume that you are buying a piece of property in which your down payment is to be a note representing 20 percent of the value of the property. The balance is to be a new loan from ABC Savings and Loan. But ABC requires you to have 10 percent cash in escrow.

Now you could make ABC happy by selling your note at discount and then using cash. Except that makes you unhappy because you had to suffer the loss. And what does it really matter, you reason, because the seller is willing to take the note without a discount and the loan amount (and interest rate) you're getting from ABC is not affected.

With this justification you find a qualified and willing escrow officer (and they do exist) who will "adjust" the settlement papers so as to show ABC that you are putting up cash. It becomes a simple matter of semantics!

A QUICK, SURE WAY OF RAISING CAPITAL

I'm sure you can think of occasions when you need a lot of money—and fast. It could be a family emergency, or perhaps you have a chance to "steal" a property that's in foreclosure and make a $10,000 profit. Only to make this $10,000 profit you need $10,000 tomorrow and not a day later.

Well, here's how you can do it—but you'll have to pay the price. If your ends justify the means, the price you pay could really be a bargain. *A word of warning, however.* This method is designed to attract an investor by possibly skirting your state's usury laws. It's done all the time—and for awhile this or similar techniques were the only practical way investors in states with unrealistically low usury rate ceilings could raise money. That was because during the late Seventies the usury interest limit was often 10 percent when the real market (albeit an underground one) was at about 15 percent. I make no statement as to whether this method may be legal or illegal in your state, I am just presenting this example as a technique which many people use and which could possibly solve a problem for you someday.

In this example a property investor borrows (on paper) $10,000 at 10 percent interest for a term of one year. In reality, however, he will only get $8,000 but make payments based upon a $10,000 note plus the interest. His true costs are $3,000. This may not be the best way for him to go, but occasionally it is the only way. And if a fairly sure $10,000 profit awaits, maybe it isn't such a bad trade-off.

Our hypothetical note investor in this example will buy the $10,000 second mortgage for just $8,000—a 20 percent discount. In addition to that he will be getting $1,000 in interest over the course of the year. That amount of interest can be guaranteed by inserting a sliding scale prepayment penalty in the event the loan is paid off early. In other words, with a combination of interest and/or prepayment penalty the note can be structured to guarantee the investor this additional $1,000. Thus the note investor will make 30 percent in this example—not a bad incentive to get someone to loan you money quickly.

To make this plan work (or to be quasi-legal) most of those who set up this kind of an exchange will use a third party. This person should be a very close and trustworthy friend or relative of the borrower. This is because the original note will be drawn in his (the third party's) favor. Without any transfer of cash, the borrower will sign, execute and record this second mortgage in favor of his friend. He will then bring in the real lender—the note investor who will pay $8,000 for this $10,000 note. The trustworthy friend then assigns his note over to the note investor and gives the money to the property investor.

The note investor, incidentally, should not be told what is going on as he is the one who normally gets punished for usury law violations.

BUYING WITH AN "INVESTOR IN THE WINGS"

Earlier I stressed the importance of cultivating private sources for secondary money. This *investor in the wings* technique will help you make a lot of good deals that otherwise couldn't be made without second money help from a source who's standing by and waiting for you to say "send in the money."

In this example our hypothetical investor, whom I'll call Ms. Venture, is told about a property which will soon be on the market. Ms. Venture contacts the owners and inspects the property and *suggests* a verbal offer of $75,000 which she feels is a fair price for both buyer and seller (but especially the buyer).

(Note: although I do not normally recommend making verbal offers, in this example it is acceptable because the property was not actually up for sale yet so the owners had not yet determined a price. So Ms. Venture suggested that she might be interested in buying the property at $75,000. If the sellers respond with a "we might be interested in that price," the stage is set for formal negotiations.)

The problem is that Ms. Venture only has $15,000 cash and she will need $25,000 plus closing costs to buy this home because the first mortgage balance is at $50,000. Although this purchase will not represent the best use of leverage, Ms. Venture feels that the total terms are worth it. The first loan, for instance, is at 7½ percent interest, and the property is really worth $85,000. Or at least Ms. Venture feels that a real estate office could probably get that price. This home will also provide Ms. Venture with a small positive cash flow. And that, she feels, is the icing on the cake.

Fortunately for Ms. Venture, she will not lose this good deal because she has an *investor in the wings.* That is someone who has already agreed to loan money via a second mortgage to Ms. Venture when the need arises.

When a seller will participate in the financing—like carrying back a second mortgage—you don't need this investor in the wings. But many times the seller says no, so if that's the case you can still go ahead with the sale if you've got an investor ready to go. Sure, you could still go through with the sale and get your secondary money from a hard money broker (if there was enough equity), but the high costs of this money might sour the whole deal.

Occasionally your investor in the wings will want a better interest rate than 10 or 12 percent, and why not, with T-Bills being as high as they are at this writing. Here's one way of doing this without paying too high a price.

Again using Ms. Venture's example, let's suppose that her investor in the wings wanted a 15 percent return or else *no deal.* And the usury limit in her state is less than 15 percent. To get the note investor his 15 percent return, Ms. Venture can pay $2,000 more for the property (that's not so bad, since it's already underpriced) and have the sellers carry back a second for $12,000 at 10 percent interest.

That's right—the sellers said they wouldn't do this; but with a little persuasion they can be convinced to do it for just a day or two until Ms. Venture's investor in the wings can buy the note at a discount. This is necessary, because as you may remember, purchase money loans do not usually come under the thumb of usury laws. And when they don't, a purchase money loan can be a vehicle for higher interest rates.

So that everything will work out okay, the note would be discounted by about 16.63 percent, giving the sellers their $10,000. The happy result would be the note investor getting his 15 percent; the sellers getting their full price without carrying back anything; and Ms. Venture still gets a good deal, although she'll be paying 10 percent interest on $12,000 now rather than on $10,000.

TERMS CAN BE TAILORED TO FIT YOUR BUDGET

There is no one correct way to set terms or to collect payments. Whatever the two parties agree to is usually okay—as long as the interest rate is within the legal limits. For instance, if you have a negative cash flow problem, why not structure a five-year note for $10,000 payable interest-only with a balloon payment like the following:

Year One . . . . . no interest payment at all
Year Two . . . . interest at 10 percent
Year Three . . . interest at 12 percent
Year Four . . . . interest at 13.5 percent
Year Five . . . . . interest at 15 percent (or top maximum allowed)

The above terms will allow an investor to get by the first year or two with relative ease. And those first couple of years are always the worst for negative cash flow. At the end of five years, when the note must be paid off or renewed, the investor should be able to refinance without a great deal of trouble.

But what about the lender? Obviously you'll need to find someone who doesn't need a lot of money during the first few years. When you think about it, however, there are hundreds of reasons why this might be the case. For instance, maybe the lender is making a lot of money now but will retire with a lower income in a few years; or perhaps he has large capital gains this year and wants no additional income during the tax year; or maybe he is saving money for a son or daughter's college education which doesn't begin for five more years.

In the above flexible monthly payment example, at the end of the fifth year the investor will get $5,050 in interest. This comes to just slightly better (by $50) than 10 percent a year. This may not be enough return for your investor—you may have to give him something additional—a *kicker*.

This kicker could be something like a favor you could bestow upon him; or an unusually high prepayment penalty which would be paid regardless of how the loan was paid off or when. I grant that this prepayment penalty (say $1,000 which would guarantee to boost his return to at least 12 percent) will probably not be legal in your state. And that's because when a five-year note is paid off during the last month the borrower cannot be penalized for an "early payment." But it is a relatively simple way of boosting your note investor's return when he needs it most . . . and when you can most afford to pay it.

The favor I suggested can be something simple like any of the following performed without charge: Gardening work for one, two or three years; painting his personal residence; teaching his son or daughter how to play the piano; doing his income tax each of the five years; repairing his automobile (free labor); or providing free or wholesale cost services or goods. The list can go on and on, but the idea is simple. Agree in writing (independent of the mortgage note) to provide something extra to help make up the monetary imbalance in the second mortgage. *I'll tell you this, if someone in my neighborhood offered me his son or daughter for free babysitting duties for a couple of years, I'd sure jump at it.*

BLANKET MORTGAGES SOLVE THIN EQUITY PROBLEMS

Sometimes one doesn't have enough equity in a single property to justify a second loan. But if an investor owns more than one real estate parcel, there is nothing stopping him but a lack of imagination, from securing the loan with two or more properties. Some lenders like the extra security of having their loan backed by more than one property, and are thus more willing to either carry back a second or to make the loan in the first place.

Don't get carried away, however, and offer more than you have to. If you don't have enough equity in one property, then offer another, but not one with lots of equity. You won't want to cut off your chances for another loan in the near future.

STACKED OR MULTIPLE MORTGAGES
MIGHT BE THE ANSWER

It's very common to find a seller who is willing to carry back a small amount of money but does not want to commit himself to a larger amount for fear he will need some or all of the proceeds before the note will come due. Thus, you can use what is known as multiple mortgages to break up an otherwise large amount and make smaller amounts due at different times. For instance, $12,000 could be repaid in three separate loans due as follows:

$3,000 second loan due in one year
$4,000 third loan due in two years
$5,000 fourth loan due in four years

You'll have a decent chance at getting these loans on straight note terms with no *interest* and *principal* payments until that portion of the note becomes due. Why? Because the holder does not have to wait four years before he gets his money. Because he gets some in the first year and again after just two years he may be more apt to let you get by without making any payments whatsoever.

These stacked "no payment" second mortgages can be a fantastic tool for the investor with several properties who can sell or refinance at least one each year. It's very conceivable that this investor could line up one or two note investors who would provide him with $40- to $50,000 of second money, stacked so that one note would become due each year. It would be paid off by refinancing or selling a property.

This method of pyramiding can get a little hairy, but it is a way of borrowing a fairly substantial amount of money which will not add to negative cash flows, and in fact can be used to reduce them. I know one investor who does this type of leveraging with seconds. He has made a lot of money and has not goofed up and lost one of his highly leveraged properties yet.

If you want to make money in real estate—then think *second mortgages* every time you buy or sell a property. Use them to raise new investment capital. Don't let idle equity slow you down—use seconds to "get it out" and make you money.

"There are many, many different ways to buy property . . . and the use of cash is only one of them. Cash is not as important as desire and drive!"
— *Charles Dorsey*
Creative investor & Realtor

15

CREATIVE FINANCING . . . STARTING FROM THE BOTTOM

What is creative financing?

The governor of California said that *creative financing* could be a major solution to nagging tight money and high interest rate problems.

Is creative financing something like a miracle drug? Can it solve all real estate financing problems? Or is it overrated? Is it just a lot of fancy talk which helps sell books and seminars?

I have not found an acceptable definition of creative financing yet. I feel the term *creative financing* is broad enough to encompass just about any type of dealing in which a buyer buys property without new financing or without paying cash down to an existing loan.

Creative financing has no boundaries. Just about anything goes! For instance, could you count how many ways or variations there are for buying real estate? I don't think so. You might not even want to know about some, as they are pretty far-fetched—the kind that work only one out of a thousand times.

Creative financing is the one area of real estate that is universal to all the parts—in other words what you read here can be applied to buying land, commercial buildings, farms, industrial property, multi-family or single family dwellings.

Does it work? Yes, when the needs of both the buyer and seller are completely satisfied in a workable agreement. And it won't work when the needs of both parties are not met or when the creative tools used to bind the agreement are faulty or illegal.

In the wrong hands some creative financing ideas are lethal . . . they are akin to fraud. So this is one area not to get too far into by yourself until you thoroughly understand real estate investing. Once you get your feet wet you can go deeper and deeper into your *bag of tricks*. Bag of tricks?

I always imagined myself entering any negotiating session carrying a big cloth bag—not unlike those the carpetbaggers used to carry—and in that sack were every imaginable phrase, statement, financing device or sales closing technique that I would never need.

If the particular sale I was trying to nail down looked as though it would work if the seller took back a second mortgage, I would imagine myself reaching into my bag of tricks and pulling out the right words, which I would then recite. Everything I know about real estate is in my bag of tricks. It gives me the confidence I need to win at the negotiations table because I can always reach (mentally) into my bag and come up with a workable plan or idea that I thoroughly understand.

Try this method yourself—it works. Take each new investing or financing idea you learn and mentally put it into your bag of tricks. It'll be there some day when you need it. But don't put anything into your bag that you don't thoroughly understand. Master each technique before you mentally file it away.

How frequently can you be successful with creative financing methods? Not as many times as I would like—yet often enough to make creative strategies a very vital part of your bag of tricks. Creative ideas sometimes fail because a lot of sellers want (and insist upon) their entire equity and will usually hold out until they get what they want.

These people aren't what you would call distressed sellers. With single-family homes they are the transferred executives or the families moving up in life and right into a bigger home—with a much bigger mortgage. Only in a down or buyer's market are you going to have a realistic chance of convincing this type of seller to participate in the sale. And that's what creative financing is all about—getting the seller to participate in the sale.

You will be successful putting together creative sales many more times than you might at first imagine. A Realtor friend of mine who earned in excess of $100,000 in commissions in 1979 did this without going to a single institutional lender for a new loan.

So some people are not responsive to your creative overtures. So what! Many others are . . . so when you want to buy property with existing paper (a second mortgage you already hold) don't waste your time with the impossible, but look for the type of situation where the odds will be in your favor. Review chapter 11. Find the seller who does not need all his cash immediately out of the sale.

A lot of sellers qualify. They include the elderly who are moving closer to relatives or perhaps into a rest home; the recently divorced; the tired land-lord; the out-of-town owner; the not-so-elderly but recently retired who want a smaller property and would like a comfortable income rather than a lump sum payment; the seller with a tax problem; the desperate seller who is about to lose his job; and on and on. Free your imagination and you'll come up with hundreds of situations where it would actually benefit the seller to sell with creative terms.

This chapter is entitled *Creative Financing . . . Starting from the Bottom.* The biggest fault I find with many creative real estate practitioners is that they take so much pride in what they can accomplish they completely overlook the basic methods which would work as well or perhaps even better.

If you can buy a property by assuming the present 9 percent FHA loan and having the seller carry back a good-sized second mortgage, why bother with a contract of sale or perhaps a wrap-around?

I have always found that the direct method is best. Many sellers expect the absolute worst when the potential buyer starts rattling off a series of ideas (wraps, lease-backs, etc.) they know nothing about. My philosophy is to be direct and as simple as possible—using the KISS principle. Keep it simple stupid! But my bag of tricks is very full . . . so if the most simple or direct method that benefits me the most is turned down, I reach deeper into the bag to find another idea, one which I presume will be acceptable to the seller.

Following my philosophy of "building from the bottom, not the top," I have already introduced what I feel is the basic bottom line of creative financing. That was second mortgages, discussed in the last chapter. Now in this chapter I am writing about what I feel is the next logical step in creative financing—*wrap-around loans, contracts of sale* and *purchase money first mortgages.*

WRAP-AROUND LOANS

A wrap-around is a mortgage or trust deed which secures a debt that in-cludes the balance due on an existing senior mortgage (or trust deed) and an additional amount advanced by the wrap-around mortgagee. The wrap-around mortgagee (who usually is the seller) thereafter makes the payments on the senior mortgage.

These loans are often called All-Inclusive Trust Deeds, overrides, or other similar names depending in part on which region you live in.

The wrap-around loan is usually the result of a purchase money trans-action (one in which the seller participates by carrying back a portion of his equity) and thus is usually exempt in most states from usury limits. Don't take my word alone, however, check it out in your state.

A wrap is also similar to the contract of sale, which I'll discuss next, except that title to the property is actually transferred and may be insured by a policy of title insurance.

Wrap-arounds really only work when current interest rates are significantly higher than older interest rates—those in effect two to six years previously. At this writing, wraps are "in" because current interest rates are in excess of 14 percent and previous rates are mainly in the 8 to 10 percent range. The why's of the excitement over wraps will become very apparent in a moment.

A necessary ingredient for a successful wrap-around mortgage is that the first loan (the senior mortgage) be totally and completely assumable. If it is not—if the loan has a due-on-sale clause—then the lender will call the loan due and payable in its entirety or at the very least will raise the interest rates to the current market level. This ruins the mathematics which make these loans work.

Remember—FHA and VA loans do not have a due-on-sale clause. Anyone can assume these regardless of their financial status. Also in California and a growing number of other states, it is now against the law for a state-chartered lender to enforce its due-on-sale clause if the basic security for the loan is not threatened. This all came about after the famous Wellenkamp vs. Bank of America decision in 1978. Thus in many states (Florida is one) you can now wrap loans made by state-chartered lenders.

I mentioned earlier that the seller must participate in the sale to make a wrap work. For a purchase money wrap as I am discussing here, yes. But there are some lenders (usually small ones) who will take the place of the seller if he doesn't choose to participate. Their rates are usually slightly below the regular going conventional rate and the loan fees they charge are usually less too. So when the seller says "no" don't automatically think you are dead—check with local Realtors to see if there are any wrap companies in your area.

Why is this type of loan so popular with sellers and some lenders? Because they are collecting interest on a senior mortgage which they do not hold. For example, let's assume that you are buying my $90,000 property with a $10,000 down payment and I'll be wrapping the current 8 percent first mortgage with a remaining balance of $50,000.

I do this by lending you (on paper) $30,000 of my equity. Because I want my property sold, I'll let you have this loan at 13 percent interest—which let's say is one to two percent less than the going conventional rates. Not bad—it beats whatever interest a bank or savings and loan would pay me if I deposited my money in one of their accounts—but it gets a lot better.

Because I am not giving you a plain vanilla second mortgage, which I could have, I am able to continue to reap benefits from my low interest rate first loan. If I didn't wrap I probably would have wanted $30,000 down instead of just $10,000. Instead I am going to let you make use of my low interest rate loan for a fee—a five percent override. That five percent is the difference between the 8 percent first and the 13 percent I am charging you on the $30,000.

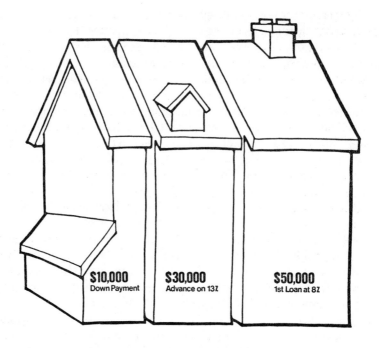

| $10,000 | $30,000 | $50,000 |
| Down Payment | Advance on 13% | 1st Loan at 8% |

On the $50,000 first loan this additional five percent which I will be collecting amounts to $208.33 a month additional income. Add that to the 13 percent I'll be collecting on the $30,000 portion of the wrap (which is $325) and I come out with an income of $533.33 per month.

If you think I am earning just 13 percent on my money—take another look. The total income is approximately $6,400 a year. By dividing that by the $30,000 that is more or less invested out of my own pocket, my yield is 21.33 percent. It's not hard, with results like that, to see why many sellers prefer wraps.

The wrap can be written on a 30-year amortization schedule or anything else desired. There are no set rules. You are free to arrange the terms and conditions to meet your (and the buyer's) needs. What is popular is to amortize the loan over a 25- or 30-year period but have it become due and payable in a shorter period of time—for instance, five years.

Don't let your mind complicate the wrap-around structure. It's really simple. For instance, we've talked about a loan with two parts. But as far as the buyer is concerned it is one loan. He makes one payment on a loan for $80,000 which carries an interest rate of 13 percent in this example. And it's just as simple from the seller's viewpoint, because he will undoubtedly have the buyer make his payment directly to a savings and loan which in turn, for a very small fee or perhaps none at all, will pay the senior lien holder and deposit the balance in the wrap-around mortgagee's account.

LET'S LOOK AT THE ADVANTAGES
AND DISADVANTAGES

Before an investor can realistically make a decision to buy via a wrap-around loan, he must analyze the pros and cons. He should also determine whether or not the sale and financing could be made by any other means—for instance, a simple loan assumption or a purchase with the seller carrying back a purchase money second mortgage. The best advice is don't try to complicate a transaction that could be handled in a simpler manner.

Here are some of the advantages that a wrap-around has for the *SELLER*:

- A great aid in selling property when money is tight. By offering wrap-around terms the seller is giving the buyer a message that you can buy this home with reasonable terms regardless of what the S&L's are doing.
- Allows the seller to get a much higher interest yield than otherwise allowed by state usury laws. However, when rates are generally low, the law of supply and demand will keep wrap-around rates low too. Note: check the laws and customs in your state before trying to obtain higher than usury interest rates.
- The holder of a wrap-around loan can get a better deal or pay less in discount when either borrowing against or selling his loan. This is usually true because of the high effective interest rate the loan provides.
- By offering to sell his property via a wrap-around loan, the seller can obtain a higher price because he can afford to give otherwise better terms. (For instance, the buyer would not pay a loan fee.)
- By accepting less than 29 percent of the sales price in one year the seller may have an installment sale rather than a capital gain; this means a lower tax bill.

Here are some of the major advantages that a wrap-around loan has for the *BUYER*:

- Often a property can be purchased for a significantly smaller down payment when using a wrap-around, therefore affording the buyer better leverage.
- The buyer can save a lot of money by buying property with a wrap-around because he will not usually be faced with new loan appraisal fees, lender's charges, etc.
- Enables a buyer to purchase property when he might not otherwise be qualified by a lender's standard.

Often the biggest advantage for both buyer and seller in times of high interest rates and tight money ... is that a transaction can be made via a wrap-around loan when the doors to conventional financing might be closed.

Wrap-around loans are certainly a good tool to have available . . . a tool which may just "save a deal" for you in the future.

THE CONTRACT OF SALE

When a buyer wants a property but is not in a position to raise all the necessary cash down payment to make the deal and secure a deed from the seller . . . a contract of sale *may* be the answer.

But as I will demonstrate, the contract of sale is not a financing tool to be taken lightly, because the buyer does not receive a deed to the property—the seller remains in title until either the end of a specified time period or until an agreed-upon amount of money has been paid through installments.

In concept, the contract of sale is like a lease with option to buy. Because the buyer does not have title (even though he will have recorded his contract of sale), in the event of default, the installment payments are usually retained by the seller as rent or liquidated damages. So in a very short space of time, a buyer on a contract can have his interests wiped out.

And if the seller dies (or disappears) before the deed is signed over (when the terms of the contract are met), the buyer can be facing almost insurmountable problems.

The contract of sale has a certain mystery about it. One reason for this is that it is known by so many names, some of which are regional favorites. These include: land sales contract; installment contract; conditional sales contract; and contract for deed. The key word is *contract.*

The other reason for its reputation is that there is no recognized form for the contract's usage. Thus each time a contract is used, the agreement must be written practically from scratch. This means that an attorney will get into the act—even in states like California where attorneys normally do not participate in real estate escrow and purchase agreements.

The contract of sale has one very important usage today in some areas. And that is to defeat the *due-on-sale clause* which the conventional lenders use. Because title does not pass with a contract, how can the lender say there has been a transfer of title or that the security has been impaired?

This usage for the contract of sale became assured in California in 1974 with the Tucker vs. Lassen decision. Basically it held that conveyance of title (specifically with a contract) did not endanger or impair the security of the lender and thus did not entitle the lender to call the loan on the basis of the due-on-sale clause.

This landmark decision helped pave the way for the later Wellenkamp decision. As I observe the happenings across the country, I see where more and more states are following the California precedents. As this matter is in constant flux, I suggest you consult with attorneys in your state to see whether or not a contract can be a device to assume (subject to) institutional loans.

192

In spite of the drawbacks, the contract of sale has some definite advantages. Here are some of the biggest from the *BUYER'S* viewpoint:

1. The best chances for high-leveraged, low-down payment deals come with a contract of sale because the seller feels secure since he retains title to the property. "Why not let me put down just $2,000," you can say, "because if I default I lose everything and you get the property back."

2. Move-in costs are lower. There are none of the often excessive charges, such as loan fees, levied by conventional lenders.

3. Closings are fast. Most contracts can be closed within one to two weeks, but don't try to get around title insurance. Contracts can be tricky, so get the best professional help you can.

4. The terms of the contract are negotiable. The interest rates, down payment and monthly payments can be (and usually are) more favorable than with an institutional lender.

5. In periods of tight money, when most conventional lenders squeeze out investor buyers, contracts can be used for non-owner-occupied properties.

SELLERS like contracts for these reasons:

1. The property can be sold for a higher sales price and without an appraisal by a lender.

2. Homes for sale offering contract terms tend to sell quickly, many times without the help of a Realtor.

3. Once a property is sold, the seller is not responsible for repairs. In fact, in many states most of the homes that can't qualify for financing because of their poor physical condition are sold with contracts.

4. If a seller receives less than 30 percent of his sales price in cash in the year of sale, capital gains are deferred on the balance until the year they are actually received.

The advantages of contracts are numerous . . . but there is also a lot of risk for the buyer because he does not have title to the property until completion of the contract. This lack of title also keeps a buyer from borrowing via a second mortgage. You just can't borrow against a property that you don't have title to!

Thus a buyer should examine a possible contract purchase from many different angles. The following questions would be in order: If the seller is elderly, how many more years might he live? Will I need to borrow against this property in another year or two? If the answers don't come out the way you would like them to, then consider alternative ways of buying the property. Would a wrap-around loan work? Most of the advantages of a contract can also be had with a wrap-around loan, but few of the disadvantages.

Sometimes, however, the buyer won't have a choice or will not be able to talk the seller into any other type of financing. Many sellers like contracts because they give them a lot more security—the buyer cannot further encumber the property and if there is a default the seller can usually get the property back fast.

In Oregon, however, the forfeiture clause found in most contracts will not stand up. The seller must go to court to repossess the property, and this often takes a year or more to do. So be sure to check out local laws and customs.

As the old expression says, "don't look a gift horse in the mouth." When you have an opportunity to buy a good property on a contract of sale . . . with a minimal down payment of $4,000 (because the seller feels secure) . . . maybe you shouldn't try too hard to change the terms, but just accept the fact that you are only risking $4,000. You can strengthen your position by convincing the seller to pre-sign the deed and then leave it with an attorney who is instructed to deliver it when all terms of the contract are met, regardless of where the seller may be.

PURCHASE MONEY FIRST MORTGAGES

How many times have you encountered someone selling his property and offering to carry back the entire first mortgage? It's a real winner in this day and age, especially as the consumer is being threatened by a new mortgage device—one which may be renegotiated every five years or less. Renegotiated, hell! These new types of loans which are supposedly coming our way will have the interest rates bumped up to whatever the current rates will be *or else*.

You may be surprised to learn that with today's rising interest rates, a fairly high percentage of sellers are carrying back first mortgages. Many of these homes never appear on multiple listings—they're too hot a deal.

And other sellers—more often than not couples over 50 years of age—can be talked into carrying back a purchase money first mortgage. When you find one who will—it'll be a good deal for both of you. You'll probably get a lower-than-market interest rate, plus you'll pay a lot less in closing costs. And the seller, well, as you read on his benefits will become apparent.

The trick, of course, is to find a situation where the seller *can* carry back the first loan. And then you must convince him to do so. It mostly boils down to what the seller's motivation is when searching for likely candidates. If his reason for selling is that he is buying a bigger home, there is probably no chance that he will carry back the loan.

However, if he is either *retiring*, suffering from poor health, moving to a smaller property, or selling off surplus investment properties, you have a good chance of getting the seller to carry back the loan. You may have to do some convincing—not only of the seller, but possibly his real estate agent, too.

Following are some tips on how to convince the seller to carry back the first mortgage.

This task will be difficult if you are negotiating with an owner-occupant of a single-family home who is over 55 years of age. That's because Congress recently passed the "over 55 rule" which gives a homeowner over 55 a one-time $100,000 tax exemption. Thus there will be some people who won't be impressed with the following tax savings ideas. But keep in mind that this exemption only applies to the principal residence and can only be used once in a lifetime. Incidentally, if the tax angle doesn't impress them, ask if they can get a better interest rate return from their friendly neighborhood savings & loan.

If the potential seller is in a lousy tax situation (because of either high income and low tax write-offs or not being eligible for the "over 55" rule), he is apt to be eaten alive by taxes, as most Americans are. You can help him!

Owner-occupants will also have special problems if sales proceeds are not put into another residence within 18 months. If this seller puts his equity into another home, then he won't pay any taxes on the proceeds and thus is not a very likely candidate to carry back the first mortgage.

So when you find a seller (like a tired landlord) who will not or perhaps cannot escape taxes by buying another residence, you may have "a live one." You must then point out that spreading the capital gains profit over a number of years also spreads out the tax liability over those years—as long as no more than 29 percent of the purchase price is paid to the seller in any one year. It is even possible the seller may have enough shelter or write-offs to completely avoid taxes by spreading his profit out by this installment method.

Thus if you can demonstrate how much the seller can save in taxes while pointing out the advantages of a steady income, you stand a good chance of convincing the seller to carry back a purchase money mortgage. One word of advice, however. Don't give the seller specific tax saving figures. Only give him approximates and tell him to get the specifics from his own tax advisor. Don't take the liability for wrong figures.

The technical side of a purchase money mortgage is easy. Escrow or the settlement attorney will draw up all the important forms—including the note and the mortgage. Most likely the seller will hold the original fire insurance policy (as do regular lenders) so as to be assured of continued protection. And probably a bank or savings & loan will collect and disburse the monthly payments.

I mentioned the tired landlord as an excellent prospect for carrying back a purchase money loan. I also indicated that "older" sellers would be more apt to do so. But consider this true story:

Several years ago, clients of mine went through a divorce. They were in their early thirties and had two children. They owned a home which was almost "free and clear." I think they owed something like $8,000 and the property was worth $40,000 then.

Here's what happened: After the divorce, the wife moved out of the area to be closer to her parents. The husband didn't particularly want to keep the home—in fact there was probably no way he could, as one-half the equity was to be paid his "ex" when the divorce became final. In addition to the equity split, he was ordered to pay $350 a month in combined spousal and child support.

His solution was to sell the home and carry back the mortgage. The buyer paid $11,000 down (less than 29 percent so my client would be eligible for installment sales tax benefits) and the sellers jointly carried back the $29,000 balance at 9 percent for a 25-year term, but with a 10-year due date. This brought in monthly payments of $243—half of which the wife was entitled to. The other half too was assigned to the wife so the support payments could be reduced $121.50 a month. By carrying back the mortgage my client was able to make an unbearable situation bearable.

The $8,000 existing first mortgage, incidentally, was paid off with the down payment proceeds received from the seller. These small existing loan balances often stand in your way when trying to get a seller to carry back a purchase money loan. But they don't need to if you can come up with a creative way to remove them.

One possible way to do this is with a substitution of collateral. This means transfer the remaining loan balance from one property to another. Now this won't be possible when that first lender is a bank or savings and loan. They won't give up their first position for a second position on another property.

But consider this technique instead. You can remove the remaining loan by: 1) borrowing the needed amount (say $10,000) via a second mortgage against either your residence or another rental property and then 2) paying off the loan with the money you borrowed (reducing the sales price by the amount you contribute to pay off the loan) so that the seller is now free to carry back a favorable purchase money first mortgage.

Be creative! But also be careful!

Remember how I said you should always reach into your bag of tricks for the simplest and most basic techniques first. In all probability, the interest rate on the remaining $10,000 loan I just described is at some ridiculously low interest rate—like 5¼ percent. If that was the case—and if that loan were assumable—then why not have the seller carry a wrap? He was ready, willing and able to carry the first mortgage if possible, wasn't he? And for probably an interest rate like 12 percent.

But if the seller wrapped instead, you would save money by not having loan fees for the $10,000, and the seller could give you 11½ percent interest (rather than 12) and his effective yield would be 12.35 percent. Both parties would be better off with a wrap in this situation.

The point I am making is this—put all these tools into your bag of tricks and be prepared to use them whenever they fit. You never know when you may need one until you get out a pencil and paper and go over the figures. One time the best way to go might be with the seller carrying back a purchase money first mortgage and the next situation might call for a simple assumption with secondary financing.

Get a little calculator that has percentages. By following the easy directions that come with the calculator you'll be able to figure out which way actually costs the most—or the least.

And then you'll be making big real estate deals just like a pro.

FOUR MORE CREATIVE FINANCING TOOLS

Following are four concepts which either I or my clients have used successfully many times. They are creative concepts and not pie in the sky wishful thinking that will only cause your wheels to spin. But as with all creative concepts—they are only going to work for you when both parties benefit from the arrangements.

1. THE LONG ESCROW OR CLOSING:

Normal real estate transfers take from two weeks to three months to complete. But in ever-changing and tight money markets an extended escrow or closing can be an important tool. For instance, a long escrow can give you the time you will need to get a new conventional loan at a more favorable interest rate, yet lock in *today's* price. Or it can buy time while you wait for more favorable conditions to refinance or sell one of your properties. Thus with a longer closing date you can buy in a favorable buyer's market (with a minimum amount of cash), yet not have to "pay the piper" until the time is right.

It's a neat trick these days, when you can pull it off. So a valid question is: Can you? The answer is *yes*, if you can locate the right seller. The right seller is one who is eager to sell but not so anxious that he needs to get his equity right away. You need a seller who can wait about six months . . . or even longer if necessary. A good example would be someone who has just retired and is planning a move to Florida. He's anxious to get going, but is not desperate enough to sell quickly and take a huge loss.

You'll be most effective in getting an extended close when you find a property that is fairly priced—not over market, nor set at a bargain basement price, either. As the seller will be braced for *offers* which might be several thousand dollars beneath his asking price, you will make immediate points when you offer to pay his asking price, or at least something close to it. His eyes might just pop out when he first sees the purchase price written in large bold lettering at the top of the purchase agreement. It's not until you discuss the less significant parts of the contract—the closing date—that you'll possibly begin to have problems. A six-months' close is enough to startle anyone —at first. But when the seller begins to think about the benefits he'll be getting, the longer close will begin to make sense to him.

This is your key to getting a longer close or settlement—SELLER BENEFITS. If he feels that he is getting $1,500 more than expected on his sales price, he may be inclined to wait an additional three or four months for it. Sometimes this benefit won't be money, but a problem-solving device. For instance, the seller may be more worried about getting to a new job in Saudi Arabia than the money. You can offer an interim occupancy agreement wherein you take an early possession and even rent out the property. Thus the seller's benefit in this example is to be relieved of his immediate problem (moving).

When asking for a long escrow, in essence you are saying "I want to buy your property, but not with today's financing of 17 and 18 percent. But I will pay your price if you will allow me up to six months to complete the purchase *if and when* interest rates drop to a more acceptable level." (Note: When interest rates are artificially pushed to 17-18 percent, then it makes sense to wait. But be careful when they are at the relatively high rates of 12 and 13 percent—because they just might not drop down from those levels.)

I realize this "if and when" might get some of your offers "kicked out the door," but if you gamble on better conditions and they don't arrive, you're caught, with a firm contract which says you *are* (not maybe) buying a property. You will probably lose your deposit and may even end up being sued. So rather than have a loose "open-ended" contract, you can state at what interest rate you will act. For instance, you may agree to proceed with the financing when the rates come back to 12.5 percent. If they don't, you are not obligated to complete the purchase; or you might put in a six-month extension option if the financing you want is still not possible.

If this long escrow technique sounds a little like an option to you, you are right. But since this technique is designed to give the seller greater security and peace of mind, he may be more apt to go for it than for an option. One problem with an option is that the mere mention of it often signals a fight over price or the method for establishing a price in the future. And the seller is often troubled over the fact that with an option, the buyer can decide at any time not to buy, and walk away.

However, this isn't so with your extended closing, because this technique generally provides for a firm contract to buy. Thus the seller does not feel threatened. Psychologically, the seller thinks "down the road" with an option. For example, he is concerned about how much his property might appreciate in value in a year or so. But with the longer close he's thinking about the good price he just got—not what the value may or may not be in six months or so.

2. TRADING SOMETHING OF VALUE:

Think! The best creative real estate transactions are the ones where you come up with something that no one else could think of—some idea that opened previously closed doors.

Things other than money can be used for barter . . . for your down payment. What valuable possessions or skills do you have that could be used to buy real estate? Maybe your wife is a former school teacher and you could offer her services—for tutoring—in lieu of $5,000 of down payment. And maybe you're good at carpentry and your wife could offer your services. Be creative! The following story ably demonstrates how creative trades can open doors.

An acquaintance of mine, a farmer in California's rich San Joaquin Valley, sold one half of his 140 acres to a city slicker who offered just $2,000 cash, a time-share condominium in Hawaii a four-year-old Ford pick-up pick-up truck and five years of free income tax preparation.

I know that sounds like a steal, but before you jump to any wrong conclusions you should know that the farmer was a widower, over 65 years of age, and had two grown sons, both of whom had left the farm for city life. Although his health was failing some, he was as stubborn as a mule and will probably go on farming until he has to be carried away.

Now along comes one smart city slicker. He had found out about the farmer's plight and approached him with the following deal: He proposed that my farmer friend, who had a $50,000 trust deed against the property, divide the farm in half. After all, it was much too big for the ailing farmer to keep up by himself. And with values then approximately $1,500 an acre he felt that the lender could be convinced to transfer (substitution of collateral) the $50,000 loan to the seventy acres he proposed to buy.

The pick-up truck was a good deal for my friend too because the one he had was over 15 years old and hardly ran anymore. The free income tax preparation was nice too, but the real kicker in the deal was the two weeks the farmer was able to spend each year in Hawaii. Before he sold half of his land, he had too little money, too much farm and too little insight to drop everything for a two-week jaunt to Hawaii. By getting rid of the deed of trust, he was left with almost $600 a month more to spend.

What did the city investor get? Rapidly appreciating farm property which in three years jumped from a worth of about $1,500 an acre to over $2,500. So in just the three years alone he made $70,000. Not bad when you consider that he only paid $2,000 out of pocket plus the $2,000 or so he paid for the pick-up. The $5,000 he paid the year before for the time-share condo didn't hurt much either, as he got to use it once and decided he really didn't like it. And the tax work was no problem, either, because the city slicker was an accountant.

Who got hurt in this transaction? Nobody! Who made out the best? It's hard to tell . . . they each liked what they got.

3. CREDITS FROM THE SELLER

In a *seller's market* the investor often has to work his tail off to find property because values are apt to be climbing so fast that every good property has buyers lined up three deep. In a seller's market the investor often does best by systematically seeking out new listings. However, the opposite can be true in a *buyer's market.*

By simply picking up the daily newspaper, scanning the multiple listing book or by reading any other periodical which advertises homes for sale, the investor has before him a smorgasbord of opportunities. His only serious decision will be how to get the most mileage for his money.

Although in a buyer's market the investor will have his very best opportunities to buy via options, wraps, contracts, etc., I am going to concentrate here on the smaller—but still important—considerations that he should be able to get from the seller. Here are just some of them:

- *Closing costs:* The seller is expecting low offers, but you may be more interested in high leverage. Ask that the seller pay all of your closing costs.
- *Six months' payments:* Have the seller pay all your principal, interest and tax payments for a six-month period.
- *Eliminate negative cash flow:* If you feel the price is $3,000 soft and you are anticipating $125 monthly negative cash flow, don't go for the price break but have seller pay your negative cash flow ($125) for 24 months.
- *Contract of sale:* Have the seller carry a contract of sale until the time you can either get a new loan or refinance one of your existing properties.
- *Extended guarantees:* Buying a fourplex? Have the seller guarantee you against any future loss due to vacancies. In other words, if you lost $1,000 in year one and $1,500 in year two, the seller would reimburse you—to a maximum limit of, say, $3,000. This guarantee (in lieu of a price reduction when buying, of course) could also be used to cover the first $3,000 of repairs that might be necessary for the property over a two- or three-year period. A great way for the non-handyman to buy a rundown property!
- *The obvious—have the seller carry back a note:* It goes without saying that you can always ask the seller to carry back a note rather than cut his price by $3,000. But don't go for a $3,000 note—go for at least twice the amount. And try for an unsecured note—so that you can later get a secured second against the property.

4. CREATE A NOTE WITH A BUILT-IN DISCOUNT

Imagine yourself in this fairly common situation. You have a residence with over $40,000 equity plus a small amount of cash—say $5,000. You want to buy rental property, but you keep running up against sellers who won't take a contract of sale, a wrap-around or carry back any portion of their equity in a second mortgage.

You are willing to use some of the equity in your home to get started, but you're not able to find cheap second money, nor have you been able to come up with a source for private money at the interest rate you want to pay.

You're discouraged and almost decide to wait until you can save another $5,000 or so. That would be a fatal mistake, however, as it never pays to wait when buying real estate.

A friend saves the day—he suggests that you create a note using the equity in your residence.

The first and obvious way to do this is to offer the seller a note secured by your residence. It's simple and it's clean! The security conscious seller receives a note for an agreed amount, terms and duration which pledges your personal residence (where there is plenty of equity) as the security for the loan.

A seller will be much more apt to take back a second mortgage on your residence than on the property he is selling with such a small down payment (the $5,000). This is good for the buyer too, because after just a year or two of equity growth he'll be able to repeat the process all over again—only this time using the expanded equity in the rental he just bought.

If the seller is reluctant to do this, you can arrange to have a third party buy the note at discount. In this example I'll assume that we're dealing with a five-year note with a $10,000 face value with interest-only payments at 10 percent. If a third party buys this note for a 20 percent discount (or $8,000), his true yield is boosted to almost 16 percent.

Here are the advantages of using this third-party approach: The buyer was only willing to pay 10 percent interest as that is all he felt he could afford. But who would have given him this rate, especially if the legal, or even underground, market rate was higher? The answer is nobody but Uncle Harry (if he has one) or a very desperate seller.

But in this example we don't have a desperate seller—just the everyday garden-variety seller who wants his best price. So the buyer creates his own discount by agreeing to pay $2,000 more for the property than he had to. Here's how easy this is to do:

Find a property in which the price is $2,000 *soft*. This is a very common occurrence. In fact most sellers price their home a little higher than they actually expect to get because "we can always come down in price." But instead of taking this $2,000 cut in price, the buyer makes it known in the negotiations that he is offering the higher or full asking price in return for a $10,000 note which will later be discounted by $2,000. Thus the note is constructed with a built-in discount which makes it readily salable to a good price with just a $5,000 down payment and a $10,000 (interest-only, 10% note) lien against his residence.

Go forth . . . and be creative!

*"Starting out in the hole every month might
be likened to wading the Florida swamps,
hoping you'll hit land on the other side before
the beady-eyed reptile with the two-foot jaws
decides to swim out for lunch."*

Bernard Hale Zick
from Impact Report
Eliminating Negative Cash Flow

16

ELEVEN WAYS OF REDUCING
OR ELIMINATING
NEGATIVE CASH FLOW

Would you describe yourself as *anxious* to buy a single-family home which will appreciate by as much as $10,000 in value by the end of a year?

Would you be less anxious if you knew that you would have to carry a $300 monthly negative cash flow on the property?

The mathematics are still on your side. When you multiply the negative cash flow by twelve months ($300 × 12 = $3,600) you find that your alligator (the property) with the negative cash flow (N.C.F.) has just eaten $3,600 of your money. But you are still left with a handsome gain ($10,000 − $3,600) or $6,400. Your investment is still a good deal . . . but getting a little too close for comfort.

Fortunately what I just described is happening only in a few areas. Mine for one, and most major California metropolitan areas, exclusive of San Joaquin Valley cities. The major reason for this has been extra-heavy pressures for housing, which has kept housing prices in these areas appreciating well above the national average. Rents are climbing—but not fast enough to make up the ground left by the almost 30 percent appreciation rate my county (Contra Costa) experienced in 1979.

If I were to buy a $75,000 home in Pleasant Hill today by paying $15,000 down to an 11 percent FHA loan, I would have a $300-a-month alligator. But in Houston my $15,000 could buy a similar home for $60,000 and my N.C.F. would be less than $100. Moving on to Pensacola, Florida, the $15,000 could buy a $45,000 home and there would possibly be a small positive cash flow. So there I might buy two homes instead of one.

What troubles the typical investor should be obvious. Most of us are on a budget ... we have only so much cash that can be allocated for alligator feeding. The family that can only afford to spend $200 a month on their investment portfolio is obviously not going to be able to buy three, four and five homes at once if the N.C.F. exceeds $200 per house.

Well, I promised I would show anyone and everyone how to *get off* the great American slide ... and how you can double your money every two years. It's obvious that I can't perform unless I demonstrate ways you can significantly reduce and even eliminate the alligator entirely.

Fortunately, there are ways. Following are eleven methods you can use. And by using these practical ways of eliminating negative cash flow, you will have no excuse for not buying as many properties as you can lay your hands on during the next few years. I'll start out by explaining methods which at best will only reduce your N.C.F. and end up with the heavies—the ones you can use to eliminate it. I'll finish this chapter by showing you some strange facts about mortgage interest rates—and how you can use this information to make bigger profits.

1. *LARGE DOWN PAYMENT*

This is the most obvious of all ways to eliminate N.C.F. I don't personally recommend it, but it works. In my area this would mean paying about $35,000 down to buy a $75,000 home. The one advantage is that the buyer using this method will be picking up 8 and 9 percent loans rather than 10 and 11 percent ones.

The reason I don't like this method is that you will run out of cash too fast unless you've got a few hundred thousand to invest. I would rather use other means to eliminate N.C.F. and buy two or three properties instead of just one. But as I have always maintained—it's better to buy just one property than none at all.

2. *BUY WAY UNDER MARKET VALUE*

In earlier chapters I told about ways of locating and buying property beneath market value. By working at this, you should be able to consistently find and buy property for as much as 10 to 15 percent beneath its true value. And unless you are assuming a loan, this savings should be reflected in a smaller mortgage with lower monthly payments than you would have if you bought at market value. By buying an $85,000 home for $75,000 you not only have bought it for 12 percent under its true value, but you will be saving $102 per month on a 12 percent, 30-year mortgage.

That gives you $102 towards reducing or eliminating your N.C.F.

3. CAREFULLY SELECT THE NEIGHBORHOOD YOU BUY IN

A few years ago I purchased a three-bedroom home in my town for $42,000. It had a family room but it was nearly 30 years old and had only one bathroom. The neighborhood was good but nothing to write home about.

About the same time I purchased another home in an excellent neighborhood of nearby Martinez. I paid $50,000 for this property, which was a six-year-old ranch-style home with three bedrooms, 2 baths, family room and built-in electric kitchen.

I rented out the first home within a week after settlement and covered my mortgage payment, including taxes. The newer home in Martinez took three weeks to rent and I ended up getting only $10 more than I was getting for the older home. It became an instant alligator. Why?

Because of the one fact that I didn't give you when I described the two buys in the two different communities. Pleasant Hill is five or six miles closer to Oakland and San Francisco than is Martinez. It is also closer to a Bay Area Rapid Transit station and the average home in Pleasant Hill sells for about $10,000 more than the average one in Martinez. That last fact adds up to snob appeal, which is common everywhere.

Because of these reasons I was able to consistently rent the older Pleasant Hill home quicker and for almost as much rent. Now would you like to guess which of the homes I still own and which I sold?

4. BUY INEXPENSIVE PROPERTY

Possibly because more poor people rent than do financially better off persons, you can often get a small positive cash flow or at worst just a small alligator when you buy *very* inexpensive property. Again, this isn't one of my favorite ways of reducing expenses because these cheaper properties usually require more maintenance and sometimes the tenant problems can be overwhelming.

But facts are facts. I'm told that in Dallas an investor can still buy (at this writing) inexpensive homes for around $25,000 and get a positive cash flow. But by going across town and paying $60,000 the investor will get $50 to $100 N.C.F.

5. THE PROPERTY YOU BUY MAKES A BIG DIFFERENCE

What do the following types of property have in common? A single-family home with an added family room, bedroom and bath; a single-family home with a separate in-law arrangement behind the garage; and a small four-unit (fourplex) apartment. The answer is that they all tend to rent for more than a standard suburban-style single-family home.

The first type home I described, with the added family room, etc. is known as an "over-built" property. These additions were extremely costly for the owner who had them done. And I can say that he also "took a bath" when he sold his property. Sometimes these costly additions bring only an extra $4,000 or $5,000 on resale, despite the fact they may have cost $15,000. There are exceptions, however, as a more expensive neighborhood to begin with (where many homes are custom-built) can better absorb the costs of remodeling. But for the most part when you are able to buy one of these homes for just a few thousand dollars more than what you would pay for a standard home in the neighborhood, this will convert into much higher rent payments—possibly as much as $75.

Finding an in-law set-up can be like finding a diamond in the rough. I know of one investor in Los Angeles who owns several of this type. He rents out each property for a positive cash flow. This is done by renting to two different groups of people, usually a family for the larger home and a single for the in-law unit. In some communities this is not legal if the property is in a neighborhood which is zoned for single-family homes. But I find that this zoning code is seldom enforced—unless you happen to put in a bunch of rowdies who attract too much attention.

Fourplexes and triplexes often bring higher rents than a single unit. And just like the single-family home, they are often exempt from rent control ordinances.

6. RENT TO SINGLES

You can often get $40 to $50 more a month in rent by renting to a group of singles rather than the standard family. This can be done by raising your rent and then placing an ad which in essence says: "Singles are welcome." But be very careful because you may lose more in problems and damages than you will actually gain in additional rent. For a complete discussion of singles and roommates, see *The Monopoly Game.*

7. HAVE THE SELLER SUBSIDIZE
YOUR NEGATIVE CASH FLOW

If you project that your negative cash flow could run as high as $3,000 over a two-year period before you'll have a chance to raise rents to narrow the gap, have the seller pay it for you.

You'll have the best chance of pulling this off in a buyer's market. You can take the subsidy, for instance, by coming in with an offer at full price rather than by going after a $3,000 price reduction.

Even in a strong seller's market, you can pull this one off. For instance, bring the seller an offer which is $1,500 more than he is asking but then stipulate that you want him to pay you $125 per month for the next two years. It's a compromise—you pay a little more if he will give some too. You'll have a good chance of pulling it off if you go after the right seller—one who doesn't want his property any more.

If you are afraid the seller may later balk at this and you don't want to bother going to court, then set up this payment in advance as follows: The seller credits your account with $3,000 which is yours at close of escrow. Even though this money is earmarked for reduction of negative cash flow, you are free to spend it in any manner you see fit. However, if you have a N.C.F. problem on top of a tight budget, I recommend you stick to the original plan.

Why not take this $3,000 and invest it in an amortized second mortgage. Make sure it repays in just two or three years. If it's a two-year note at 10 percent interest you'll get $138.44 per month. If it's a 15 percent note you'll get $145.46.

You can get in the habit of doing this with every property you buy. You don't have to buy a property unless the seller, in some way or another, is subsidizing your N.C.F.

8. *SET THE MONEY ASIDE*

Coping with alligators is actually a mental problem. The following solution to the N.C.F. problem is truly the simplest and most effective one you'll probably ever have available. But it won't work unless you learn to handle yourself first. Here's what I mean.

Whenever you buy a property, set aside monies which will be used only for helping you to cover your N.C.F. For instance, you are ready to buy your second rental property. The money is coming from a property you have owned for several years; you decide to refinance it and use the proceeds to get started on a serious investment program. You get $40,000 and decide to buy two rental homes. But wait! Have you allowed for negative cash flow? I strongly suggest you do so by *always* (no exceptions) setting aside at least twenty percent of the money to cover your monthly deficits. In this case that amount would be $8,000, leaving $32,000 to buy two properties—still an ample amount when coupled with selective creative financing techniques.

As in the last example, I think the best thing you could do with the money would be to invest it in a second mortgage. You can easily do this by dealing with a hard money lender who normally handles a lot of small, short-term amortized loans. You might even decide to go one step better, and learn how to buy discounted notes which can boost your effective yield to 20 percent or more.

Sounds easy, doesn't it? The hard part is to make yourself do this. But when you do you can buy almost unlimited properties and either fully eliminate or greatly reduce your negative cash flow. It's a mental process you must *work on yourself* if you want to be a winner. Don't get hung up with thoughts like: "But I still have the N.C.F.—I am just paying it off with *my* money in a different way." If you think like that you'll be a loser!

The net results are that you have gotten rid of your negative cash flow ... and your budget isn't being strained ... so you can buy more property when the next opportunity arises.

9. *USE A BALLOON PAYMENT NOTE*

Remember the "balloon payment" straight note I talked about in Chapter 14 (Second Mortgages)? This type of note with a long enough duration is one of the best ways of taming alligators. If you can come up with an unending supply of this money you can buy an unlimited number of homes. Nothing would stop you from making a very quick fortune.

But back to reality. Ponce de Leon didn't find the Fountain of Youth and

I am betting you will not find an unending supply of straight note money. If you seek it as I directed, from time to time you will come up with this balloon payment money. However, let's look for a more practical source—the seller.

Following is an example of how one investor, with a little creative effort, got a seller to carry back a straight note.

The investor, whom I'll call Bill, was in the market for his first rental property. He had just $12,000 to spend and was prepared to handle up to $150 per month negative cash flow. After several weeks of inspecting homes, he decided to go after a FISBO who had an attractive two-bedroom home for sale at $65,000. The seller claimed, and Bill's comparables backed it up, that the property was really worth $70,000. Bill would have liked to have assumed the current 8½ percent FHA loan of $40,000 with total monthly payments of $398—but he was just too short on cash and the seller said he would carry back only a small second.

Bill's first logical choice was to go after a new conventional loan. At the present time he could get 75 percent financing at 12 percent interest. The seller would carry back 10 percent of the sales price with a 12 percent interest-only payment second mortgage.

Here is how it looked on paper for Bill:

Cash Out of Pocket
15 percent down payment	$ 9,750
Estimated closing costs	2,000
	$11,750

Total Monthly Obligation
$48,750 first mortgage at 12%	$568
$6,500 second mortgage at 12%	65
Taxes and insurance	110
	$743

Something was obviously wrong! What has happened to the second great American dream—that of every investor owning at least a half dozen rental homes? Bill did his homework and he knew that he could rent the property for $400 a month the first year. But $343 negative cash flow was a little hard to take ... in fact Bill thought it was impossible to take. So he started thinking creatively.

Here is what he came up with: He had one solid fact in his favor—that he could buy the property $5,000 beneath its true market value. So even before he signed the contract he had one important trump card. Then he approached the seller and asked "If I give you more money for the property, will you carry back a larger second?"

The seller thought for a moment and then said, "Sure, why not? What do I have to lose."

Bill said, "I mean a lot more . . . like will you carry back a note for $24,000 at 10 percent interest if I agree to pay you $75,000 for the home rather than $65,000? That's $5,000 dollars more than the property's full value."

The seller thought for a moment and then said, "I think so." He was tempted by the extra money.

Being well schooled in investment practices, Bill brought out a purchase agreement and started writing. He wanted to capture that "I think so" on paper with an accompanying signature before any minds were changed.

But more importantly, Bill had momentum on his side and there was one other key concession he wanted to get. And that was a straight note for at least five years duration. That would leave him with just the $398 first mortgage payment and a virtual "break-even" the first year of ownership.

"By the way," Bill said as he filled out the agreement, "what are you going to do with the money?"

The seller thought for a moment and then said: "I want to pay off a few bills and then I'll probably put the rest in the bank and eventually into time certificate accounts."

"If I paid you 12 percent interest instead of 10 percent—that's an extra $480 a year or $2,880 over six years—would you give me this note without any payments whatsoever until it's due six years from now?"

The seller was no dummy. He said "Heck no, I won't go six years. Two years is all I'll go."

"Why?" Bill asked.

"I don't know," the seller retorted. "What if I need the money before six years?"

Bill got out his pocket calculator and did some figuring and then said, "Will you give me five years if I give you 13 percent interest?" He got his wish. Thus in five years Bill will need to pay back $24,000 in principal and $15,600 in interest for a grand total of $39,600.

How will he most likely pay it back? . . . By refinancing the property.

And how much will the home be worth in five years? It will be worth $112,000-plus if property continues to appreciate at just 10 percent annually. And in the very unlikely event that the property only appreciated by 6 percent annually, it would be worth about $93,500.

By getting the seller to carry back a straight note, Bill was able to get a home which would give him a positive cash flow by the second year, when he could raise the rent $20 to $30.

The seller was happy too, because he picked up the $11,000 down payment and could then look forward to collecting $39,600 in five years. He considered it as a forced savings and probably a good idea, too, because if he had gotten his hands on the money monthly, he probably would have blown it.

Here is a recap of the final figures:

Terms of Sale
Price Paid $75,000
Down Payment $11,000
2nd Mortgate 24,000
1st Mortgate 40,000
$75,000

Cash Out of Pocket
Down Payment $11,000
Closing Costs 500
$11,500

Total Monthly Obligations
$40,000 first mortgage at 8½% $398
$24,000 second mortgage at 13% 0
Taxes and insurance
(included in first mortgage) 0
$398

Now let me ask you a question. Would you take Bill's deal? Well, you don't need to take Bill's because there are thousands upon thousands more just like this one out there in the market place, just waiting for someone with enough brains to figure out what Bill figured out.

10. *USING AN OPTION*

Remember the lease option I talked about in Chapter 6? Even though you don't get title to real property until an option is exercised, it is one of the best ways I know of to eliminate negative cash flow. Here's how:

You find a quality property owned by a seller willing to deal. Preferably you'll find property owned by someone who just doesn't want it any more—probably a tired landlord. You offer to take over the property on a lease option, take care of all management and upkeep for five years, and then exercise the option after the fifth year. You'll probably need to take out a new conventional loan at that time. But you can also sell the property right after taking title . . . and thus not get caught in another round of negative cash flow.

With an option you don't even have to take out a new loan and then sell. You can simply sell your option . . . and take a reasonable profit without ever worrying about negative cash flow.

If there is any negative cash flow in a deal like this it won't be yours to worry about. For instance, the optionor may have a mortgage payment of $450. But in the terms of your lease option you should agree to something like this: You will lease option the first year for $400 monthly; the second for $450; the third for $500; the fourth for $550; and the fifth for $600.

The optionor's negative cash flow will be wiped out after the first year and any repairs, etc. that pop up will also be out of his hands. Repairs and upkeep will be your concern.

The optionee should not agree to a contract which will give him any serious N.C.F. For instance, the property should be rentable for about $400 a month during the first year. And after that depends upon the optionee's skills in raising rent.

11. MAKE THE SELLER A PARTNER

When all else fails—take a different approach.

Buy a property—any kind will do, with any kind of loan and any type of seller, even one who needs every nickel out of the property so he can buy his bigger home with the even bigger mortgage.

Let's suppose that you found a reasonable assumption and you put $15,000 down to take over a 10 percent VA loan with monthly payments of $550. You estimate the property will rent for $400 the first year and thus you'll have a $150 negative cash flow. Not bad—except for the fact that you already have a combined $500 negative flow on other properties.

What can you do? You can offer a percentage of ownership in the home to the seller, or anyone else, for that matter. You could offer 1/10th interest or even a 1/7th interest. You do this by taking title as tenants in common. By this method each party named in the deed gets a specified undivided interest in the property.

In order to get the seller (who still has an emotional attachment for his former home) to go along with this idea you must project what the property will be worth in five years. If you use a 10 percent appreciation figure, simply multiply the value of the home by 0.10. Then add the results to the price of the home and repeat the process. If you find that a particular property projects out to a $50,000 gain in five years, you can easily determine that a 1/10th interest would come to $5,000.

Will $5,000 in five years be enough incentive for the former seller to feed your alligator for five years? Possibly not! But you can correct this problem in any of several ways.

For instance, you can offer a better return—say a 1/7th interest or even a 1/5th interest. Or you can stick by your original 1/10th offer but limit the junior partner's liability. Ask him to pay only $150 the first year, $100 the second year, and nothing after that. In this way he will only have paid $3,000 into the property but will stand a good chance of getting $5,000 or more.

But what if you don't want to sell or refinance in five years? Instead, you can give the former owner a note and second mortgage against the house for an agreed-upon amount; say $5,000 due and payable in five years. And when is the note executed? It can be drawn and signed but held by a neutral third party (an attorney, for instance) until the last payment is made. At that point it would be recorded. Of course, a lot can happen in two years and the new owner could have slipped in another second in the meantime, thus relegating this note to third position.

Mutual trust is needed in this kind of situation. A fairer and more equitable solution is to have the note recorded immediately, but with the stipulation that it cannot be foreclosed upon until after a lengthy period of time—say eight years. Thus if you do not receive all the payments equaling the $3,000 sum, you can sue to have the note invalidated. But if you sell or refinance prior to five or eight years, the note will be paid off at that time.

All of the above solutions to the negative cash flow problem will not work all the time. Like any creative financing tools, you'll have to pick and choose which concepts you want to ask the seller to go along with.

The important point is that negative cash flow can be kept in check. The alligator's appetite can be satisfied. There is truly a way that you can double your money every two years.

BEATING THE SYSTEM
WHILE YOU LINE YOUR POCKETS

Figures don't lie! Mathematical formulas don't lie either! But why then are consumers—you and I—being taken to the cleaners all the time?

Because nobody bothers to tell us the *complete truth* unless we ask—and even then sometimes we don't get it. For instance, consider the following: You are undoubtedly aware that the cost of housing is climbing to record heights . . . a cost that is eliminating more and more people as buyers. I know that you've heard that before! And you've probably heard or read that the primary cause for the higher costs is the speculator/investor who is driving prices up. This reason heads most lists which political experts claim cause the higher costs.

That cause, however, is a distorted quarter truth. Many other things—such as smaller but greater numbers of family units—are more responsible for higher costs. But the biggest villain is higher interest rates—rates which the government often keeps artificially high so that inflation (and higher costs) can be kept in check. How hypocritical!

$60,000 borrowed at 9 percent interest, for instance, with a 30-year due date, is amortized at $482.78 a month. But at 13 percent the monthly figure jumps to $663.72. That's nearly a $200 monthly increase.

If interest rates remained at 9 percent this loan could have been increased to as much as $82,000 before the $663 payments of the 13 percent loan were equalled. This means that if the rates were still at the lower 9 percent figure, a borrower could have paid $22,000 more for his home for that difference. That's about three years worth of appreciation!

What's the solution? Some say we should extend the term of a typical mortgage from 30 to 40 years. Think about that for a moment before you read the next paragraph. Would you want a longer mortgage term to spread out your monthly payments? After all, some lenders recommend this.

Here is a partial answer to that question. Later I'll get deeper into the subject. Interest rates aren't 18 percent yet, but they are now listed in most new amortization books up to that amount. In the long run we seem to be headed in that direction . . . so I'll use that amount in my example.

If you borrow $100,000 at 18 percent with a 30-year mortgage, your monthly payments will be $1,507.09. But if you spread our your payments and take out a 40-year mortgage, your monthly obligation will be reduced to $1,501.19. The difference? A RIDICULOUS $5.90 A MONTH.

And don't tell me it doesn't matter because hardly anyone keeps his home (and the loan) more than ten years. It does matter . . . and I'll show you why later. Here's a hint: After five full years of making $1,501.19 monthly payments, you will have paid the loan down (increasing your equity) by only about $100. By contrast, a smaller $75,000 loan at 10 percent and amortized for 30 years will pay down by $2,569 after five years . . . and with monthly payments of just $658.18.

As I said . . . figures don't lie! And mathematical formulas don't lie. Lenders just don't tell the whole story. The problem is that as interest rates and loan terms increase, the figures begin to change dramatically from what we could once expect in the days of 7 and 8 percent loans.

We don't always have to be strangled by high interest rates. In some instances they can be beaten. After going into more background on the subject, I'll demonstrate a practical way that many investors can harness what I call hidden mortgage power—and be able to earn 12 . . . 15 . . . and even higher percentages per year on your loan. In fact you'll almost be able to earn as much as the lender does on the same loan.

But first study the following chart which shows declining principal balances for various terms and interest rates on loans in the original amount of $75,000.

LOAN REDUCTION EXAMPLES

Interest/Term	10% 30 yrs.	10% 20 yrs.	13% 30 yrs.	13% 20 yrs.
Monthly Payment	$658.18	$723.77	$829.65	$878.68
Reduction of Principal Balance After:				
1 Year	$74,583	$73,759	$74,781	$74,156
5 Years	$72,431	$67,351	$73,561	$69,448
10 Years	$68,203	$54,768	$70,814	$58,849
15 Years	$61,248	$34,064	$65,571	$38,617
20 Years	$49,804	—0—	$55,563	—0—

The preceding chart contains a wealth of information. Some of it might just be classified as "interesting," while much of it can be used to your monetary advantage. Here are just some of the things this chart tells us:

- The difference in monthly payments between the 20- and 30-year loans is relatively little. The $49.03 difference in payments between the 20- and 30-year 13 percent loan really amounts to no more than the savings a businessman could pick up by packing his lunch three days a week rather than eating out.
- The higher the interest rate, the less the difference between the monthly payments. The variation with the 10 percent loans is $65.59 while the difference drops to $49.03 between the 13 percent loans. At 15 percent the difference shrinks to just $39.26.
- All loans pay little on principal and a lot on interest in the early years. That's because you're always paying interest on the remaining balance—and if the remaining balance is only lowered by $17.15 (as with the 13 percent, 30-year loan) then interest on the next payment is calculated on the just slightly reduced balance of $74,982.85.
- Paydown begins quicker on the 20-year loan because not only do you get the $17.15 principal reduction of the 30-year loan but your entire additional payment of $49.03 is also applied to principal reduction. Thus with the shorter term loan a snowball effect (gathering of bigger principal reductions) takes place much faster. Check the chart.
- On the 13 percent loan, a borrower with a 20-year loan will have paid $8,825 more out of pocket in fifteen years than will the person with the 30-year loan. But his loan will have been reduced by $36,383 vs. $9,429 for the 30-year loan. Even after subtracting the extra $8,825 out-of-pocket from the $36,383, this borrower with the 20-year loan comes out $27,558 ahead.
- Again the higher the interest rate (not the loan amount) and the longer the duration, the more this principle is accented. For instance the 40-year, 18 percent loan pays down only about $100 after five years and only to $91,360 after a full 30 years of paying $1,501.19 monthly.
- The difference between the monthly payments on an 18 percent 40-year loan vs. the 30-year loan is only $5.90 per month or $70.80 a year or just $2,548 for the 30-year period. However, after 30 years it's paid off; but the balance on the 40-year loan is $91,360. *Aren't you getting the feeling that someone has been taking advantage of you?*
- The less interest you pay the quicker the loan balance is paid down. If you plan to keep a rental and not refinance it for seven or eight years, you might be better off paying an extra $1,000 to the seller who is carrying back a purchase money first mortgage in return for a lower interest rate.
- The 13 percent, 30-year loan pays down to $58,849 after 10 years, building an equity of $16,151—significantly better than the higher rate

loans (refer to the 18 percent loan above).

- But a 13 percent $75,000 loan for a term of 15 years will pay down to $41,700—building a 10-year equity of $33,300. And this is done with a monthly payment which is just $119.29 more per month or $14,314 over the ten-year span. But what is truly exciting is that in the next (and last) five years the $41,700 balance will be completely paid off. That's an average of $695 per month being put into your pocket. And this money isn't merely going from one hand to another, because it's your tenants who are really making this possible.

HERE'S HOW YOU CAN STRETCH A PROFIT FROM BOTH ENDS OF A REAL ESTATE TRANSACTION

"What's the significance of all this?" you may ask? Just that maybe the next time you take out a new conventional loan you'll stop to analyze whether a twenty-year loan would suit your purposes better than a thirty-year one. Or perhaps you'll take a second look at a property you can wrap because you realize that the loan is in the tenth year of a twenty-year amortization and its monthly principal reduction is $238 instead of the $20 to $30 you might have otherwise assumed. Here is another way you can harness this interest rate phenomenon if you've got a few extra bucks to invest.

For this example I will use a deluxe fourplex in which each of the two-bedroom units rents for $325 or $1,300 total. Our hypothetical investor buys the building for $200,000 and makes an extra large down payment of $80,000. Not very good leverage but, as you will see, done with a purpose. The $120,000 balance comes from a new conventional loan at 12 percent interest and for a term of 10 years. That's right . . . 10 years.

The monthly cost of this loan will be $1,722. Including taxes and insurance this investor will start out with a $700 monthly negative cash flow. But with projected rent increases of 10 percent each year this negative cash flow will be eradicated in five years.

Why would an investor do this? One reason is for growth—not so much in appreciating value as in equity reduction. In ten years the investor's $120,000 loan will be paid off. That guarantees him a $120,000 profit regardless of what happens to the value of the building. He'll make an average of $12,000 a year this way . . . that's a 15 percent yearly profit (based on his original investment of $80,000) all made possible by his nice tenants who faithfully paid their rents over this period of time.

But here is the best part of this story . . . THIS 15 PERCENT ANNUAL PROFIT IS TAX-FREE. That's right, in ten years time Mr. Investor has picked up an additional $120,000 on which he will not have to pay taxes. Debt reduction is not a taxable event and it doesn't matter whose money (his or the tenants) really paid off the loan. The only taxes he will pay are on the profit made on the gain over and above the $200,000 he paid for the building. And that only happens when the building is sold.

What this investor could do is sell the building after ten years and take a very small down payment (certainly less than 30 percent to qualify for installment tax sale). After ten years at less than an annual appreciation of 10 percent, the building will have a $400,000 value. With a $40,000 down payment he could carry the balance ($360,000) for 20 years at 13 percent interest and receive for himself a nice little retirement income of $4,218 a month. Not a bad return for $80,000, a little negative cash flow and an idea.

Why not try this or a similar idea yourself? But if you do, let me warn you of one thing. Many lenders will tell you you're crazy! They'll point out the higher monthly payments and tell you nobody does it this way. The bottom line is that the lender makes a bigger profit with the long-term loan.

But what counts is the profit you'll be making.

"The successful investor doesn't take 'no' for an answer. The successful investor doesn't believe the agents and other investors who say it can't be done."
                                      —Jack Reed,
                                   investor and lecturer

17

HOW YOU CAN DOUBLE YOUR MONEY EVERY TWO YEARS

Can I really double my money in real estate every two years?

Yes!

How?

By doing it! I am, friends of mine are, and hundreds of people who have read *THE MONOPOLY GAME* have written or called to tell me of their success.

What do all these people have in common? They are *doing it* in real estate. The key here is DOING IT. You won't make penny number one unless you get off your duff—now—and get busy and *DO IT*.

The *HOW TO* is what this book is all about. In this final chapter I'll review some of the important success ingredients from the earlier chapters and add another key dimension—a workable pyramiding strategy. I will have done my part . . . the rest is up to you. But remember this one key point—if you don't get busy *now* and get started *doing it*, you probably never will.

Don't wait . . . home prices aren't going to come down! Here's why.

WHERE WERE YOU IN 1970?

If you are over 35 years of age, what is your excuse for not having made a million-dollar profit in real estate? What will be your excuse in 1990?

Following is an article which I clipped from the Oakland Tribune in May, 1970. The headline boldly proclaimed "HOME PRICES WILL DOUBLE IN DECADE."

> *Each spring for the last five years the current president of the Associated Home Builders of the Greater Eastbay has predicted that home prices will increase substantially during the ensuing year.*
>
> *In retrospect these forecasts have been invariably accurate except when the president takes too conservative an approach and the home prices increase even more than he said they would.*
>
> *Such may be the case again this year, but final verification will have to wait until 1980 because president Tom Gentry decided for the sake of variety to make a 10-year forecast.*
>
> *"TODAY'S $33,000 HOUSE WILL COST $58,410 BY 1980," he said flatly as he advised: "Move up to the best you can afford and—particularly if you are under 40—buy to the hilt. Not only will the house almost double in dollar value but it will provide many extra pleasures."*

WHAT GOOD ADVICE!! And it was free advice . . . abundantly available in the newspapers of the day . . . in all parts of the U.S. The only problem was that the predictors missed on the prices by a mile. The Bay Area's $33,000 home in 1970 is now selling for something closer to $97,481, the median price of a single-family home in California as of February, 1980.

So what is really different today from 10 years ago? The knowledgeable predictors—those closely associated with the building industries—are at it again, despite today's current recession. They say that home values will again double or better by the end of the next decade. One—Ben Bartolotto, research director of the Construction Industry Research Board—says that home prices a year from now may be 18 percent higher.

Will these predictors be right again—maybe even a little too conservative in the estimates? I for one think they know what they're talking about, if for nothing else but the following reasons:

NEARLY 32 MILLION AMERICANS REACHED 30 YEARS OF AGE DURING THE '70's. DURING THE '80'S, 42 MILLION WILL REACH THIS PRIME HOME-BUYING AGE. And if that fact by itself is not enough impetus for another housing boom, consider that because of ill-advised policies, the federal government has tightened the screws on credit, and the effects are temporarily crippling the housing industry. It is predicted that 1980 housing starts (all kinds) may be just a little over 1 million.

Vacancy rates are already at an all-time low . . . we need approximately two million new units each year just to keep even. Now here is the corker: AS MANY AS 600,000 LEGAL ALIENS COME TO THIS COUNTRY

EACH YEAR. And those figures don't include the rising tide of temporary visitors (students, etc.) and waves of illegal aliens whose total numbers are now estimated to be as high as six million.

Is the picture any clearer? For the time being, this country may not even be producing enough housing for immigrants, let alone those 4.2 million Americans reaching the prime home buying age this year.

And so what are the politicians—especially the so-called liberals—doing about it? They are calling for rent control! That's right, the short-sighted politician is listening to the cries of his constituents . . . the cries for decent and affordable housing.

Mr. Politician wants to be re-elected, so he acts. "We must have rent control," he says.

Now if Mr. Liberal Politician had any brains at all, he would look beyond the next election and do something about the problem. The solution is simply to remove red tape and unnecessary restrictions which hamper new construction starts; he would remove rent control to help bring in more investor money and therefore competition; and he would do everything in his power to see that interest rates could remain at decent levels. I mean 8 and 9 percent—not 12 and 13 percent. How? I don't have all the answers, but when T-Bill accounts offer over 16 percent interest (as they did in early 1980) where the hell do you expect all the money to go? So maybe a good starting place is with less government competition for the dollar.

Don't look for any fast changes, however. Instead, look for a major housing crunch in the mid-eighties. Politicians are slow learners. In the meantime, look out for your own interest.

Where will you be in 1990? Enjoying life on your private yacht . . . or still commuting back and forth to work in bumper to bumper traffic? Can you believe you have a second chance to make good?

GET THE VITAL INFORMATION YOU'LL NEED

By reading DOUBLE YOUR MONEY, THE MONOPOLY GAME and HOW TO GROW A MONEYTREE, you'll be able to get about ninety percent of the knowledge and information you'll need to be successful.

The one big missing ingredient is . . . the experience and confidence you can only get from *doing it.*

Most successful investors I have met read everything they can get their hands on about real estate investing. Even though I claimed that you can get about 90 percent of the know-how just from my three books, it's a big wide world out there and it would be in your best interests to keep learning . . . and to keep yourself exposed to new ideas, trends and philosophies.

One good way to do this is to attend one or two good seminars which will come your way. Or else keep reading. One good book which will provide you with a lot of creative ideas plus a slightly different philosophical slant than mine is *NOTHING DOWN*, a Simon and Schuster book by Robert G. Allen.

The best book I have ever read on management and tenant relationships is *LANDLORDING*, by Leigh Robinson. And for those of you who are impatient for success, try THINK LIKE A TYCOON by Bill Greene. It's not only humorous and acid, but it's full of good real estate advice.

All three of these excellent books, and then some, are available from Impact Publishing Company and can be purchased by mail using the handy coupon in the back of this book.

My favorite *how-to* tool for investors, however, is a meaty subscription service of which I am the editor. It's called IMPACT REPORTS and UPDATES.

The IMPACT REPORTS are fairly lengthy in-depth Reports (about 8,000 words each) which go into subjects vital to the small investor. Each one is written by an expert. Past Reports have been written by such people as Jack Miller and John Schaub of Fortune Seminar fame; nationally syndicated real estate columnist Bob Bruss; previously mentioned authors Leigh Robinson and Bill Greene; plus numerous nationally known creative real estate people like Charles Dorsey, Barney Zick and Jack Reed.

The topics of the past and of the future will all pertain to real estate investing but will not go into the "heavier" type investments such as shopping centers, R.E.I.T.'s, or industrial property. They are basically designed for the investor who is into single-family homes and small multiples. Nearly half the issues are about creative ways to buy and own property. Many are about different aspects of real estate in which you might want to invest—like condominiums, duplexes and the how-to of converting a single-family home into a small office building.

The *UPDATE* is an eight-page newsletter which I basically write. It also covers creative real estate topics, in addition to everyday problems like termite inspections, evictions and money market conditions. Short range as well as long range predictions are also found in the *UPDATE*.

Is the service expensive? Not if you are going to be spending—and making—a lot of money in real estate. The cost is $59 for a one-year subscription or $99 for two years. You'll get your *REPORT* and *UPDATE* 10 times a year, with the July-August and December-January issues combined.

Of course I heartily recommend it—but then I'm the editor. And space here doesn't permit printing any of the numerous endorsements from happy subscribers. But you don't have to gamble, because your money will be refunded in full if you are not satisfied after you get your first two issues—and you'll keep what you were already sent.

So if you are ready to make big money in real estate, order now by either sending in the coupon you'll find at the back of this book or call us collect at (415) 935-4370 for credit card orders.

Enough commercials! Following are the 10 steps which (if you *do it*) can lift you out of the doldrums and let you double your invested money every two years . . . and then some.

DOUBLE YOUR MONEY PLAN

STEP NO. 1

MAKE THE DECISION TO DO IT. Devise a workable yet challenging goal and then religiously chase after that goal. Keep it posted where you can see it each and every day. A word of warning—you had better get the full and whole-hearted endorsement of every member of your family. If you don't you are going to have a hard, if not impossible, task in reaching your goal. At the very least, if your spouse is passive, have him or her read *THE MONOPOLY GAME*. Then ask for a pledge that he or she will support your endeavors and put up (at least for a couple of years) with your absence while inspecting property, etc.

STEP NO. 2

DECIDE ON A REAL ESTATE AGENT. As you will remember from the earlier chapters, there are a lot of considerations you must sift through when picking an agent. You may not find one to your liking right away, and that's okay. Don't rush in and take the first one you meet. But at least settle in your own mind how you will work with real estate agents.

For instance, will you go it alone entirely? Or will you *only* work through a real estate agent? The decision is yours, and it should be one you'll be comfortable with. Personally, I lean towards the combination approach. Most successful investors I know do this. They let one particular agent (a good guy) cover listed property and help with many of the more complicated details and forms. They in turn do-it-themselves when it comes down to unlisted property, such as FISBO's and foreclosures.

STEP NO. 3

SEEK OUT AND BUY YOUR FIRST PROPERTY. This is the *doing it* I talk a lot about. Any dummy should be able to figure out that if you never do it, then you'll never make it. So why wait?

Now if you presently have little or no money, it's going to take you a little longer to catch up with the investor who starts out with $20,000 to $30,000. That's okay, because *you will* eventually catch up. In the first part of this book I devoted a lot of pages to ways people without money could get started. Go back and review that material and then *get started*—if nothing else, go out and get a lease option. But I don't want you to get discouraged, so be sure to pick on the right property and owner—one who doesn't really want his property and who doesn't need his cash right away.

Now if you are more fortunate and have a good size chunk of beginning capital—then get busy and buy. In most parts of the country you should be able to secure one property for about $10,000. In some lower cost areas you'll spend less, and in higher priced areas it may realistically take $15,000 or more.

Buy one property at a time if you so choose, but don't waste any time between those purchases. Prices are only going in one direction—and that is up. So if you refinance your residence, cash in some semi-worthless stocks or borrow money from Aunt Henrietta, go out and spend that money by buying as many properties as you can realistically afford to buy.

As discussed in Chapter 16, you may want to hold a portion of that money aside—invest it in a high yield amortized and discounted note and use the proceeds to cover your negative cash flow.

(Note: For sake of the ongoing example I am going to use in this chapter to demonstrate how you can double your money every two years, I am creating a hypothetical investor whom we'll assume has just purchased his first rental property. It's a newer three-bedroom home which took $15,000 out-of-pocket to buy. The price was $70,000 and the current loan (which was assumed) is $55,000. I am also assuming that our hypothetical investor—whom I'll call Jim—spent all of his available money on this first purchase. I'll use a continuing appreciation rate of 10 percent: if anything, that rate may even be a little conservative.

STEP NO. 4

SEEK COMPETENT TAX ADVICE. Either about the time you are buying your first rental or certainly before filing your income tax return, get together with a competent tax advisor who is thoroughly familiar with real estate.

Why? Because the method you choose to depreciate your properties will have a profound impact on how much tax shelter you are able to get from your rentals. You may want to get as much as possible by taking accelerated depreciation—but Uncle Sam has what is called *recapture*. This recapture principle basically means that some day Uncle Sam will take back from you—or your estate—much of the shelter that he gave you in the early years of portfolio growth. I am a Realtor and not a qualified tax advisor. So seek out professional advice before you get too far along.

While we are on the subject of tax shelter, let me point out that each property you own will provide you with a fairly large amount of shelter. In simple terms this means that each property worth approximately $70,000 will give you between $2,000 and $3,000 to deduct (on paper) from your income for tax purposes. With an added $3,000 deduction, if you are in the 50 percent tax bracket, you will save half of that amount, or $1,500. When I say save I mean that you won't be paying that amount to Uncle Sam, or you may be getting it back in a refund if you pay taxes the painless way—through withholding. If you are presently paying about 20 percent of your income in taxes, this new $3,000 deduction will save you 20 percent, or $600 out of pocket.

It builds up, believe me. I can earn up to $30,000 and not pay one red cent in income taxes.

I said that each $70,000 home you buy will normally give you $2,000 to $3,000 in added tax shelter. Here is how that works:

1. The government lets you depreciate (write off) the investment property (less the value of the land) over a set number of years. New buildings, for example, can be written off in 45 years, but with new property you can use the fastest method of depreciation possible—the double declining balance (200 percent) method. These guidelines, incidentally, are not compulsory. An older property can be depreciated from between 20 and 40 years.

For our ongoing example, we'll assume that Jim bought a 6-year-old home and he chooses to write it off in 35 years. Jim and his tax advisor also decide to depreciate the property at $55,000, leaving $15,000 for the lot, which cannot be depreciated. Dividing $55,000 by 35 years gives Jim an annual $1,571 straight line depreciation deduction. If Jim had bought an older home, he could have written it off in 25 years and gotten a bigger $2,200 deduction.

2. In addition to the scheduled depreciation (which can't change once the method is chosen), the government also lets investors write off actual expenses. Equity build-up is not considered an expense. For our example, Jim will pay a mortgage payment of $400 a month which includes $25 to principal which cannot be deducted. But he does pay $375 a month in interest charges which are deductible, plus annual taxes of $840 which amount to $70 a month. If Jim had to replace a water heater during the year at a total cost of $250, that would be a repair expense.
replace a water heater during the year at a total cost of $250, that would be a repair expense.

Here is what Jim can deduct on an annual basis:

Interest	$4,500
Taxes	840
Fire Insurance	210
Repairs	250
	$5,800

If he rented out the property for $400 a month during the year for an annual total of $4,800, then by subtracting the income of $4,800 from the expenses of $5,800, Jim would have surplus expenses for the year of $1,000.

This $1,000 would then be added to the $1,571 straight line depreciation Jim is taking for a grand total tax deduction of $2,571. In Jim's ongoing example I am not considering the tax shelter benefits at all. And that's because I don't want to get you and me bogged down in figures. I'll show you how to double your money every two years without even considering this very real benefit.

If you want to learn more about taxes before meeting with your tax advisor, I recommend that you purchase the Impact Report entitled THE

TAX BENEFITS OF INVESTING IN REAL ESTATE, by Robert J. Bruss. It is an excellent 38-page Report (our biggest ever) that covers all tax aspects of real estate ownership, from your residence to your rental property. In addition to writing a syndicated real estate column, Bruss is an attorney and licensed real estate broker. See the coupon and additional information at the back of this book.

STEP NO. 5

DON'T STOP NOW—FORM A PARTNERSHIP. Jim has just bought his first home and has it rented out to his very first tenant. He is also out of money. If he used the lazy man's way to make a moderate long-term profit, he would merely sit back and wait for his equity in the property to grow large enough so that he could borrow against it or refinance, and then buy another round of property.

But Jim decides not to go the slow and easy way. His next most logical step is to seek out a friend or acquaintance and form a small real estate partnership.

Small two- or three-person partnerships are the "wave of the future" in real estate investing. They are the perfect match of "time" and "money." As prices continue to escalate, when the average home is priced at $150,000, and home ownership is reserved for the wealthy, partnerships will be a very logical way for investors to own property. It is now, without waiting for higher prices.

Thus Jim takes the step and locates a friend who has the money, the interest and the belief in real estate—but not the time. Jim is short on cash but has a fair amount of time. They form a partnership and buy one home.

(Note: Jim could keep doing this. If his first partner ran out of cash or wanted to take it easy, he could locate another partner. There is no law preventing a person from taking part in as many partnerships as he wants. Only the sky is the limit. But for our ongoing example demonstrating how investment money can be doubled in real estate every two years, I am not going to consider what Jim is doing with his partnerships. After all, when one invests zero cash and then harvests a $10,000 or so profit four or five years later, how do you compute it? Is it infinity or is it a 10,000 percent gain? Whatever it is—it's nice!

STEP NO. 6

CONTROL PROPERTY NUMBER TWO. One full year has now gone by since Jim bought his first property with his initial $15,000. At a steady 10 percent appreciation rate, that property is now worth $77,000. Without being *very creative*, there is no practical way Jim can use his equity to buy a second property—a second home that isn't part of a partnership.

This is the ideal time for Jim to *control* the future of a property without actually taking title. There is no better way for him to do this than with a lease option.

Here's how he did it. After the first year Jim felt that it would take about one more year for him to get enough equity out of his first home so that he could buy a second property. He didn't want to sit idly by, however, and watch property values climb steadily higher. So he gave up a half dozen hours of television each week and began looking for a situation in which he could get a one-year lease option on a property.

It wasn't that hard. Jim had to zero in on an owner who didn't really want his property and who didn't need any significant amount of cash up front. Within a month's time Jim had found several properties which fit the bill. Most were owned by absentee owners—some had simply moved out of state and others were tired landlords.

Jim conveniently found a home which he could buy for $77,000 (convenient for us—so all the figures easily match in this example). It needed painting and other repairs which he estimated would cost about $2,000. It also came with a tenant who was paying $425.

The owner agreed to take $1,000 option money and give Jim a lease for one year. Technically, Jim would sub-lease the property to the tenant who was already in the home on a month-to-month tenancy.

All the terms for the eventual sale were spelled out in advance. Rather than worry about hiring appraisers and determining the value one year down the road, Jim convinced the seller to let him buy the property for $80,000—just $3,000 more than its current estimated value. To make the deal go, Jim had to also agree to lease the property for $475 a month—giving him a $50 negative cash flow on a property that he didn't even own yet. But he seriously intended to buy it at the end of a year, so he carefully negotiated terms he could live with.

He got the seller (the optionor) to allow $175 of each month's lease payment to be credited to the eventual sale. This would give Jim $2,100 towards the sale. But in return for this concession and the relatively low price, Jim had to agree to paint and repair the property. That way if he did not exercise his option at the end of the year, he would return the home to the optionor in better condition than when he received it.

The painting and repairs were easy for Jim to resolve. He paid $300 out-of-pocket for supplies and convinced the tenant (who had the skills) to do the painting and make other minor repairs. For this Jim had to reduce the monthly rent from $425 to $375 for a one-year period. Thus for $600 (the amount of lost rent) and $300 for supplies Jim was able to take care of what he felt to be a $2,000 problem.

The main question was that of financing. Being astute, Jim realized that he would be much better off assuming the current loan than he would be taking out a new and expensive bank loan. The problem was that the existing loan balance was only $28,000. The loan was an 8 percent FHA. The total payments including impounds (taxes and insurance) were only $350. There was no practical way that Jim could assume that loan as $52,000 (minus his credits of $2,100) would be needed for the balance of the purchase price.

A wrap-around, Jim thought, would be ideal. And why not? Anyone who would give a lease option on his property would have to be a good candidate for a wrap. Even if the seller did not want to carry it, because of the high rate of return these loans provide the mortgagor, they are highly salable at a modest discount. If this were the case, Jim could have agreed to raise the price another $3,000 to $4,000 to cover the necessary discount. But in this example, Jim didn't have to offer a higher price, as the seller agreed to carry the wrap as long as Jim would pay $15,000 down. Here is a recap of what Jim will be getting:

Sale price in one year $80,000
Less down payment 15,000
New loan balance (with wrap) $65,000

Jim still will have a $2,100 credit coming when he buys the property. Jim decides to keep that liquid and use it to supplement the negative cash flow he'll have. (Remember that even in the option year he will have $100 N.C.F.—the difference between the reduced rent of $375 and the $475 he is paying the seller-optionor.)

What will Jim's new payment be after he exercises his option? That depends largely upon how well Jim was able to negotiate with the seller as to what the interest rate would be on the wrap. Without question, Jim should be able to get from between 1 and 2 percent less than current market rates. For this example, we'll assume Jim ended up with 11 percent. This would make his new payment, excluding taxes and insurance, $595.83. With taxes and insurance he'll be paying about $700 a month.

How much negative cash flow will Jim have? When he takes title to the property he will be able to raise the rent to about $475, leaving him with $225 N.C.F. If that seems like a large rent increase, keep in mind it only reflects an annual jump of $25 or 5.5 percent. Remember the tenant was paying $425 and instead of being hit with an increase was given a $50 reduction in lieu of doing work on the property. That agreement has expired and another year has passed, making an increase to $475 both fair and logical.

What can Jim do about this N.C.F.? When you start out with just $15,000 total cash as Jim did, some of his options that could reduce the N.C.F. are lost. In this case he will have an alligator costing him $225 a month—but he also has his credit of $2,100 less the $600 he spent on closing costs to buy the home or a grand total of $1,500. Now that $1,500 isn't going to keep the alligator at bay forever. But it can help feed him until more help arrives a year or two hence. Thus Jim decides to use $125 of that money each month for almost 13 months (he will have collected some interest) to reduce his negative cash flow to a manageable $100 a month level.

And by the way, what does the seller get out of this? He gets $15,000 cash (he didn't pay a commission on this one) plus a net monthly income of $409.

Incidentally, this deal Jim made does not represent a particularly good one or a bad one—but what I would consider an average lease option buy. IT IS A VERY PRACTICAL EXAMPLE OF WHAT CAN BE DONE AND WHAT MANY INVESTORS ARE ALREADY DOING.

STEP NO. 7

BORROW FROM THE FIRST PROPERTY PURCHASED. In step number 6 Jim took control of a property via a lease option. That sale cannot be completed, however, until Jim comes up with $15,000 from some source. This money could have come from an inheritance, a life insurance policy, Uncle Harry, an unsecured bank loan or by knocking over the local bank. But to make this example as practical as possible, we'll have Jim get the $15,000 from his first property two years after buying it.

Why two years? The following diagram demonstrates how Jim's equity has been "growing" in the first property.

Jim's Equity Position After One Year

```
Value @ 10% appreciation
      for one year . . . . . . . . . . . . . . . . . . . . . $77,000
Less loan amount which reflects
      equity pay-down of $300 . . . . . . . . . . .  54,700
Jim's equity (28.9% of value) . . . . . . . . . . . $22,300
```

After Two Years

```
Value @ 10% appreciation
      for two years . . . . . . . . . . . . . . . . . . . . . $84,700
Less loan amount which reflects
      additional $300 equity pay-down . . . . .  54,400
Jim's equity (35.7% of value) . . . . . . . . . . . $30,300
```

Jim's equity position of 35.7 percent of the property value will allow him to borrow up to $13,300 from a hard money broker who wants at least 20 percent equity in the property. From a more lenient private source, Jim should be able to get up to $17,500 and still leave 15 percent equity in the home.

There is really no practical choice. Not only is a hard money source expensive but, except for an unusual broker, Jim couldn't get enough money. So Jim elects to go for a private source.

```
Property value ....................... $84,700
Less 15% of value .................... 12,705
                                       $71,995
Less loan balance .................... 54,400
Potential loan ....................... $17,595
```

Remember the commitment Jim made one year earlier when he decided to give up six hours of television each week so that he could use the time to find a property he could buy with an option? Looking back on that decision, Jim feels that he didn't miss anything but gained a lot. (Incidentally, the average American supposedly watches 40 hours of television a week. Need I say more!) Thus Jim decides to continue with the six hour a week program and use the additional time to find a private source for the money he will need for exercising the lease option. In one year this additional six hours a week comes to 52 weeks × 6 hours equals 312 hours. Even with taking time off for holidays, vacation and illness, Jim will be gaining about 250 productive hours.

Now here is a question I have for my readers. Being very realistic, don't you think that in 250 hours almost any dummy could have found *one* property that could be tied up with a lease-option contract and *one* benefactor who would have made a well-secured second mortgage loan—even on a straight note? I know that you know the answer.

Step No. 7 comes to a successful conclusion with Jim borrowing just $15,000 from the father-in-law of a business associate. He gets it on a straight note at 12 percent with the balloon payment due in four years. With the money Jim exercises the lease option in step No. 6. He doesn't go after any additional monies to take care of negative cash flow because he reasons he will soon be raising both rents and that the total for both properties (less than $200) will be very manageable. Without a straight note he could not have done this.

STEP NO. 8

REPEAT THE LEASE OPTION PROCESS. As Jim goes back into the market place to find a second property he can control with a lease option, the fourth year of his investment program is just beginning. He now owns two properties outright— both valued now (for our convenience) at $93,170.

Jim will now lease-option another property. Its projected value in one year, when Jim exercises the option, will be $102,487. However, Jim's use of the lease option allows him once again to split the difference between today's and next year's value. Thus he will eventually buy the property for $97,500 with a $20,000 down payment.

Frankly, someone putting in 250 hours a year devoted mostly to finding one good lease option buy should really be able to come up with a winner—

something closer to $10,000 under market. But to keep this example realistic and to show you how some stumbling blocks aren't really such bad obstacles, I am holding Jim back from making any super deals. I want the reader to see how relatively easy it can be to make big money in real estate—that the main key to success is just plain *doing it*.

STEP NO. 9

BORROW TO BUY THIRD PROPERTY. Step No. 9 concludes with Jim borrowing $25,000 so that he can exercise his second lease option which was arranged a year earlier in step No. 8. The loan is a blanket mortgage secured by his two existing rentals. This time Jim was not able to get a straight note so he went for the next best thing—a $25,000 interest-only note at 10 percent with a five-year due date. He borrowed an extra $5,000 so that he could use it to defray the cost of the new note and some of his negative cash flow.

Along with an extra $2,000 that he had saved—mostly due to his new tax shelters—Jim bought at discount a fully amortized three-year note. The interest rate was 10 percent and the face value of the note was $10,000. Jim got it for $7,000. His monthly income will be $322.70. On the $25,000 he just borrowed, he will only be repaying $208.33; however, the entire principal amount will be due in five years.

LET'S TAKE A LOOK AT WHAT JIM HAS
AFTER FIVE FULL YEARS

At the end of five years Jim will own three properties. And that is not even considering what he may or may not have done with the partnership concept he began in step No. 5. The three similar homes that Jim bought are each worth $112,735 at the end of five years. Is that unrealistic? Consider that the 10 percent appreciation figure we're using is lower than what most of the country experienced from 1977 through 1979. Also consider that this country is quickly slipping into a serious housing shortage problem. It might have been even more realistic in this example to use a higher figure than 10 percent. Maybe in five years the $70,000 home Jim started with will be worth $140,000?

JIM'S EQUITY POSITION AFTER 5 YEARS

The First Home Bought At Beginning Of Program

Current value	$112,735
1st mortgage now	$53,800
$15,000 2nd mortgage with interest	
accumulated to date	20,400
½ of $25,000 blanket mortgage	12,500
	$86,700

Equity in property $26,035

The Second Home Bought At End Of Third Year for $80,000

Current value	$112,735
1st mortgage now	$64,400
½ of $25,000 blanket mortgage	12,500
	$76,900

Equity in property $35,835

The Third Home Bought At The End Of The Fourth Year For $97,500

Current value	$112,735
1st mortgage now	$77,200

Equity in property $35,535

Jim's Total Net Worth In His Investment Portfolio Is:

First home	$26,035
Second home	35,835
Third home	35,535
	$97,405

Jim originally started with $15,000. For him to have doubled that money every two years he would have needed to make an annual 50 percent return on his original investment; or by the end of five years he would have had to have made $52,500. But he didn't make $52,500 did he? He instead has equities of $97,405. And he did this without using half the principles stressed in this book. For instance, Jim didn't:

- Buy any properties at foreclosure sales
- Include any partnership properties in the example
- Option properties and then sell the option two or three years later
- Buy any property at significantly under-market prices

If anything, Jim's example is conservative. I know of many people who are doing much better than what I outlined. But instead of taking the risk that my example would be too unbelievable, I kept it conservative. Following is a brief synopsis of a real success story.

In December, 1979, I received a thank-you note from a *MONOPOLY GAME* reader who bought his first home in 1975. The note gave the figures for the homes, condominiums and duplexes he and his wife bought and told me what the end results were. The note ended with: "YOU ARE RIGHT! IT WORKS!"

This investor started in '75 with money borrowed from his credit union and a local savings and loan — enough to start out with three properties that year. After a full five years this investor had property valued at $760,000 and equities estimated at $357,000. He also told me he and his wife had taken some of the investment money and enjoyed three pleasure cruises in that time span.

STEP NO. 10

REFINANCE RATHER THAN SELL. Jim's story isn't over yet. The next logical question is, what happens next? Obviously, he should keep going. He could keep up the same successful approach he has been taking and lease-option another property or even two for that matter. Or he could slow down a little and keep his negative cash flow in check.

But however fast or whatever approach Jim may decide to take, there is one thing for certain — he is going to have to consider refinancing eventually. In one more year — at the end of his sixth year — his three homes will each be worth $124,000 and will all have sufficient equity to refinance. He also has a four-year straight note which will be due and payable in the sixth year. That means he will certainly either have to 1) sell; 2) refinance; or 3) renegotiate and extend the note; or 4) participate in a tax deferred exchange.

By the end of the sixth year Jim will be in the enviable position of being able to begin this profitable investment pyramid all over again — except this time he'll be starting with three homes instead of basically the one he bought for $15,000. It's when one plays this investment game with bigger numbers that the results quickly get very interesting. At the end of another six years, by repeating the first ten steps over and over again, Jim will have made well in excess of one-half million dollars. And this profit will have basically come from his initial $15,000 investment plus perhaps another $15,000 added along the way for such things as option money or negative cash flow.

I favor the refinancing method if—and this is an important *if*—the property in question is worth keeping. In other words, if the particular home or property is in a declining neighborhood, or if it is going to require several thousand dollars of repairs and maintenance over the next couple of years, I would be in favor of selling. If a roof is currently leaking you are obligated to reveal this to the buyer, and he'll probably negotiate you into a corner and have you pay for the replacement. However, if the roof is only getting old and may have to be replaced in a few years, that's the buyer's problem. Also keep in mind that a cedar shake roof, for instance, can cost up to $4,500 to replace on just a 1400-square-foot home.

So if the property is in good condition and if you feel that it will be good for another several years, by all means refinance rather than sell.

But I haven't even mentioned the best reason for refinancing—and that is, it is not a taxable event. That's right! If you sell, you pay capital gain on the profit. But if you refinance you simply put off the day of reckoning with Uncle Sam. You can do this as many times as you want and go to your grave and let your heirs worry about settling up with Uncle.

FREE AT LAST

There you have it! A detailed road map which can lead you to more fun, excitement and riches than you ever dreamed was possible.

All you have to do is *believe* and get off your duff and *do it*. That's my challenge to you.

It doesn't much matter how you make your money. I've shown you my way. A tremendous number of people buy houses, as I've described, and are making a literal killing. Yet others buy large apartment buildings or farmland or commercial property. They too are making money . . . and they too will achieve financial independence.

Most Americans will never get off the great American slide. They'll just keep on going downhill. But I'm not like that . . . I am a John Wayne fan and would rather fight than submit. The poorhouse will never get me because I won't let it. How about you?

You don't have to be a slave to your investment portfolio. Only plan to buy as many properties as you will be comfortable with. Tailor your program to co-exist with your budget and your take-home pay. Believe me, you can be just as happy some day by owning three rentals as you might be by owning 23.

And if you go after the higher number of properties, competent management services can always be found. In fact, that's what I sometimes like best about being an investor—the knowledge that there is no one right way to do it but many ways.

The rewards of investing are many. For me it's freedom.

I am free to do as I please. I can change jobs . . . and I can go where I want to when I want to. I am not saddled with an unfair tax burden any more. And I don't need to scrimp and save every nickel and dime I earn to put something away for a rainy day. Why? Because my properties (and their appreciating values) do the saving for me.

My old age will be taken care of . . . I won't need to depend upon you, my children, Uncle Sam, the State of California, or anyone else. That's a good feeling . . . I hope you too will be able to experience it someday soon.

The biggest problem you should have as an investor is *what to do next?* Like Jim in the preceding example. He'll most likely want to repeat the 10 steps until he owns a dozen-plus properties with over a half million dollars equity. He'll then have to decide which road to take. He'll have to decide whether to just sit tight and *enjoy*, or take in a partner, or trade up for larger units.

But that's the fun of making a lot of money, isn't it? Trying to decide how to spend it. Well, that can be your problem in the very near future. I hope it is.

DOUBLE YOUR MONEY IN REAL ESTATE
EVERY TWO YEARS

☐ YES, Please send me _____ additional copy(ies) of Dave Glubetich's *DOUBLE YOUR MONEY IN REAL ESTATE EVERY TWO YEARS.* I'll keep this one for myself and let friends read the dog-eared copy. (NOTE: We pay fourth class, book-rate postage: for quicker 1st class mail add $1 per book up to 4 books only.)

PRICE LIST (Check one category)

☐ **Soft Cover** Edition $12.00
3 to 4 books @ 8.75 each
5 to 9 books @ $7.50 each
10 to 19 books @ $6.75 each

☐ **Deluxe Hard Cover** Ed. $14.50
3 to 4 books @ $11.00 each
5 to 9 books @ $9.75 each
10 to 19 books @ $9.00 each

☐ I am enclosing $1. per each soft cover book ordered and/or $2 extra per each hard cover book for special first class postage and handling.

Amount enclosed $ _____
(Cal. residents please add 6% sales tax)

Name _____

Address _____

City _____ State _____ Zip _____

CREDIT CARD ORDERS SIGN HERE _____

☐ Master Charge   ☐ Visa/Bankamericard   **Expiration date** _____

Credit Card Number _____

MAIL TO: IMPACT PUBLISHING COMPANY
1601 Oak Park Boulevard
Pleasant Hill, CA 94523

For quicker service call (415) 935-4370

Special Note: You will receive our current catalog of exciting real estate products with each order. And even if you don't order now you may write or call for a free catalog.

THE MONOPOLY GAME
and
HOW TO GROW A MONEYTREE

THE MONOPOLY GAME, The How-To-Book of making big money with rental homes, by Dave Glubetich. Currently in its fourth revised edition, 147 pages. *The Monopoly Game* goes into the complete story of investing in single-family homes, taking the reader through his first purchase to the first tenant; and goes into management, selling and refinancing, taxes and a workable pyramiding strategy. Not available in hard cover.   PRICE $10.95

HOW TO GROW A MONEYTREE, the Magical Book of Making Big Money with Second Mortgages, is the second book by Dave Glubetich. 117 pages, only available in soft cover. How one can successfully invest in second mortgages and trust deeds—every detail you'll need to know. It also supplies the technical knowledge of notes and secondary paper which every property investor should fully understand.   PRICE $10.95

☐ YES, please send ____copies of *The Monopoly Game* and/or ____ copies of *How to Grow a Moneytree*. PRICE IS $10.95 PER SINGLE COPY or as indicated below for multiple copies. (NOTE: We pay fourth class, book-rate postage: for quicker 1st class mail add $1 per book up to 4 books only.)

Amount enclosed $ _____
(Cal. residents please add 6% sales tax)

Combination orders are accepted with the following discounts:
3 to 4 books @ $8.00 each
5 to 9 books @ $7.00
10 to 19 books @ $6.35 each
Please call for further discounts — (415) 935-4370

Name _____

Address _____

City _____ State _____ Zip _____

CREDIT CARD ORDERS SIGN HERE _____

☐ Master Charge   ☐ Visa/Bankamericard   **Expiration date** _____

Credit Card Number _____

MAIL TO: IMPACT PUBLISHING COMPANY
1601 Oak Park Boulevard
Pleasant Hill, CA 94523

INDIVIDUAL
IMPACT REPORTS

Following is a description of three *IMPACT REPORTS* which are being made available to non-subscribers. As a subscriber to *Impact Reports* these back issues may be purchased for $4 each or two of them may be chosen as your free bonus when you subscribe.

The regular price for non-subscribers is $9 each; however, as an introduction to the service, the following special prices will apply with this coupon offer only.

Any One Report $7

Any Two Reports $13

All Three Reports $18

☐ SYNDICATIONS AND PARTNERSHIP by Thomas Binford. Goes into the ABC's of small syndicates, limited and general partnerships. Learn how to form your own profitable investment group . . . or how to find a reputable group to join.

☐ WINNING METHODS . . . A Close Look at the Investment Techniques that Three Average People are Using to Create Million-Dollar Equity Portfolios, by Dave Glubetich. The title of this one says it all—read the interesting success stories of three investors and learn how they did it—and how you can duplicate their success.

☐ THE TAX BENEFITS OF INVESTING IN REAL ESTATE by Robert J. Bruss. It's all here—almost everything you'll ever need to know about real estate taxes. It's complete with interesting and *understandable* case studies.

☐ PLEASE SEND ALL THREE OF THE ABOVE REPORTS

I am enclosing $ _____

(California residents please add 6% sales tax)

Name _____

Address _____

City _____ State _____ Zip _____

CREDIT CARD ORDERS SIGN HERE _____

☐ Master Charge   ☐ Visa/Bankamericard   Expiration date _____

Credit Card Number _____

MAIL TO: IMPACT PUBLISHING COMPANY
                       1601 Oak Park Boulevard
                       Pleasant Hill, CA 94523

IMPACT REPORTS
and
UPDATES

IMPACT REPORTS and *UPDATES* are a powerful two-part investor service designed to assist the small investor in buying, managing and making more money with single-family homes and small multiples.

Each Report is written by an investor who has achieved an unparalleled degree of success in his or her field . . . and each reveals ideas, techniques or new concepts which are designed to help you make a lot more money.

The *UPDATE* brings you important real estate news plus timely how-to information that is too brief to be included in the lengthier Reports. *IMPACT REPORTS* and *UPDATES* cost just $59 (tax deductible for most) and are issued 10 times a year. Your complete satisfaction is guaranteed or your money back.

☐ Yes, I would like to sharpen my investing skills by learning many inside tips and techniques from pro's who are making a lot of money themselves. Please begin my subscription immediately for the number of years I have checked below. AS A FREE GIFT I UNDERSTAND THAT I WILL BE SENT A BONUS CERTIFICATE WHICH I MAY USE FOR TWO FREE BACK ISSUE REPORTS OF MY CHOICE. (Note: A list and description of back issue Reports will be sent to you upon receipt of your order.)

☐ One year for $59   ☐ Two years for $99 (I save $19)

Name _____

Address _____

City _____ State _____ Zip _____

CREDIT CARD ORDERS SIGN HERE _____

☐ Master Charge   ☐ Visa/Bankamericard   **Expiration Date** _____

Credit Card Number _____

MAIL TO: IMPACT PUBLISHING COMPANY
                  1601 Oak Park Boulevard
                  Pleasant Hill, CA 94523

For further information call (415) 935-4370

REAL ESTATE AMORTIZATION BOOKS

AVAILABLE FROM IMPACT PUBLISHING CO.

REALTY BLUEBOOK, from Professional Publishing Corporation
The Realty Bluebook, which is designed as a daily reference tool for use in every phase of real estate, is commonly referred to among professionals as the "real estate Bible." In addition to amortization schedules and various tables, the *Bluebook* contains a treasury of other valuable information including checklists and specific wording for various contract clauses and financing techniques. The information is so specific and concise that the *Realty Bluebook* can actually be carried in one's pocket for use during a business transaction. A new edition is published each Fall. You will be sent the current edition.   **PRICE $14**

THE COMPLETE REFERENCE GUIDE FOR REAL ESTATE,
from Delphi Information Sciences
The Complete Guide for Real Estate is a complete, easy to read amortization book with 221 pages filled with understandable tables and charts which are indispensable to the real estate investor or salesperson. The Delphi book doesn't have the contract wording that comes with the *Bluebook* but it does come spiral bound for easy table top use. Both are excellent books and at least one of them is a must for every investor.   **PRICE $8**

PLEASE SEND ME THE BOOK(S) I HAVE CHECKED BELOW

☐ Realty Bluebook
☐ The Complete Reference Guide

Amount enclosed $ _____
(California residents please add 6% sales tax)

Name _____

Address _____

City _____ State _____ Zip _____

CREDIT CARD ORDERS SIGN HERE _____

☐ Master Charge   ☐ Visa/Bankamericard   Expiration date _____

Credit Card Number _____

MAIL TO: IMPACT PUBLISHING COMPANY
                        1601 Oak Park Boulevard
                        Pleasant Hill, CA 94523

REAL ESTATE BOOKS AVAILABLE

FROM IMPACT PUBLISHING COMPANY

LANDLORDING, by Leigh Robinson.

It will be a joy to manage your rental units . . . when you know the "tricks of the trade." And you'll learn these tricks (and make more money too) after you read the exciting and expanded third edition of *LANDLORDING*. It goes into every detail you'll want to know to be a smart property owner— *how to* select the best tenants, write airtight contracts, prevent property damage, avoid costly eviction (but how to if you must), raise rents and much, much more. PRICE $15

NOTHING DOWN, a proven program that shows you how to buy real estate with little or NO money down, by Robert G. Allen. You'll learn how to get from where you are now to where you want to be financially, and you'll learn how to get there in the shortest possible time. Learn how to find the best buys, how to negotiate and how to manage your properties. Allen covers apartment unit investing more than smaller units but the principles generally apply to all real estate. PRICE $13

THINK LIKE A TYCOON, by Bill Greene

Humorous yet full of solid real estate tips—even though some of the writer's advice may sound pretty far-fetched. But Bill "Tycoon" Greene has become a multi-millionaire by doing the unusual in real estate and he'll show you how you can accomplish the same. PRICE $16.

PLEASE SEND ME THE BOOKS I HAVE CHECKED BELOW

☐ LANDLORDING ☐ NOTHING DOWN
☐ THINK LIKE A TYCOON

Amount enclosed $ _____
(Cal. residents please add 6% sales tax)

☐ I am adding $2.00 **per** book for special first class postage and handling.

Name _____

Address _____

City _____ State _____ Zip _____

CREDIT CARD ORDERS SIGN HERE _____

☐ Master Charge ☐ Visa/Bankamericard **Expiration date** _____

Credit Card Number _____

MAIL TO: IMPACT PUBLISHING COMPANY
1601 Oak Park Boulevard
Pleasant Hill, CA 94523

DOUBLE YOUR MONEY IN REAL ESTATE
EVERY TWO YEARS

☐ YES, Please send me _____ additional copy(ies) of Dave Glubetich's *DOUBLE YOUR MONEY IN REAL ESTATE EVERY TWO YEARS.* I'll keep this one for myself and let friends read the dog-eared copy. (NOTE: We pay fourth class, book-rate postage: for quicker 1st class mail add $1 per book up to 4 books only.)

PRICE LIST (Check one category)

☐ **Soft Cover** Edition $12.00
3 to 4 books @ 8.75 each
5 to 9 books @ $7.50 each
10 to 19 books @ $6.75 each

☐ **Deluxe Hard Cover** Ed. $14.50
3 to 4 books @ $11.00 each
5 to 9 books @ $9.75 each
10 to 19 books @ $9.00 each

☐ I am enclosing $1. **per** each soft cover book ordered and/or $2 extra per each hard cover book for special first class postage and handling.

Amount enclosed $ _____
(Cal. residents please add 6% sales tax)

Name _____

Address _____

City _____ State _____ Zip _____

CREDIT CARD ORDERS SIGN HERE _____

☐ Master Charge   ☐ Visa/Bankamericard   **Expiration date** _____

Credit Card Number _____

MAIL TO: IMPACT PUBLISHING COMPANY
1601 Oak Park Boulevard
Pleasant Hill, CA 94523

For quicker service call (415) 935-4370

Special Note: You will receive our current catalog of exciting real estate products with each order. And even if you don't order now you may write or call for a free catalog.

ABOUT THE AUTHOR

Dave Glubetich is a fourth-generation Californian. Born in Oakland, he now lives in Pleasant Hill. He graduated from San Jose State College with a degree in journalism/public relations, is married and has six children.

In 1965 he went into real estate and two years later he received his broker's license. He bought his own company in 1969 and sold it in August 1977. He then devoted his full attention to family, writing, portfolio management and some real estate sales.

He founded Impact Publishing Company in 1977, which besides his own books *The Monopoly Game, How to Grow a Moneytree* and *Double Your Money in Real Estate Every Two Years*, publishes a monthly newsletter and Report service for real estate investors. It is called *Impact Reports* and *Updates*.

As the first edition of this book goes to press, Mr. Glubetich begins another adventure. He is starting a new real estate company for investors only. Utilizing many modern techniques, this new and yet unnamed company will counsel clients and then set them up with homes or packages of investment property which best suit their needs.